In a Queer Voice

Introduction

The Importance of Being Heard

> To have a voice is to be human. To have something to say
> is to be a person. But speaking depends on listening and
> being heard; it is an intensely relational act.
>
> —CAROL GILLIGAN, *In a Different Voice*

> Jumping off the gw bridge sorry.
>
> —Rutgers University freshman TYLER CLEMENTI, eighteen,
> posted on Facebook the day of his suicide

To grow up lesbian, gay, bisexual, transgender, or queer (LGBTQ) in the United States is to be aware of a profound silence in our relationships, our society, and in many cases even ourselves. Despite recent political and social gains such as the legalization of same-sex unions in some states, glimpses of LGBTQ (or at least gay and lesbian) visibility on television and in other media, and the growing support for some LGBTQ rights among segments of the U.S. population, we still live in a culture in which presumed heterosexuality and traditional messages about gender dominate us from birth. Children and adolescents who violate these norms get the message that they need to keep aspects of themselves hidden, or at least alter them, if they want to be accepted across all aspects of their relational world: their families, their peer groups, their schools, their communities, and the larger society.

In early childhood, girls and boys are socialized, sometimes quite forcefully, to wear the clothes, choose the activities, and display the interests "appropriate" to their biological sex. Even when parents make deliberate efforts not to impose gender-based limitations on their children, messages at school, in the media, and elsewhere compensate to reinforce the cultural binary: boys do this, girls do that, and shame on the child who crosses the line or does anything in between. In the waiting area at my auto repair shop recently, I saw a boy of about three years old get excited about a toy truck that was being advertised on television. He then momentarily—and quite visibly and abruptly—checked his enthusiasm to make sure his father thought his liking the toy was acceptable. After the boy's initial outburst of excitement, he asked in a hushed voice, "That's a boy thing, right?" Of course, the toy truck passed the test, but when children develop interests and proclivities that run counter to the unwritten laws of gender, they learn quickly that silence is the order of things. They learn to conceal aspects of themselves that may expose them as violators, and they learn to expect silence from the adults around them about anything that deviates from what is considered normal gender behavior.

Of course, when children reach adolescence, it is not only gender boundaries but also sexuality that is subject to "policing," as some researchers and theorists have called it (e.g., Pascoe 2007), both by adults and by adolescents themselves. (Evidence suggests that even in the early elementary grades, many peer groups use the language of sexuality to harass and bully each other, but this practice is rampant by the time students reach middle school; see, for example, Poteat and Espelage 2005.) Several of the case studies in this book begin with stories of middle school, with young people experiencing intense gender- or sexuality-based harassment—sometimes even before they are out to others or even to themselves as gay, lesbian, bisexual, transgender, or queer.[1]

---

1. When discussing the issues that affect people who identify themselves as lesbian, gay, bisexual, transgender, or queer (LGBTQ), language can be a problematic issue. Before the 1990s, most studies about LGBTQ people referred only to gay and lesbian individuals, but researchers have become increasingly aware that bisexual people are a distinct group with specific concerns (Lewis et al. 2009). More recent research also has recognized the special issues that affect transgender youth and adults, those who do not conform to traditional man/woman or boy/girl gender norms in a variety of ways. (Some transgender people also identify as gay, lesbian, or bisexual, while others do not. See note 1 in Chapter 5 for a more detailed definition of transgender.) In addition, some individuals identify as *queer*, a designation that implies a rejection of societal norms and/or labels associated with sexuality and gender. (Again, some individuals who adopt a queer self-designation also self-identify as lesbian, gay, bisexual, or transgender, and others do not.) Finally, the letter Q in LGBTQ is also used to designate "questioning" in many contexts to refer to individuals who are unsure of their sexual orientation or gender identity, but I do not use it as such in this book because it was not a focus in our project's original research design. (See Lipkin 2008 for a more complete discussion of the various self-identifications used by youth with regard to gender and sexuality.) When speaking of the participants in this study, I refer to them using the identifier they used for themselves at the particular time being discussed in the interview (e.g., in Chapter 1 David says he came out as "gay," so I use this word in that context). I use the abbreviation LGBTQ to avoid placing a participant or group of participants in a specific category, especially since many interviewees used multiple self-identifiers at various points.

The Silencing Effects of Hostile School Climates

A recent national survey of more than 7,200 middle and high school students (mostly LGBTQ-identifying) conducted by the Gay, Lesbian and Straight Education Network (GLSEN) paints an alarming portrait of the many ways school environments and experiences silence many youths' open expression of a lesbian, gay, bisexual, transgender, or queer identity. GLSEN found that 89 percent of the students they surveyed heard anti-LGBTQ language regularly in their schools and that 85 percent had been direct targets of harassment for reasons associated with their actual or perceived sexual orientation and/or gender identity (Kosciw et al. 2010). For the past decade, GLSEN's biennial surveys have found this at-school harassment to be pervasive in middle and high schools, but more recent administrations of the survey have also found that technology, such as the Internet and text messaging, provides a wider forum for school harassers to target LGBTQ students even while they are at home. More than half (53 percent) of students who participated in the GLSEN survey said they'd experienced cyberbullying, defined by GLSEN as "using an electronic medium, such as a mobile phone or Internet connection, to threaten or harm others," in the past year.

For many youth, anti-LGBTQ language and harassment have a dampening effect on their presence and performance in school. Most of the students GLSEN surveyed said they were distressed either "extremely" or "pretty much" by the homophobic language they heard at school. Some skipped certain classes or even entire school days because they felt unsafe or uncomfortable; others said they avoided certain parts of the school (e.g., the locker room, the cafeteria) for similar reasons (Kosciw et al. 2010). For David, profiled in Chapter 1 of this book, the fear of harassment led him to stop raising his hand in class ("I never talked, unless I was called on, pretty much") and discouraged him from joining certain activities he might otherwise have enjoyed: "I never tried out for a play or musical, because I guess I thought if I was onstage, somebody might yell something out from the audience at me."

Contributing to the silencing effect of anti-LGBTQ language and harassment in many schools and peer groups is a complete lack of representation of LGBTQ identity, history, or people in most school curricula. Despite a society in which LGBTQ issues are included more frequently in news reports and public discourse than ever before, the latest GLSEN study found that only 13 percent of the youth surveyed reported that LGBTQ issues were discussed or covered in any of their classes (Kosciw et al. 2010). Clearly little has changed since 2004, when a student at a public forum I cochaired before the Massachusetts Governor's Commission on Gay and Lesbian Youth testified:

> The gay rights movement is not even mentioned during the civil rights chapter in my American history textbook. I have yet to read a book in English class with anything more than the implication of homosexuality, and in all my classes when we talk about discrimination, we stay to race issues between black and white communities. . . . With all these people in my life ignoring an issue that is a significant part of me, it is easy to feel that I don't matter. (Massachusetts Governor's Commission on Gay and Lesbian Youth 2004)

I am by no means suggesting that all middle and high schools have a uniformly silencing effect on LGBTQ adolescents. Many teachers and school personnel address anti-LGBTQ language and harassment consistently and effectively, serve as important allies and role models for LGBTQ students, offer open support and communication, and include LGBTQ issues in curricula in thoughtful and creative ways. The work of some of these educators and the difference they have made in individual young people's lives play significant roles in the case studies included in this book. In addition, more and more schools now have gay-straight alliances (GSAs), school-based groups in which LGBTQ students and their "straight allies" support each other, plan events, and discuss LGBTQ issues in a "safe space" where they are free to be themselves. (As this book went to press, more than four thousand GSAs across the country were registered with GLSEN, according to the organization's website.) Still, evidence from national surveys like GLSEN's and other sources suggests that most middle and high schools in the United States *still* do not have GSAs and that most LGBTQ adolescents attend schools where LGBTQ issues are discussed infrequently or not at all, except for the insulting, uncontrolled, and ultimately silencing language and harassment that take place in hallways, cafeterias, and in some cases even classrooms.

In addition to the fear of hostile encounters with peers, many LGBTQ young people have another reason to be silent: they learn that if they "come out" and are targeted for it, adults will not necessarily be there to protect or defend them. The latest GLSEN survey showed that most teachers intervened inconsistently or did not intervene *at all* when homophobic language was used at school (Kosciw et al. 2010). Moreover, 62 percent of students harassed for reasons associated with their sexual or gender identities said they never reported the harassment to school staff, and the reason they cited most frequently was that they believed such reporting would produce no effect.

Strikingly, almost as many (55 percent) never reported these incidents to family members either, underscoring how the silence in which many young people cope with anti-LGBTQ harassment can cut across multiple aspects of their lives.

The Silence at Home

Numerous participants in the study profiled in this book, all of whom were "out" on at least some level to their parents or other family members, nevertheless talked about the silence that pervaded their families about LGBTQ issues. Travis, profiled in Chapter 4, was one of a number of participants who, even though they had come out to family members, were discouraged from talking about it: "Most of my family has been—it's kind of 'don't ask, don't tell,' you know? If we don't talk about [my sexuality], it's better." Jordan, profiled in Chapter 5, felt the need to be silent after coming out as transgender because of the distress that resulted from conversations with family members: "My mom pretty much cries whenever I talk about [being transgender]."

For some young people, the silencing of their LGBTQ identities was more forceful than unspoken "don't ask, don't tell" rules and took the form of verbal abuse. Lindsey, profiled in Chapter 2, says her older sister called her a "fag" and her stepfather insulted her with terms such as "dyke" and "carpet muncher" even before she came out as lesbian. The abuse and shaming Lindsey endured at home magnified what was going on at school and resulted in her not feeling safe coming out in either context. Lindsey ultimately came out to her family and peers after a suicide attempt, and her family relationships improved considerably. For youth who *never* feel safe coming out to family members, the costs of this silence are immeasurable, given the importance of family support and communication in helping young people build resilience to cope with many of the challenges of growing up (Resnick et al. 1997; Scales and Leffert 2004).

A Relational Catch-22

At the heart of the silencing—and self-silencing—of LGBTQ youth is a "Catch-22" of relationships that is analogous to one that feminist psychologists such as Carol Gilligan, Jean Baker Miller, and Irene Pierce Stiver have said affects girls and women as they are initiated into a male-dominated society. In their 1997 book *The Healing Connection: How Women Form Relationships in Therapy and in Life*, Miller and Stiver (1997) termed this predicament—which scholars in the field had been writing about for roughly a decade—the "central relational paradox": the need to sacrifice *relationship* with significant aspects of oneself (feelings, thoughts, knowledge, perhaps even a true sense of one's own identity) in order to maintain *relationships* with others. Without this sacrifice of the self, significant relationships are at risk; but with the sacrifice, they are also at risk—of becoming inauthentic, unfulfilling, and ultimately isolating.

The research of the Harvard Project on Women's Psychology and Girls' Development, led by Gilligan and involving hundreds of girls and women across numerous studies in the 1980s and 1990s, found this paradox to be especially prevalent among girls at the onset of adolescence. To synthesize one of the project's recurrent findings, the researchers consistently found that in early adolescence, when girls were faced with the realization of their subordinate position in a patriarchal society and the accompanying expectation that they be "good girls" (Taylor, Gilligan, and Sullivan 1995, 25), many consciously or unconsciously drove aspects of their true selves "underground" (Brown and Gilligan 1992, 7). This self-silencing was manifested in a variety of ways: the girls stopped raising their hands in class, chose not to speak up when their rights or personal boundaries were violated, and pretended everything was all right when they were in emotional distress. While this sublimation of the self obviously came at great personal cost, it allowed the girls to maintain seemingly harmonious but ultimately inauthentic relationships with others, particularly those whom they were expected to please (e.g., boys, men, parents, teachers, and other authority figures). In her 2005 book *The Disappearing Girl: Learning the Language of Teenage Depression*, psychologist Lisa Machoian drew on her clinical work and research to document the more extreme risks to adolescent girls of relational disconnection and self-silencing, including depression, self-mutilating behaviors (e.g., cutting), and suicide attempts. Without license to express their true thoughts, feelings, and selves in the world, the girls Machoian interviewed found alternative ways to communicate, ultimately placing themselves at tremendous risk.

No major published studies have applied feminist psychological theories about relationships, voice, and silence specifically to research with sexual minority youth, but the parallels between the Harvard Project's findings on women and girls and the issues affecting LGBTQ young people are many. LGBTQ youth are members of a culturally dominated group (and, in many cases, several such groups based on gender, race, sexuality, gender identity, and other factors). Their ability to bring all aspects of themselves authentically into relationships with family members, friends, teachers, and others is compromised by societal homophobia and culturally enforced notions about appropriate and inappropriate gender and sexual behavior. They are therefore often silenced in these key relationships and, in turn, silence their own voices in order to maintain some semblance of "relationship" with the key people and institutions in their lives. Finally, as in the cases of the adolescent girls Machoian interviewed, this silencing can be associated with serious risks.

The Costs of Silence

Numerous research findings and several recent, high-profile news stories underscore the urgent need to understand more thoroughly the factors that contribute to risk behaviors among LGBTQ youth, particularly those related to suicide. Data from the Massachusetts Youth Risk Behavior Survey (MYRBS), which draws on the responses of 2,707 students attending randomly selected high schools around the state, showed that 25 percent of the gay, lesbian, and bisexual students responding to the survey had attempted suicide in the previous year. This figure is an improvement over the 40 percent of sexual-minority youth who reported a suicide attempt on the 2003 survey, but it is still more than four times the rate of reported suicide attempts for other adolescents, which in the 2009 survey was 5.6 percent (Massachusetts Department of Elementary and Secondary Education 2010). Vermont's 2009 Youth Risk Behavior Survey also found dramatically higher rates of suicide attempts for sexual-minority youth: 24 percent of the students who identified themselves as gay or lesbian said they had attempted suicide in the previous twelve months, eight times the percentage of heterosexual students (Vermont Department of Public Health 2010). Sexual-minority youth in the Massachusetts survey, the Vermont survey, or both were also significantly more likely than their heterosexual peers to be involved in physical fights, skip school because they felt unsafe, abuse alcohol and illegal drugs, and experience depression.[2] While it is obviously difficult for researchers to connect risk

---

2. Massachusetts and Vermont have some of the country's most thorough and long-standing practices of assessing suicidal behaviors and other risk factors among lesbian, gay, and bisexual youth through their Youth Risk Behavior Surveys. As this book goes to press, forty-seven states administer Youth Risk Behavior Surveys under the federal Centers for Disease Control and Prevention's Youth Risk Behavior Surveillance System (along with a national survey, four territory surveys, two tribal government surveys, and twenty-three local surveys), but only five states (Delaware, Maine, Massachusetts, Rhode Island, and Vermont) include survey items asking participants to self-identify their sexual orientation, and just seven states (those listed previously plus Connecticut and Wisconsin) include questions about same-sex sexual activity. Only these states can therefore assess the specific risks of lesbian, gay, and bisexual youth. No states collect data on suicidal behavior or other risk factors among transgender students, the most understudied population among

factors to any specific causes, several of the accounts profiled in this book suggest associations between relational problems such as isolation, self-silencing,
and emotional, physical, or sexual abuse and risks such as severe depression,
self-harming behaviors, and suicidal tendencies.

National awareness of the issue of LGBTQ youth suicide reached a peak
in September 2010, a month during which as many as nine teenagers around
the United States are believed to have committed suicide after being bullied for reasons associated with their actual or perceived sexual orientation.
In the most highly publicized of these cases, Rutgers University freshman
Tyler Clementi, eighteen, jumped off the George Washington Bridge after
his roommate video-recorded an intimate encounter between Clementi and
another man and posted descriptions of it online. Many in the media specu-
lated that the humiliation Clementi experienced played a significant role in
his emotional distress and perhaps his decision to take his own life.

Clementi's suicide and those of other youth who had been harassed
prompted a new national focus on bullying, new antibullying initiatives in
several states, municipalities, and schools, and the online "It Gets Better"
campaign, in which celebrities, political figures, and others provide video-
recorded messages of hope to LGBTQ youth struggling with harassment
and isolation. These initiatives are highly commendable and no doubt make
a lifesaving difference to many young people. The accounts presented in the
following chapters, however, raise questions about whether approaches focused on protection and encouragement are enough, and they illustrate how
a voice-centered approach to nurturing positive LGBTQ youth development
may be needed to complement existing efforts.

Hearing the Voices of LGBTQ Youth

The research described in this book began with a project at the Harvard
Graduate School of Education led by Lisa Machoian and me that focused on
using voice-centered research methods to examine the relational dynamics
of LGBTQ youths' lives. Our team was interested in learning how relationships in family, peer group, and school contexts may be associated with both
risks among LGBTQ adolescents and their resilience to these challenges.[3] For

---

all gender- and sexual-minority youth. For the first-ever federal report synthesizing LGB-specific
data from these seven states' Youth Risk Behavior Surveys and those of several large school districts,
see Kann et al. 2011.

3. Other researchers involved in the data collection and/or analysis were Steve Anderson, Stephen
Chow, Constance P. Scanlon, Andrea Sexton, and Travis Wright.

this initial project, which I refer to subsequently as Phase I of the research, we recruited participants at a community-based LGBTQ youth group in a large northeastern U.S. city beginning in 2003 (hereafter called CityYouth), and I repeated the research protocol at a smaller, rural LGBTQ youth group (hereafter called YouthWest) approximately one year later. In all, thirty young people completed questionnaires, and twenty of these participants ages fifteen to twenty-one[4] participated in in-depth, open-ended interviews about their relationships in three contexts: family, peers, and school—as well as a fourth relational "context" our research team called "relationship to the self." Phase I interviews were conducted and analyzed using the Listening Guide, a "voice-centered relational method" developed through the work of the Harvard Project on Women's Psychology and Girls' Development (Gilligan et al. 2003) that focuses on how participants talk about themselves and the various aspects of their relational worlds. (See Note on the Listening Guide Method at the end of this book for a more thorough explanation of how the methodology was used in this study.)

During Phase I of the research, participants described a wide range of experiences. Youths' relational experiences at home, in school, and among their peers ranged from receiving open and unconditional support and affirmation to severe relational violation, sometimes including emotional, physical, or sexual abuse. Despite the fact that questions about voice and silence—or about harassment or other forms of abuse—were not part of the interview protocol, participants described in disturbing detail the ways in which they were silenced in family, school, and other contexts. Many participants directly associated the harassment, rejection, and other relational violations they experienced with their own self-harming behaviors such as cutting, suicide attempts, and dropping out of school.

Another pattern we saw across many of the interviews, however, was that young people seemed to develop more positive "relationships to the

---

4. While in the legal sense young people are adults upon reaching age eighteen, I use the words *adolescents* and *youth* to define participants up to age twenty-one in this study. (The LGBTQ youth programs from which we recruited participants serve students through age twenty-two, but no twenty-two-year-olds enrolled in the study.) The National Institutes of Health (1999) defines childhood as the period from birth through age twenty-one, since this age range "spans the period when many individuals are still within the education system and are dependent on their families." For example, numerous young people over age eighteen with whom we spoke were being supported by their parents while in college, and a substantial number were still living with their parents or other adult family members when they were interviewed. For the purposes of this book, I generally use the terms *adolescent* and *youth* to refer to young people participating in Phase I of the study; their ages ranged from fifteen to twenty-one. I refer to Phase II participants, whose ages ranged from twenty-one to twenty-seven, as *adults* or *young adults*.

self" when their relationships in one or more of the three other contexts improved. Finding spaces such as school- or community-based LGBTQ youth groups *that felt genuinely safe* and relationships in which they could *communicate openly, be themselves, and have their identities affirmed* was associated for many with the cessation of risk behaviors and a greater sense of self-acceptance. One key indicator of this self-acceptance, to draw an analogy to Gilligan's findings about women's development, was that participants spoke "in a different voice" (Gilligan 1982) than they had at other points in their interviews—one that reflected optimism about the future, a sense of pride about their identities, a rejection of self-destructive attitudes and behaviors, and a willingness to challenge gender and sexuality norms. Said another way, each participant's narrative reflected the emergence of a positive, self-affirming, and in some cases even defiant "queer voice."

After project colleagues Stephen Chow, Constance P. Scanlon, and I published an article in the *Journal of LGBT Youth* that synthesized our team's findings and highlighted three case studies we found to be illustrative of central themes (Sadowski, Chow, and Scanlon 2009), I began to wonder how the nascent queer voices we heard in our research had evolved as participants took on the challenges of adulthood. Because of the highly personal, in-depth nature of Listening Guide methodology, whereby the researcher's experience of the interview makes up a central aspect of the analysis, I limited my outreach for what I hereafter call Phase II of the study to participants whom I had interviewed personally, had met and interacted with (e.g., the president of the urban LGBTQ youth group, who was key in approving our team's entry into the site), and/or whose Phase I narratives I had already studied closely. From this group of thirteen—after numerous e-mails and telephone calls (many to addresses and numbers that were no longer valid) as well as searches of several social networking sites—I located six participants from Phase I who agreed to be interviewed as adults. These interviews took place in different parts of the country between the fall of 2009 and the fall of 2010.

Organization and Content of the Book

Case studies of the six participants interviewed for both phases of the research make up Chapters 1 through 6. Based on the ways in which the themes in each case unfold, I have chosen to present some chronologically and others in "flashback" form. Each chapter ends with a section in which I offer a "listening" to the participant's voice and discuss the unique contribution I believe it makes to an understanding of the issue of queer voice development in adolescence and young adulthood (with a recognition that many such listenings and interpretations are possible).

In all six chapter-length case studies, we hear various manifestations of the central relational paradox, of participants keeping the LGBTQ aspects of their voices *out of relationship* in order to stay *in relationships*, and the costs of this silencing. But we also hear how various forms of resistance help each participant survive and discover her or his own queer voice. In Chapter 1, David employs what Jill McLean Taylor, Carol Gilligan, and Amy M. Sullivan (1995) have called both covert and overt political resistance in order to survive, first quietly planning his escape from his rural community, then becoming an outspoken advocate for LGBTQ rights and his own right to be himself. In Chapter 2, Lindsey gives up self-destructive forms of indirect communication such as cutting and attempting suicide and learns how to "talk to people" and place honest, communicative relationships at the center of her life. Ruth, profiled in Chapter 3, draws on support from institutions and on the power of mentoring, both as a mentee in adolescence and as a mentor in adulthood, to cope with a difficult family situation and ultimately to find her voice as an LGBTQ scholar. In Chapter 4, we hear Travis respond to unspoken "don't ask, don't tell" policies with his family and at school by adopting a stoic voice of rugged individualism, which transforms in adulthood through loving relationships with a partner and with friends. As a transgender youth, Jordan in Chapter 5 attempts to balance the need for self-fulfillment with a desire not to hurt the people she loves and emerges as an adult with her own, unique expression of gender that is ever-evolving. Eddie's coming-out story, related in Chapter 6, represents the gradual integration of an LGBTQ identity with a more expansive view of himself as a citizen of the world.

Although I could not locate six of the study participants whom I had interviewed personally for Phase II of the research, Chapter 7 includes mini-profiles of these youth that focus primarily on how aspects of family and school relationships either supported or silenced their emerging queer voices. The accounts in this chapter include efforts by abusive teachers, an "ex-gay" conversion therapist, sexual harassers, and others to silence these young people, but they also illustrate how supportive family, peer, and school relationships made a positive difference in their lives.

In Chapter 8, I synthesize the patterns and themes found across the case studies and mini-profiles and discuss their practical implications. In so doing, I envision what *some* of the foundations of a voice-centered approach to supporting LGBTQ youth might look like, in the hope that future research will build on these foundations. Finally, in the interest of transparency, basic fairness, and the relational nature of Listening Guide methodology, I attempt in the afterword to capture my own experience listening to the stories participants in this research so generously shared, in particular their resonances with my own history. As I do for the research participants, I discuss the ways in which I believe my own queer voice has evolved—and continues to evolve—through the writing of this book.

In both the case studies and the mini-profiles, I have attempted to capture the authentic voices of the study participants as accurately as possible. Accordingly, interview excerpts are verbatim, with all "ums," "uhs," and "likes" included—in some cases to illustrate possible tentativeness, hesitation, or uncertainty about a particular topic and in others simply to depict with authenticity contemporary adolescent speech patterns. Ellipses in interview excerpts indicate where participants' responses have been abbreviated for clarity, and dashes illustrate midsentence changes in participants' lines of thought.

"Queer Voice": A Note about Terminology

It is with some caution and, admittedly, a fair amount of discomfort that I apply the term *queer voice* to the narratives of the adolescents and young adults profiled in this book. Having come out as gay after graduating from college in the 1980s, I am a member of what may be called the "pre-queer" generation—those who came of age after the AIDS crisis emerged but before the LGBTQ community started pushing back en masse against government inaction about AIDS and the dominant heterosexist culture through organizations like ACT UP (AIDS Coalition to Unleash Power) and Queer Nation. When I hear the word *queer*, I still have difficulty separating the political and prideful uses of the term from its history (and from *my* history with it) as a demeaning epithet.

I certainly know people my age and older who have embraced *queer* as a self-identifier, or at least as a way of describing the community. Conversely, even among the "post-queer" generation, represented by the adolescents and young adults profiled in this book, the adoption of *queer* is far from universal. While some of these young people—David in particular, profiled in Chapter 1—adhere adamantly to *queer* and its variants as important foundations of their self-definition, others—Lindsey and Travis, for example, in Chapters 2 and 4—reject these terms in favor of pre-queer self-identifiers such as *gay*, *lesbian*, and *bisexual*.

As I listened to and read the interviews, however, it became clear that something collectively "queer" was emerging, and this included the participants who do not think of themselves in those terms. In her 1982 book *In a Different Voice* (which paved the way for much of the research on girls and women cited here as well as the Listening Guide qualitative research method), Gilligan reported that women brought a different voice into conversations about self, relationships, and morality—one that challenged the gender binaries and hierarchies that are integral to patriarchal social structures. In my interviews with LGBTQ individuals, particularly in adulthood, I heard a new but strikingly analogous "different voice" in response to patriarchal—and heterosexist—social structures, a way of living in and speaking about the world that challenged and contradicted the strict rules about sexuality and gender that had silenced them as children and adolescents.

My use of the term *queer voice*, then, is not to imply that each of the individuals profiled herein *is* queer; we all are the utmost experts on the identifiers that help us make sense of who we are. Rather, across all of their narratives one can hear *ways of thinking and being* that may be considered queer according to the term's most agreed-on definitions. Each individual profiled in this book, deliberately or not, speaks in ways that, to borrow from theorist Michael Warner's definition of queer, "challenge the common understanding of what gender difference means" (Warner 1993, xiii).[5] In this sense, each represents at least some aspect of a queer sensibility, especially if we recognize that merely living as lesbian, gay, bisexual, transgender, or queer constitutes a "queer" challenge to the silence about LGBTQ identity that still pervades American society.

A central aspect of *queer* as it is defined in most theoretical texts involves *resistance*—a current that runs deeply through all the participants' narratives in different but related ways. Several youth tell stories of severe harassment and ostracism from peers, a lack of support (and in some cases abuse) from adults, and the silencing of their LGBTQ identities in the relationships and institutions that were most important in their lives during adolescence. These oppressive experiences at first led some youth to direct their resistance inward, using various forms of what Lyn Mikel Brown and Carol Gilligan (1992) and others have called *psychological resistance*: keeping silent, harming themselves through cutting and other self-destructive behaviors, and even attempting suicide. Ultimately, however, they all found unique pathways toward a healthier *political resistance* (Brown and Gilligan 1992) in later adolescence and/or young adulthood: speaking out for the equal rights

---

5. For further discussion of queer challenges to socially constructed gender and sexuality norms, see Butler 1993.

of LGBTQ people and other oppressed groups, working to make schools and communities safer for younger LGBTQ youth, advocating for and being part of same-sex unions and families, and simply asserting and defending their right to express sexuality and gender in whatever ways they choose. Just as feminist psychologists have highlighted resistance as a key adaptive strategy that resilient girls employ to fight against the silencing of their voices in adolescence (Brown and Gilligan 1992; Taylor, Gilligan, and Sullivan 1995), there is evidence that these LGBTQ young adults, despite the different life challenges each of them continues to face, have developed over time the personal and relational resources to "push back" against the forces that would hold them down and keep their voices from being heard.

Imagining the Possible

The small number of young people profiled in this book obviously cannot in any general way represent the experiences of all LGBTQ adolescents or young adults in the United States. Especially when one considers the often vastly different experiences of young people who adopt the various self-identifiers under the LGBTQ umbrella, overgeneralizations are misleading at best and dangerous at worst. One thing that the case studies illustrate, for example, is how the experiences of Lindsey, a young woman whose family and friends ultimately accept her lesbian identity after initially rejecting and harassing her for it, are vastly different from those of Jordan, who describes an internal "war" between a strong desire for gender reassignment and an equally powerful desire to spare her family emotional pain. These profiles show how both Lindsey's and Jordan's experiences, as well as those of all the other research participants, are unique to them based on the individual circumstances of their lives.

Moreover, a serious limitation of this research project thus far is that all Phase II case studies in Chapters 1 through 6 are based on white young adults raised in the Northeast, and only one youth of color is profiled in Chapter 7 (Clark, an African American youth from a Southern U.S. city, who could not be reached for participation in Phase II). To an extent, this limitation reflects the difficulty that some LGBTQ youth groups, including those to which our participants belonged, have had in connecting successfully with communities of color and making youth of color feel welcome. Rather than conduct additional outreach to include more youth of color in this study—and thus place an unrealistic burden on these new participants to represent somehow the experiences of youth of color within a limited sample—I have chosen to maintain the original two-phase research model and draw only from participants in the original Harvard study. Thus, I present this book as the first overture in what I hope will be an ongoing conversation about voice and LGBTQ youth.[6]

While the experiences of the LGBTQ young people profiled in this book are in some ways unique to their social locations with regard to race, ethnicity, gender, socioeconomic status, education, and other factors, I also believe they speak to many issues that affect LGBTQ youth regardless of these categorizations. At the same time, the accounts in this book admittedly leave unaddressed other important issues related to what theorists have called the "intersectionality" (Crenshaw 1991) of homophobia, heterosexism, and transgender oppression with racism, sexism, classism, and other forms of oppression. A colleague and I are in the planning stages of a subsequent phase of this research that will focus specifically on the development of queer voice among LGBTQ youth of color in New York City, thus extending—though by no means completing—an ongoing research conversation that must ultimately involve the voices of LGBTQ youth from all around the world.

Another limitation of this book, a tragic but also inevitable one, is that the voices of the many LGBTQ young people who have been lost to suicide remain unheard. News accounts following Tyler Clementi's death suggested he had little to say between the time his peers humiliated him online and his fatal leap into the Hudson River. (His Facebook posting read simply, "Jumping off the gw bridge sorry.") We can never presume to know what Clementi was thinking and feeling in the hours before he died, or what—if anything—might have made a difference in his decision to take his own life. In one sense Clementi's "voice" was heard loudly and clearly after his death, when people around the world were suddenly focused on the injustice he had suffered and on the harassment and humiliation that so many young people

---

6. The retrospection inherent in these interviews (and, to some degree, in all interviews), whereby participants reflect on experiences that have taken place in the past, is another limitation of this research. Certainly a wave of this study conducted while participants were in their early teens would have been highly informative, but other researchers have noted significant obstacles to conducting research with younger LGBTQ youth, including those associated with self-identification and parental consent (Elze 2003). LGBTQ-identifying youth in their early teens who could obtain parental consent to participate in research studies would likely represent a highly skewed subsample of young people who (1) self-identified at an early age and felt ready to talk about it, and (2) had high levels of parental support for their LGBTQ identities. While I acknowledge that one's attitudes about experiences inevitably change in retrospect, I argue that the nature of the inquiry involved in this study—particularly the *development* of queer voice—is such that participants' attitudes about their past experiences are highly relevant to the analysis. Moreover, the high emotional salience of participants' past experiences in school, family, and community contexts, even several years later, is evident across these interviews.

endure every day. Still, it is hard not to wonder what might have happened if we had listened sooner.

This book has two primary purposes. The first is to listen closely to the voices of a small number of LGBTQ young people and, in so doing, begin to understand the factors that can help a voice silenced by oppressive gender and sexuality norms break free. The second is to use what we understand—incomplete as our understanding might be—to work toward a better future. How do teachers, parents, counselors, mentors, and others who work with and care about LGBTQ youth create opportunities, spaces, and relationships in which they can "talk back" to the forces that threaten to silence them? The voices heard in these chapters cannot provide all the answers, but the process clearly needs to start with listening.

1

David: The Slow Build
of a Voice of Resistance

"I think it was like eighth grade when I told myself, 'I
know what I'm going through—I know where I live—
isn't normal.'"

When David[1] first enrolled in the Harvard study on the relational
lives of LGBTQ youth, he was well into his junior year at Carpenter College, a well-known urban liberal arts institution, even
though he was only nineteen years old. An intelligent, articulate young white
man with blond hair and bright blue eyes, David was remarkably forthcom-
ing in our first interview about the harassment that led him to transfer districts during secondary school and then enroll at Carpenter a year early,
during what would have been his senior year.[2] David's memories of middle
school and high school—and the feelings these evoked for him—were fresh
as he related a story of virtually constant taunting based on other students'
perceptions of his sexual orientation:

> The first day of seventh grade I started getting harassed. People, the
> older students, started calling me "faggot" in the hallways, and it just
> kind of trickled down so that—so that several people in every grade
> called me "faggot" in the hall, and, uh, on the bus, people would
> throw things at me [and] throw things at me in the hall; they started
> pushing me. By eighth grade it got really bad. I got death threats, I
> got my gym clothes urinated on in the bathroom, I started skipping

1. All names of research participants are pseudonyms, and the names of places and organizations,
as well as other information that could potentially be used to identify them, have been changed.
2. By the time David was interviewed, he had recently turned twenty.

school a lot. . . . I just had a horrible time, more and more harassment every day; like, it got to the point where it was constant, like all day, people would be saying things in class, between classes.

Unlike many other participants in the study, who attended high schools where gay-straight alliances (GSAs) helped ensure at least some visibility of LGBTQ issues, David says there was no affirmation or even recognition of lesbian, gay, bisexual, transgender, or queer identity at either of the secondary schools he attended. There was no GSA or other student group dedicated to supporting LGBTQ students and their allies; nor were LGBTQ issues ever discussed in any of his classes or with any of his teachers. Even David did not disclose that he was gay (the identifier he used for himself at the time) until well into his high school years, and then only to a few select friends. But this did not stop his peers at the first secondary school he attended, North Jackson County Junior-Senior High, from labeling him before even he understood what his feelings of being "different" meant: "At North Jackson, I was 'the faggot,' like, people didn't even know my name." David tried a variety of strategies to reduce, or at least cope with, the harassment he faced daily at school. Ultimately, however, he says these strategies were futile because in the minds of his peers his identity as "the faggot" was fixed:

> I mean, after three years [of being harassed], you use any method you can think of. You ignore it, you fight back, you, you know, walk with your head down, walk with your head up, walk with—however. Dress a certain way, don't dress a certain way. . . . I ended up not camouflaging who I was too much, because I found that even when I did try to dress like a stereotypical redneck or hick or try to join a sports team, it didn't really help. Like, I still got harassed.

Adults at School: A Collective Silence

Despite the severity and constancy of the harassment David experienced at North Jackson, the teachers, administrators, and guidance counselors there did virtually nothing to address it. One guidance counselor even suggested that David himself was responsible for what was happening to him:

> I went to the guidance counselors; some people that saw [the harassment] happening went to the guidance counselors, who did nothing. Teachers did nothing. I had several teachers at that school even witness me being in physical fights and turn around and walk away.

Um, one guidance counselor told me not to walk around in school like a little puppy dog—that maybe that would deter some of the harassment, if I just acted a little more masculine in the hallways.

Predictably, David says he had no strong, positive relationships with teachers or any other adults at North Jackson. He had minimal support from a music teacher, who allowed him to attend voice lessons in order to avoid gym class (which he found particularly threatening) and who urged him to press charges against a student who had spit on him. David says he was not "out" to this teacher, although "I'm pretty sure she knew."

Another example David shares demonstrating the complete silence about LGBTQ issues at North Jackson involves a closeted gay Spanish teacher, about whom David says, "If he came out at that school, he would be fired." David believes he had a tacit understanding with this teacher about their both being gay, but he says the teacher was "completely in the closet," and because the subject was taboo at school, the two never discussed issues related to sexual orientation:

It's hard to say if that helped me or hurt me, because he was so closeted that, you know, he didn't do a lot to support me. He talked to me, I think once or twice, and said—he told me that he thought I should press charges against certain kids because he had heard what happened. But that's the—the degree of our conversation about anything. You know, the "G word" was certainly never mentioned between us.

Evidence suggests that LGBTQ students can benefit from having openly LGBTQ teachers and administrators (Mayo 2008). It is unclear, however, whether David benefited in any significant way from knowing a closeted gay teacher at North Jackson. If anything, David seems to feel some resentment toward this teacher because, despite the fact that David believes the man was gay, he failed to deal with David's homosexuality or the harassment he suffered in an openly supportive way. David says the teacher's actions were especially troubling to him when one of his class projects, which he had placed in a school display case, was vandalized with antigay graffiti:

It was just, like, a Spanish project I did, a craft thing. . . . And someone wrote, like, "David loves men," or, and, "David is a faggot"— stuff like that on it. And I had to go open the display case and take it out. . . . But the whole thing was just horrible. So, but I—I don't know. I guess I forgave him [the Spanish teacher] for that. I—I don't know. I kind of understand where he is, but I wish he could come out and, like, make a big change there. It would help—yeah.

This incident is especially illustrative of the risks involved when David made himself visible in any way at North Jackson. In putting the Spanish class project in the showcase, David immediately made himself vulnerable to antigay harassment. The risks that David perceived were associated with "going public" were also the primary reason he says he chose not to become involved with drama, even though he was interested in being in one of the school plays or musicals: "I guess I thought if I was onstage, somebody might yell something out from the audience at me." Clearly, one of David's main self-silencing strategies for dealing with the harassment he endured at North Jackson was to keep a low profile, even if that meant not participating in a class or pursuing an extracurricular activity in which he was interested.

More Silence at Home

Although David grew up in a rural, conservative area, he describes his parents in our first interview as "democratic" and "liberal" and says somewhat proudly that his family has always been viewed by neighbors as "the quirky people who live up on the mountain." In addition to his parents, David's immediate family consists of one married older brother, who David says "fits all the straight stereotypes." When David and his brother were children, he says his brother "used to make fun of me for being girly . . . almost to the point of physical abuse" but adds that their relationship has become much more mutually respectful since then.

Despite feeling somewhat connected to his parents ideologically, David says in our Phase I interviews that he has struggled all his life to make emotional connections with them: "They don't show a lot of emotion or even, like, excitement or whatever, very—kind of muted." When David was growing up, his parents noticed his tendencies toward gender-atypical behaviors (such as trying on makeup and showing little interest in sports), but they never openly discussed them with him. He says his mother tried on several occasions to guide him toward more typically male behaviors, encouraging him to "do sports" and "wear certain clothes," but otherwise issues related to sexuality and gender were avoided.

David came out to his parents as gay at age fifteen. He describes their reaction to his disclosure in generally positive terms, although it provoked an unusual display of emotion from them, particularly his mother:

I haven't seen my parents cry, like, ever, but my mom cried then, and I—I don't know why she was crying with a lot of emotions. Um, my dad has a brother that's gay, and we talked about that then. I came out to my mom in the car, and then I came out to both of them after we got home from my grandma's house. . . . So we talked about my gay uncle, and they said they still loved me and supported me, and that was about it.

Despite the fact that David referred to his parents as "very supportive" on his initial survey for the study and repeats this assessment in our first interview, he says his parents avoided discussing his homosexuality for a long time after his initial disclosure. Eventually, David started bringing up the fact that he was gay at home and "forcing" his mother to talk with him about boys he was dating and other issues related to his sexual orientation. The only conversation David relates having had with his father about his gay identity is one in which David's father forbade him to continue writing "pro-gay" articles for the local newspaper, since he feared David's writings would jeopardize the business he owned in town. One topic that David says his parents never discussed—despite the fact that David feels sure they were aware of it—was the antigay harassment he experienced on a daily basis at school:

What I wish they would've said [when I came out] was, "What can we do to help you be safe? What have you been going through in high school?" Things like that. But they didn't. It just kinda ended with, "We love you; we support you." We talked a little bit about my uncle, and then that was it.

David's parents seem to have been living under the same "code of silence" as his high school teachers. Although they were ostensibly supportive of him, their inability to discuss the antigay harassment he was experiencing with any degree of candor precluded their ability to protect him in the way he needed to be. In subsequent interviews with David, it becomes apparent that the factors behind his family's silence about LGBTQ issues may be considerably more complex than mere discomfort. In a second interview about a year later, David shares with me his suspicion that both his parents might be gay—he is especially certain about his father—and that his father has had sexual relationships with several men in their hometown. By the time I interview David six years later for Phase II of the study, his relationship with his parents, especially his father, has changed dramatically in ways deeply connected to sexual orientation. These changes are described later in this chapter.

Risks in David's Adolescence

The portrait David paints of his life at school, with his family, and among his peer group during Phase I of the study is thus one of extreme verbal, emotional, and at times even physical abuse, with no deeply supportive relationships to buffer these experiences. While it is impossible to draw definitive causal links between the antigay taunting David suffered and any risk behaviors he engaged in during adolescence, David reports strong suicide ideation, thoughts of inflicting violence on his peers, and several other risk factors (including a possible eating disorder) during this period of his life. From his perspective, these behaviors were closely connected to the harassment he experienced and the feelings of "depression and loneliness" that accompanied it.

According to David, "Thoughts of suicide were running through my head since seventh grade—like every method of ending the harassment ran through my head." In addition to hurting himself, David says that at times he contemplated harming the peers who abused him: "I remember thinking about taking a gun to school. I remember thinking about shooting myself, along with other, less violent methods of deterring the harassment."

David's suicide ideation reached a peak on one of his last days attending school at North Jackson, when he had faced an unusually intense day of harassment:

> I sat on the edge of my dad's bed and held his gun up against my head that was in his closet. Um, again, it's a rural area, there's hunting, there's—guns are a part of the culture. Even if you live in a liberal family, like, you definitely grow up in a house with guns. I don't know anyone that doesn't have guns in their house. So we had a pistol in the closet, and I knew right where it was, um [clears throat], and the bullets were there, too. I loaded it, I sat on the edge of my parents' bed, and I held it to my head for—probably [sighs], like, I don't know, it seemed like forever; it was probably like half an hour. And I was too afraid to shoot the gun because I was afraid of not dying, and I was afraid of, like, the physical pain. Like, I didn't want to lay there and suffer in case I didn't die instantly.

It is difficult to determine exactly how close David came to committing suicide in the incident he relates here. He believes he came very close to killing himself, and the primary reason he did not do so was simply that "I was afraid of not dying." In the second Phase I interview I conducted with David about a year after our initial conversation, I asked him to reflect again on the factors that led to his near suicide attempt with his father's gun. His description is consistent with his previous account, but he provides additional details about the events leading up to the incident and shares more insight into his mental and emotional state at the time:

> Well, I was just like a mess, you know? My parents weren't home, my father had forgotten to pick me up at the bottom of the hill, and I had to walk up the mountain again. And I had just ridden the bus for an hour, and I had a terrible day at school; I was getting harassed a lot. Um, on the bus, too. And, um, I really just wanted to get out, or to escape to a different place or a different world, and—but I was too afraid to shoot myself. One, because of physical suffering. Like, I didn't want to suffer physically, or I didn't want to fuck it up and not die. And, um, and then I also did definitely think about how it would affect my family. And those two things combined, I think, prevented me from shooting.

While David says that he no longer has violent or suicidal thoughts (and has not had them for a long time), he indicts homophobia in the school community as having played a major role in his suicidal and violent ideation.

Although David does not believe he had an eating disorder in middle and high school, he discusses a period in which he engaged in some unusual behaviors with regard to food. Studies have shown that gay and bisexual men are disproportionately likely to develop eating disorders relative to heterosexual men (Andersen 1999; Boisvert and Harrell 2009; Strong et al. 2000), but there is less published research examining this phenomenon among gay male adolescents (Austin et al. 2009). As David explains:

> There was one time when I ate an entire bag of Hershey Kisses, and then I took the—this ipecac; I don't know if you know what that is—like a medicine you drink and it makes you throw up. . . . Well, I took that and threw up the—the Hershey Kisses. I don't even know why I did that; like, it's so weird. Like, I don't know why I held a gun up to my head. . . . But, looking back, I think I was kind of body-conscious, though I was conscious of everything: not just body-conscious but conscious of the way I talked, conscious of the way I looked, walked, everything. Because when you're being

harassed every second about everything, you can't help but, like, evaluate everything about you. So, I was conscious of, like, everything. . . . And it wasn't that I was trying to control how I looked, but it was like controlling—being in control, period. . . . So I would eat a little bit of breakfast, I would eat a salad for lunch, and then go home and sleep and not eat dinner. And that was my routine for probably seventh and eighth grade, but that kind of got better.

Although David says he does not believe he had an eating disorder, the accounts from this period in his life suggest at least some pathological behaviors with regard to food, especially his "routine" of eating very small amounts of food during seventh and eighth grade and his bulimic incident with the Hershey's Kisses and syrup of ipecac. He also describes an extreme form of self-consciousness ("I was conscious of the way I talked, conscious of the way I looked, walked, everything") and a diminished sense of control that seems in some way connected to the antigay harassment he experienced. The period David describes here seems to have been relatively short, and he emerged from it without any serious risk to his health; nevertheless, this part of his story raises questions about the extent to which David may have been at risk for a serious eating disorder during early adolescence.

Platteville High: "Much More Open and Liberal"

After enduring the harassment at North Jackson for several years, David persuaded his parents to allow him to attend Platteville High School, located in a college town in another county, and says his mother drove him more than two hours round-trip to and from school each day. While David found Platteville a more comfortable and accepting environment, he still faced harassment there, although it was not as intense as that he experienced at North Jackson:

The kids at the new school still harassed me, but it wasn't near the severity of the last school. Like, not even close. I got—um, after I could drive, after I turned sixteen and I could drive, I got some death threats under my windshield wiper and stuff, but I hardly missed any school, and I kinda liked it. It was more challenging than my last school; the teachers there were much more open and liberal.

The fact that David considers death threats placed under his windshield wipers to be a relatively benign form of harassment underscores the severity of what he had experienced at North Jackson. By the time he arrived at Platteville, he had clearly come to expect harassment simply as a part of what it means to be a gay high school student in a rural community, even one in a "college town." David says he was more open about his sexual orientation at Platteville but still did not feel safe being completely "out": "At the second high school I wasn't in—in the closet, and I wasn't out of the closet. But if somebody asked me if I was gay, I would usually say yes." David did disclose his sexual orientation to three fellow students in a support group at Platteville High and to his cousin Debbie, who also attended the school. For the most part, however, the isolation David experienced as a gay student continued until he left Platteville at the end of his junior year. As he explains, "I always viewed college as my way out, like ever since the end of sixth grade. College was how you left Jackson County."

College and the City: David's "Way Out"

For many adolescents, college is a major life transition they anticipate for a long time, one that brings increased autonomy, independence, and, for some, the forging of a new identity far away from the constraints of home. In David's case, the urgency with which he anticipated this transition was greatly heightened both by the hostility of his high school environment and by the isolation he felt in a rural setting where LGBTQ issues were discussed either negatively or not at all. In the following interview excerpt, David's first-person statements (italicized)[3] highlight the stark contrast between the isolation he felt in Jackson County and the hopes he had for what his life could be if he could move to an urban area:

> *I felt isolated; I felt alone* [in Jackson County]. *I grew up on a mountain* in the middle of nowhere, um, so *I didn't know any other out gay people.* Um, *I knew that—I suspected that my uncle was gay,* but he was in the closet until after *I came out.* Um, and so, you know, *I felt really alone,* and that's what caused a lot of depression. Feeling alone.
>
> What *I did know is that there were gay people* in the cities and *I had to get to a city,* and *I only knew of other gay people online* on the Internet . . . so *I found tons of gay people,* and *I realized that I wasn't alone.*

---

3. The analysis of participants' "I" statements is a central step in Listening Guide methodology. For more information, see Note on the Listening Guide Method.

David's voice immediately changes from despairing to hopeful when he shares his realization that there were openly gay people "in the cities." Like a number of other youth interviewed for this study, David's access to the Internet seems to have played a significant role in breaking through at least some of his isolation. As an adolescent, he used the Internet as his main resource for knowledge about places beyond Jackson County where gay people lived openly.

Along with hope, David's voice is marked at this point in the interview by determination as he explains that, from sixth grade on, his "mission" was to find a way out of his high schools and out of Jackson County: "I had to get to a city." Clearly, David was effective at applying himself to this mission: when the harassment at Jackson County had brought him to the brink of suicide, he persuaded his parents to allow him to transfer schools. Similarly, when he still was experiencing harassment (though less severely) at Platteville, he took the necessary steps to apply to college early and left for Carpenter College during what would have been his senior year.

David describes his first year of college in terms that are vastly different from those he uses when discussing either of the high schools he attended. For the first time in our interviews, his voice exudes enthusiasm as he describes his initial encounters at Carpenter. He describes with excitement the location of the school in a "liberal" urban center, the presence of out gay people on a panel during the college's preview sessions, the "liberal" curriculum that even includes a "queer class," and the presence of a gay student group:

> Yeah, it's like the polar opposite of the first day of high school. I— you know, I just felt like, "This is a liberal atmosphere." I remember going for April preview sessions, and there was a panel of students, and they talked about things going to Carpenter, and one of the kids in the big, huge audience asked someone on the panel what it was like to be a gay student at Carpenter. . . . So it's just been awesome, very supportive atmosphere. They had a gay group at the school, and I got involved in that, and then a friend told me about CityYouth, and I got involved in that, and the gay speaker's bureau, and I got involved in that.

It is clear from David's language in this passage (for example, his repetition of the phrase "I got involved in that") that he became significantly more positively engaged with his LGBTQ identity when he moved to the city and enrolled at Carpenter. His LGBTQ identity, instead of being silenced and hidden as it was during middle and high school, became a central aspect of his education, his extracurricular activities, and his personal relationships. This period seems to have been the first time in David's life when he felt accepted as an openly gay student, both by his school as an institution and by his peers. And, through involvement in LGBTQ youth groups in college and the community, he developed many affirming, supportive relationships that resulted in his actually feeling *fortunate* to be gay, an attitude that seems to have been unimaginable in his earlier surroundings:

> I feel, like, really, really good about it [being gay], because I feel like if I wasn't gay, but I was still different than everyone growing up, I wouldn't have found such a supportive, understanding community to help me deal. But because I was gay, I found this community of loving people who understood what I went through and understood who I was and were there to support me every second. I know I could call anybody at CityYouth if I needed them. I know I could call almost any known gay activist person in [the city], and if I needed them, they would be there. And if I wasn't gay, I don't know who—who I would call, and I know a lot of straight friends who don't have that kind of community. . . . I'm so happy that I am queer. I've made the best friends I'll ever make being queer; bonds that I think some people never make in their lives I've made because I've found people in the community. So, I love it.

The contrast between the level of support David receives from peer relationships in his college years compared to that he received in middle and high school is especially striking. While his childhood friends, he says, "kind of just faded away—they didn't want to be around me because it would embarrass them to be around me while I was being harassed," David's current friends now support him *because* he is gay, and they affirm his identity as such: "I've made the best friends I'll ever make being queer." This is also the first time in our interviews that David uses the word *queer* to describe himself, an identifier on which he elaborates in more sophisticated ways when we meet again during Phase II of the study.

In addition to introducing David to a different way of interacting with school, peers, and his community, David says the move to Carpenter and to the city has given him a new perspective on his previous circumstances and how they may influence his future career choices:

[After I moved to the city,] I just started getting really involved in everything, which really helped me heal. And it helped me feel like I was making a difference in other gay youths' lives because—I think it was like eighth grade when I told myself, 'I know what I'm going through—I know where I live—isn't normal.' Because I had access to the Internet, I had chat rooms and websites about queer youth in cities, and I had relatives that lived in Washington, D.C., and New York City, so I knew where I lived was atypical and everyone there wasn't the norm. . . . So I kind of made it my goal then to make a difference in the lives of other gay youth that were going through what I was going through, and that's why I'm so involved now with gay youth groups and stuff. And my experience in high school will definitely, like, stay with me forever and be a major—kind of like the engine that drives me to keep working to stop harassment and violence among gay youth. You know the suicide statistics; they really ring home because I know that was me, and I know other kids where I live are probably contemplating suicide right now because that school didn't change, and Jackson County didn't change, and—and so, hopefully I'll have a career in gay stuff.

Like several other youth who participated in the study, David expressed a strong commitment to social justice, the motivation for which he associates largely with the severe harassment he experienced in his earlier adolescence. When I met David for our second interview during Phase I, he was in fact beginning his career in what he called "gay stuff." He had accepted a staff position at CityYouth, he had started a website urging LGBTQ youth to become involved in community activism, and he had participated in and even planned several protests against political and religious institutions that had anti-LGBTQ policies. By the time we met a third time during Phase II of the study, David's career in "gay stuff" was well under way and had become an even more central component of his identity.

David as an Adult: An Established Career in "Gay Stuff"

Nearly seven years after David first became involved in the study, I met him again at age twenty-six, more than three thousand miles from the location of our previous meetings. He is now living in a large West Coast city known for its strong, politically active LGBTQ community and, as his original interviews foreshadowed, one of the central aspects of David's life on the West Coast is a career in LGBTQ issues. David is now a key staff member in an organization that supports families headed by LGBTQ parents. He also is the founder of an online LGBTQ activism network with more than six hundred members, a project he began while still living in the Northeast, and he has spoken about LGBTQ issues at dozens of rallies and educational events since our previous meetings. David's deep personal investment in LGBTQ issues is evident when he talks about the online network he started and his plans for its future:

> My dream [for the network], my hope is to get a fiscal sponsor underneath another nonprofit so that I can start taking donations and then grow it and have programs. . . . And one of the main roles of [the network] is to (a) build coalitions with other movements but also (b) to challenge the mainstream gay rights organizations to address the needs of the most oppressed in our community. . . . There's not a lot of gay groups out there that are loud and challenging the other gay rights groups. And so people call us divisive, or they, like, marginalize us as too radical or whatever, but we just keep doing what we're doing.

Thus, since his first LGBTQ-related job at CityYouth, David's sexual and gender identity has been a central component not only of his sense of self but also of his career and his politics, all of which he views as linked:

> It's [being queer is] still as big a part of my life as it was the last time we spoke, you know, if not more. I mean, it never has been a—that's never going to change. . . . And of course, my job is queer again. I had a couple of years there where my job was—I worked for a health-care organization one or two years after we spoke. And now I'm really happy to be back in the LGBT, nonprofit world where I can feel a little more—more fulfilled in my daily work and connected to it more. I mean, a lot of my time and a lot of my identity is still very much around queer [issues].

In his Phase II interview, David also expresses a much more complex and nuanced view of his gender and sexuality than he did when he was younger. Specifically, he explains that the word *gay* fails to express adequately who he believes he is and that *queer* and *gender queer* do a much better job of encompassing the many aspects of himself that he views as important to his identity:

I still think of myself as queer, and that, to me, really defines my
sexuality and my gender and my politics. That's how I describe it
to people when people ask me what *queer* means at a training or
something. I always divide it into those three categories. I say, sexually queer, kind of open-minded about sexuality and pro-sex positive
and, you know, kind of being willing to explore and challenge ideas
and my own thoughts about sexuality.

And then gender queer: I just don't identify as manly or a man.
I don't think many people view me that way. And I don't walk
through my life like a typical man, so that whole, like, man/woman,
blue/pink thing is messed up. So I challenge that, and I identify really as gender queer. I wear clothing that is—sometimes it's women's
clothing; sometimes it's men's. But it's gender queer.

And then politically: obviously, you know, I think *gay*—*gay*
leaves a bad taste in my mouth politically because now, I think especially, it's just come to mean gay marriage and, you know, kind of
the mainstream thing—like "we're just like everybody else" type of
stuff. And more and more I reject that and I identify my politics as
queer, and I think these issues are all—social justice issues are all so
intertwined. . . . I think I'm too gay to be gay. I have to be queer.

In addition to his nuanced adoption of the terms *queer* and *gender queer*
to describe himself, David also tells me in our Phase II interview that he has
a tattoo on his arm of the word *sissy*, which he had done several years before
moving to the West Coast. Clearly, this word also carries significant meaning for him as a defiant response to the ostracism and harassment he faced as
a teenager about his sexual and gender identity:

I think of that word [sissy] and what it means when it's used against
me and used against, you know, effeminate males. And it was kind
of like my reclaiming it and being like, "I'm strong, and I'm going to
put it on my arm, and if somebody calls me a faggot or a sissy, like,
I own it, and it's mine, and I—and I'm proud of it." And it's kind of
my challenge to the binary gender system and my little "fuck you"
to that system. . . . And it kind of reflected—it kind of symbolized
my moving on and my overcoming from, kind of the pain of, like,
oppression and kind of confronting it head-on.

Another central aspect of David's new life on the West Coast is his relationship with his partner, Jay, who moved with him from the Northeast.

David describes Jay as "the best thing in my life ever" and then quickly adds with a smile, "And I think I'm the best thing in his life ever." One of the many things David's relationship with Jay provides for him is balance amid the hectic world of LGBTQ advocacy and activism, which David admits sometimes exhausted him when they lived in the Northeast. Since their move west, David has learned to balance a busy work and activism schedule with more time for self-care and the nurturing of his relationship with Jay:

> I make more of an effort to go to the beach and relax and just have
> fun with my partner, whereas [back east] I—a lot of my time was
> just consumed with, like, activism nonstop. And so here—I said
> when we moved here I'm going to take a year or so to, like—I'm not
> going to overcommit myself to other organizations or volunteer work
> and stuff like that. I'm just going to cool off and, like, take care of
> myself. So I think I'm doing that.

David's relationship with Jay, however, seems to conform to a pattern that is seen in other areas of his life in that, when good things come his way, he is anxious about losing them:

> I think now we're in a really good place in our relationship, and we
> just keep growing our relationship, and it only gets better, you know?
> We talk about having—adopting kids one day and all that stuff. So
> that's really, I would say, the shining light in my life. Like that's the
> best thing in my life, and I think maybe that's why I can't help but
> fall into this kind of trap of, like, anxiety of, like, him dying or, like,
> awful things like that.

During our Phase II interview, David relates a shocking turn of events that began about a year before, one that has clearly been a significant source of stress for him and may even be related to the generalized feeling of anxiety he expresses about losing Jay and at various other points throughout our interview. David explains that his father, Andrew, is currently serving a three- to six-year prison term for a sex-related crime. According to David, Andrew was arrested as part of an undercover raid for attempting to solicit sex with a police officer who was posing online as an underage boy. In our Phase I interviews, David had expressed suspicions that his father was gay and was sexually involved with several men, including some David's own age, but even in this context David's revelation is surprising. Although David does not condone his father's actions, he maintains that Andrew was "entrapped" and says the incident has "caused a lot of despair," both for him personally and for the family:

> He's in jail now, yeah. So I have to deal with that on kind of a daily basis. Like thinking about my dad in jail and what he must be go-ing through, and I can't be there for him. The struggle he's going through trying to figure out his gay identity—since he's been in jail, he has come out to me as gay. I don't know that he's specifically said it to anyone else. He asked me not to really talk about it with my family. . . . I mean, I feel like now I'm really able to support my dad and his discovery of his identity and becoming comfortable with being a gay man and showing my dad there's a lot of other gay men here that I know about. And he wants to meet here [on the West Coast] if he's able, but there's a lot of obstacles to figure out how we could get him here after he's out of jail, if it's at all possible. I've always told him what I was doing around gay stuff, and I think he likes to hear it and, you know, just helping him, putting him in touch with stuff.

The fact that Andrew's sexuality has been forced into the open by his arrest also gives David some new perspectives on the dynamics of his family, particularly on his parents' silence about LGBTQ issues while he was grow-ing up. For David, Andrew's internal struggle with homosexuality, especially in the context of the rural community in which they lived, contributed to his parents' inability to address openly David's sexual identity and the ha-rassment he was facing at school. In light of this, David adopts a more for-giving tone than in his previous interviews when he considers the factors behind his father's silence:

> This, I believe, is partly why he never really talked about my gayness when I was struggling with it. He never really openly supported me or, like, helped me deal with what I was going through in high school. And I think it's because he was struggling so much with his own identity, or it was too much for him. But yeah, like, I'm trying my best to support him now.

The support David feels he must provide since his father's arrest and in-carceration also involves a change in his role with his mother, who has filed for divorce from Andrew. Although David now finds it extremely difficult to visit his mother and her relatives, who he says "always bring up negative stuff about my dad and my dad's side of the family," David was planning to go back east for Christmas shortly after our interview to try to support his mother because "she's been through a lot, too." Still, as David explains, this "parenting of his parents" takes an emotional toll on him:

> A lot of the support has to come from me, and it's a lot of pressure. And I always felt like I was parenting my parents, and now I'm parenting them even more, and that's frustrating, you know? . . . I can't take on all of my mom and dad's problems. You know, I just can't. And it's hard to detach from it, but I try.

Given the obvious stress associated with this difficult family situation, it is perhaps not surprising that the high level of satisfaction David expresses about his current life circumstances—his partner, his job, his online activism, and his new life on the West Coast—is tinged with a considerable level of anxiety. When I ask David to estimate on a scale of one to ten how happy he is with his life, he replies:

> Like an eight. I'm pretty happy with my life. But how happy I am is different than how happy I am with my life. Happiness is hard. That I would say fluctuates a lot. . . . Happiness is kind of fleeting. I don't know. I think what—I think what makes it hard to be fully happy would be the—kind of the anxiety about stuff. It's hard to be like—feel really whole and happy when you're anxious. And given what's going on with my parents and things like that, it's hard to be—to feel a sense of ease or happiness as well. Um, but with my life and the decisions I've made and my—in general, like, I feel really happy to be in [the city] and to have created kind of this perfect little modern gay life, you know? Like, I think a lot of people would be jealous of what I have now. Like, I live in a queer city with my partner, and we've been together for years, and I have a queer job, and I get to go—we get to travel together and have fun together, and so I feel really fortunate and happy about kind of the way that we've designed our life. I feel really good about that.

Even with the anxiety David feels about his father's current circumstances, he seems to have come to a point where he views his own feelings and experiences, his family-of-origin relationships, his relationship with his partner, and his work with a new sense of integrity that is firmly rooted in his LGBTQ identity:

[My father's situation] justifies the work that I've always been doing around queer activism. Like, I feel this is why I'm doing this work, and now it's so deeply ingrained in my life and my family. Like my queer identity, like you said before—that's why I was like, gosh, it's even more a part of me now. My dad's gay. My uncle's gay. And when this was all coming out, my brother said that my uncle said maybe their dad was gay. So that means my grandpa might have been gay. You know, it's just this creepy thing that has, like, trickled down and affected my life so deeply. And luckily, for whatever reason, I was able to process it and use it for activism.

Listening to David: A Silenced Adolescent Finds a Voice in Adulthood

David's experiences as a middle and high school student in rural America are all-too-representative of the isolation many rural LGBTQ youth report in research studies (Kosciw, Greytak, and Diaz 2009; Pearson, Wilkinson, and Muller 2007; Yarbrough 2003).[4] Except for the antigay harassment David says he experienced on a "constant" basis, he saw no reflection of his gay identity anywhere around him; the silence about LGBTQ issues in his world was pervasive. Despite many adults' having witnessed the taunting he endured at school, his teachers were silent. With no gay-straight alliance or discussion of LGBTQ issues in the curriculum, his school as an institution was silent. Except for one conversation that took place immediately after David came out to his parents as gay, his family was silent. And, perhaps most disturbing, David silenced himself in various ways during this period in order to survive in a heterosexist school, peer culture, and society.

At the most basic level, David's decision not to be out to most of his peers and none of his teachers during high school was one way in which he disengaged from an important aspect of his identity in order to survive in a homophobic context. It is certainly not uncommon for LGBTQ adolescents to delay coming out to others when they are unsure how the disclosure will be received, but David's self-silencing also took other forms and is thus illustrative of how LGBTQ youth may be vulnerable to what Miller and Stiver (1997) called the "central relational paradox" in their writings about the psychology of women and girls. Paradoxically, David kept central aspects of himself—his thoughts, his feelings, his voice—*out of his relation-*

---

4. For a discussion of the ways in which rural LGBTQ youth use resources in their communities to construct their identities and advocate for change, see Gray 2009.

ships with others, especially those he perceived had greater social power (or at least greater numbers), in order to remain *in these relationships*, despite how inauthentic or unsatisfying they may have been.

Although David did well academically at North Jackson, he spoke very little in his classes there: "I didn't even talk at North Jackson. I didn't— I never talked, unless I was called on, pretty much." David's censoring of himself in class is related to his choice not to audition for the school plays and musicals for fear that someone "might yell something out from the audience at me." Both decisions seem motivated by the desire to maintain a basic, survival-based level of "relationship" with the people at his school by not drawing any additional attention to himself. Yet these kinds of adaptive strategies cost David more than authentic relationships with his teachers and classmates (assuming these might even have been possible under the circumstances). They cost him things to which he was entitled as a student in a public school, such as the right to be an active participant in his own learning and the right to develop his talents through extracurricular activities.

The isolation that pervaded David's life while he attended North Jackson was exacerbated by a lack of communication and emotional connection in his family relationships. Although David found his parents to be financially supportive and ostensibly supportive of his identity as a gay youth once he came out at age fifteen, there was considerable emotional distance in this relationship, and little or no communication about the harassment he was experiencing at school and the emotional distress it was causing him. The "code of silence" under which David's family operated is especially evident—at least according to David—in his parents' denial of his father's homosexuality, a silence for which the entire family pays a heavy price later on.

Although David reports having had a few positive relationships during his middle and high school years, even these relationships seem to have been compromised by a lack of open communication. For example, among the few teachers David cites as having been supportive of him in middle and high school—including the closeted gay Spanish teacher and his choir teacher, who allowed him to skip gym class and attend voice lessons with her—David did not disclose his sexual orientation or discuss LGBTQ issues openly in any way. Thus, with few peers, school adults, or family members with whom he could share his thoughts and feelings—and given the ineffective response of his teachers, counselors, and administrators to the harassment he experienced at school—David seems to have largely been alone in coping with the daily abuse he faced, as well as any other issues related to his sexual orientation and gender identity he may have been going through at the time. Not only did this isolation serve as a source of emotional distress for him, but it also seems to have been connected in some way to serious risks such as suicidal and homicidal ideation and a possible eating disorder.

Despite the tremendous risks David faced as an LGBTQ youth living in a homophobic rural community, there exists throughout his story a consistent strain of resistance to the harassment and isolation he experienced as an adolescent. At first, David's response to his world was to draw inward: he considered suicide, developed what may have been an eating disorder, and fell silent at school. As discussed in the Introduction, this kind of *psychological resistance* helps a young person cope with the forces of oppression, but since the response is self-directed, it can also have devastating consequences for her or his mental and/or physical health (Brown and Gilligan 1992).

Fortunately for David, as early as middle school he also seems to have had awareness of a world outside his school district and hometown, and this awareness allowed him also to develop a resistance that was focused outward—a *political resistance*—over time (Brown and Gilligan 1992). During high school, David's political resistance took primarily nonpublic forms: he strategically navigated life at both of his high schools (modified his ways of walking and talking, kept his hand down in class, avoided certain activities) in order to survive in these homophobic contexts, while he secretly planned his escape from Jackson County. Jill McLean Taylor, Carol Gilligan, and Amy M. Sullivan call strategies like those David used in high school ones of *covert political resistance*, whereby a person subject to oppressive social conventions "outwardly appears to comply with the conventions but does so as a conscious strategy of self-protection" (1995, 26). Through his access to the Internet, David was able to envision a life for himself after high school where he would find relationships in which he could be accepted for who he was and to recognize that "I know what I'm going through—I know where I live—isn't normal."[5] Obviously, the extent to which David could act on this knowledge was limited by his age and other factors, but his ability to plan for a better future—thanks both to his family's financial resources and to his own powerful mindset of political resistance—may well have saved him from the more self-destructive ways of thinking and behaving in which he was also beginning to engage.

Once David left Jackson County and came to a supportive college and urban environment at age seventeen, his political resistance went public, and much of David's story can be read as a gradual evolution from private forms of resistance such as self-silencing and self-monitoring to *overt politi-*

---

5. See Harper et al. 2009 for a discussion of the Internet as a resource in the sexual identity development of gay- and bisexual-identified boys.

cal resistance (Taylor, Gilligan, and Sullivan 1995), acts aimed at demanding recognition and respect not only for himself but for other LGBTQ people. At this point in David's story—quite suddenly, it seems—many aspects of his day-to-day life turn around. For one thing, the severe relational violation he experienced in high school ends when he enrolls at Carpenter. (He gives no indication that he continued to experience harassment in college.) In addition, the isolation and silence about LGBTQ issues that David felt while attending the Jackson County and Platteville schools are replaced by open dialogue about issues central to his identity (including a "queer class"). Instead of peer relationships based on harassment and violence, David has friendships based on open communication, support, and acceptance in his new urban collegiate environment.

Again, while it is impossible to draw causal links between these relational experiences and other changes in David's life—David's greater maturity and independence as a college student obviously also play some role—it is notable that at this point in his interviews David says he feels "really, really good" about being queer, that he no longer has suicidal or violent ideations, and that he has committed himself to a career in public service. He takes on a leadership role at CityYouth (and eventually becomes a staff member there), becomes a speaker at educational and political events, and begins an online LGBTQ political network. Concurrent with the changes in David's relational world, a strong queer voice begins to emerge, which becomes even stronger in adulthood.

In David's voice today we hear many echoes of his life as an adolescent. David's decision to move to "a queer city" on the West Coast can be read in itself as an act of resistance against his past, since it represents a polar opposite to the life he lived as an isolated, primarily closeted queer youth in conservative Jackson County. David's current nuanced definition of his queer/gender queer/sissy identity is another overt form of resistance in defiance of the harassment, rejection, and silencing he experienced as an adolescent. In articulating his identity as such, David is, in very public ways, claiming the queer voice that was silenced in him years before. And, with his "sissy" tattoo, he is in a sense permanently writing this aspect of his identity on himself, challenging the way the word has been used as a weapon against him and the validity of binary conceptions of gender.

The strongest aspect of David's overt political resistance to his own and others' oppression is perhaps seen in his commitment to social change and in the centrality of LGBTQ issues to his vocational life: his speaking at educational events and rallies, his institution and maintenance of a large online LGBTQ activist network, and his current job working on behalf of families with LGBTQ members. David's resistant queer voice is especially evident in the specific role he plays within the LGBTQ activist world: "challeng[ing] the mainstream gay rights organizations to address the needs of the most oppressed in our community." Even within LGBTQ circles, David is attempting to "queer" the work of activists and resist what he sees as the oppression and exclusion of groups within the LGBTQ community.

David's long-term, committed relationship with Jay could be viewed as yet another act of resistance to his past, particularly when viewed in light of his adolescent experiences in Jackson County, where same-sex relationships were neither visible nor discussed. Within what David calls his "perfect little modern gay life" are obvious stress factors, including the verbal harassment he says he continues to experience occasionally in his home city and when he and Jay travel. In contrast to when David was an adolescent, however, he gives no indication that these experiences encourage him to censor his behavior or appearance to avoid drawing attention to himself: "When it happens now, I just feel bad for the people who are doing it."

The general anxiety David says affects his otherwise "perfect little modern gay life" as an adult raises questions about the extent to which David's past experience of prolonged and severe antigay harassment may still resonate with him today, but it is impossible in research of this nature to determine if it is related to any type of post-traumatic stress. The incarceration of David's father, Andrew, on sex-related charges obviously is a major source of stress in his current day-to-day life, one he says contributes significantly to his anxiety. Although David says he does not condone many of his father's past actions, however, the strength of David's queer identity serves, somewhat ironically, as an important asset in this anxiety-producing situation for the family. David's knowledge about and involvement in LGBTQ issues, his unambiguous embrace of his own sexuality and gender expression, and his empathy for Andrew's struggles in coming out as gay in Jackson County allow him to serve as a role model and mentor for Andrew and a source of support for his mother as they try to put their lives back together. And while David says that he sometimes resents having to "parent his parents" in this way, the experience also seems to give him a new perspective on his identity and his evolving role within the family. David's queer voice is now not only something in which he takes pride; it is something he uses to be of valuable service to some of the most important people in his life.

2

Lindsey: Learning a New Language

"I can talk to people now. Like, I never used to be able
to talk to people. . . . I never talked to anybody, and that
was hard."

S itting on an old sofa in the "hangout" room at YouthWest on a Saturday
afternoon, fifteen-year-old Lindsey is an open book. With her straight
brown hair flowing down to the middle of her back, baggy untucked
shirt, and fluid way of walking and moving, Lindsey exudes ease—that rare
teenager who seems extremely comfortable in her own skin—and the forth-
coming way in which she tells her story is in keeping with her physical presentation. Lindsey checked the boxes "female" and "bisexual" on the study's
preliminary survey, but when I ask in our first interview how she identifies
herself in terms of her gender and sexual orientation, she simply says in a
confident and self-possessed voice, "I don't identify. . . . I'm Lindsey."[1]

As Lindsey tells me later in this first interview, however, being at ease
with herself and trusting that others would accept her did not always come
easily: "Like, if you would have met me a year ago—I'm a totally different
person." Unprompted by questions about "voice" or any other concepts that
would much later become organizing themes of this book, Lindsey names
honest and open communication with others as the major factor in her turnaround: "I can talk to people now. Like, I never used to be able to talk to

---

1. Because Lindsey uses the term *gay* when describing her coming-out process and the harassment
she experienced at school, I also use that term to discuss those incidents. During high school,
Lindsey first came out as bisexual and, in her Phase II interview, she identifies as lesbian, so I use
those terms in those contexts. Otherwise, I use the term LGBTQ to describe Lindsey in order to
avoid placing her into a distinct category.

people. I just—I didn't care. I never talked to anybody, and that was hard. I feel so much more open and so much more free now."

Harassment, Family Rejection, and a Suicide Attempt

The story of how Lindsey learned to "talk to people" begins in middle school where, like David in Chapter 1, she endured extreme harassment because of perceptions about her sexual orientation, even before she was out to others or herself as lesbian, gay, or bisexual. Lindsey's older sister, Kelly, was one of the chief perpetrators of this abuse, taunting Lindsey both at home and at school and acting as a ringleader among her friends:

> And, um, my older sister, she was just—oh, I hate her. When I was, like, in sixth grade, she had, like, all of her friends that were—all her friends on the bus. . . . They'd pick up rocks and throw them at me and call me a dyke, and, like, they'd pull my hair and try to trip me and stuff. And Kelly would just laugh with them and just, like, have a good old time. She was like, "Yeah, I call her a fag. She hates it." It was horrible.

In addition to Kelly and her friends, Lindsey says that other peers in middle school bullied her and that this made school "really hard" for a long time. To make matters worse, when Lindsey came home, the harassment continued, leading her to doubt whether she could ever safely come out to the family. In addition to Kelly, Lindsey's stepfather verbally abused her, calling her names like "dyke" and "carpet muncher." Lindsey associates her inability to escape from this abuse with a suicide attempt she made when she was thirteen years old:

> School was, like, really hard. Everybody was always, like, you know, calling me things. . . . I had a lot of friends, but there was always, like, that group of people that liked to call me a dyke and just—I was, like, I was goth and everything. So I used to dress different, and people'd just, like, pick on me and just, you know, say shit. And so, I was like—I just got really fed up with it. And then, like, I'd go home, and I'd have to listen to my stepdad calling me things. And him and my sister would, like—my older sister—would start, you know, saying things, and I would just like—I couldn't take it anymore; it was horrible. And my mom, like, found some of my poetry or something, and my poetry talked a lot about death and dying and

stuff like that. And she was really worried, I guess, and I, like, tried to slit my wrists or whatever, and she stopped me, and all this crap happened. Um, it was really hard.

Upon discovering that Lindsey was suicidal, Lindsey's mother had her admitted to a local crisis center and, subsequently, to a mental hospital in a city about a two-hour drive from the family's home. Although Lindsey did not attempt suicide while in the hospital, she continued the wrist and forearm cutting in which she says she engaged throughout her middle school years. As Lindsey explains it, the cutting sometimes resulted from a desire to kill herself but at other times was precipitated by the need to find an outlet for her emotional distress:

> If I was mad or—you know, I had to—I can't express myself, or I couldn't express myself very well. I couldn't talk to people. I wasn't very social at the time, and I couldn't talk to people, so I couldn't—I couldn't find a way to get the pain out, so I just took it out on myself when I was mad; if I was sad, you know, I just marked it on myself to get the pain out, you know? I wanted to show the pain that I was feeling on the inside on the outside, to make it kind of go away. So it kind of made it feel—I don't know. It made me know that I was alive still. I don't know how to explain it, really.

The fact that Lindsey begins her explanation of the thought process that led to her cutting with statements like "I couldn't express myself very well" and "I couldn't talk to people" underscores her unmet need to communicate her experience to others. In one sense, Lindsey's cutting could be viewed as an expression, albeit a self-destructive one, of her voice, a desire to reach out and communicate where words—and, perhaps more importantly, her relationships—failed her. Since at this point she was still unable to talk or write about what she was experiencing and feeling, she "marked it on myself to get the pain out." Paradoxically, while at times Lindsey associates this wrist cutting with suicidal thoughts, she also describes it as something that "made me know that I was alive still," a coping strategy that helped her survive amid a failure to make the kinds of relational connections she so desperately wanted.

Lindsey remembers her experiences at the mental hospital as extremely stressful. She says she was on multiple medications "and none of them worked" and that one of the doctors made sexual advances toward her. Also, she still has scars from the cutting she engaged in while an inpatient.

Nevertheless, the hospital seems to have represented a sort of "rock bottom" experience for Lindsey, after which her life slowly began to turn around and she was able to make more positive connections with a number of people in her relational world.

An Improvement in Lindsey's Family Relationships

One of the relationships that underwent the most dramatic turnaround after Lindsey's hospitalization, which ended about fourteen months before our first interview, was with her stepfather. As Lindsey explains:

> I guess our relationship's changed a lot, like, in the past year. Um, we've gotten a lot closer. I ended up, um, getting really depressed and, um, everything that was going on, just like, everything was getting really bad, and then when he found out I tried to commit suicide. And I went to a mental hospital, and that's when our relationship started to build and we started getting really close. And I guess that's when he started appreciating me for me.

Like many of the participants my colleagues and I interviewed during Phase I of the research, Lindsey mentions her parents immediately when I ask her to identify the most important relationships in her life. Whereas some participants described parental relationships with ambivalence, emphasizing both deep connections and disconnections, Lindsey describes her relationship with her mother in exclusively positive, even effusive terms: "I have a really close relationship with my mom, which is kind of weird, but, um, my mom is like my best friend, and I talk to her about everything, and she's just a part of me—and that's, like, the best relationship right there."

When I ask Lindsey what makes her relationship with her mother as strong as it is, she first mentions her mother's acceptance and support when Lindsey ultimately came out to her as gay. One of the ways this support was most evident was the ultimatum Lindsey says her mother gave to her stepfather at this crucial moment in Lindsey's life:

> She told him, you know, like, "Either you're gonna appreciate my daughter and love her, or you can leave." . . . So she supports me in any way she can, whether it be school, whether it be with my—my girlfriend; she takes me over there. I mean, she does everything she can for me. You know, my father left me when I was little. And my

mom has been, like, my mother and my father. She raised me, and she's like my backbone, and just like I can—you know, that's, um, I don't know. She's just the person that I can talk to about anything, and she just—I—I love her to death, and, uh, I don't really know what to say about her. But she's just there for me no matter what. I could tell her anything.

In addition to Lindsey's mother's insistence that her husband "appreciate my daughter and love her," Lindsey speaks here to a number of other ways in which she believes her mother now "supports me in any way she can": taking her to her girlfriend's house (which Lindsey realizes is something not every parent of an LGBTQ youth would do), helping her with schoolwork, and serving as "both my mother and my father" since Lindsey's biological father left the family. Lindsey says of her mother three times in our initial interview that she can "tell her anything." As is evident throughout our interviews, both in Lindsey's adolescence and young adulthood, this ability to communicate "about anything" is central to all of the relationships she views as closest and most supportive.

Lindsey's Transition to High School

Following Lindsey's release from the mental hospital, she completed eighth grade and then enrolled in her region's technical high school that fall. At first, Lindsey says, she once again faced harassment based on her sexual orientation similar to that she endured in middle school:

Well, my first day—um, we had orientation the first day, but my second day of my freshman year, which was this year, um, I was walking down the hallway with one of my friends, and some of the seniors started calling me "Butch." And I was like, "Uh-oh." And then they were like, "Hey, President Butch!" And I was like, "Oh, that's very—that's original!" And it was like, you know, that wasn't helpful at all, and, like, it was horrible. Like, my first five months of high school were horrible.

Directly after describing her first five months of high school as "horrible" (the same word she also used to describe her middle school experiences and the harassment that went on there and at home), Lindsey describes how a friend's recommendation resulted in a major turnaround:

And, um, my friend Sam told me about the GSA, and, um, I was like, "What the hell's a GSA?" Like, we never had 'em around here, because I go to a vocational school. And um, so I talked to the school nurse, who was the leader of our GSA or whatever, and, um, she was talking to me about it, and I came to a couple of groups [meetings], and, like, I was talking to them about [the harassment]. . . . And, like, they're like, "Oh, we'll talk to them [the bullies]," and they did, and eventually everything just stopped. Like they just—[*snaps fingers*]. Everything stopped.

According to Lindsey, the juniors and seniors in her school's gay-straight alliance (GSA) spoke to the students who had been harassing her and "just made them realize that that wasn't okay and that it was hurtful." From this point on in the interview, Lindsey discusses her school experiences almost exclusively in positive terms and says she has found connections and friendships not only in the GSA but also with adults in her school community and with other groups of students in both academic and nonacademic settings.

Lindsey attended Clay Technical High School (Clay Tech), a school she depicts as generally accepting and supportive of sexual-minority students, although she says some of her classmates are still "closed-minded and racist and homophobic." Lindsey believes her school's climate is aided by the presence of faculty who are either openly LGBTQ themselves or "out" in their support of LGBTQ students. Lindsey feels an especially close relationship with Janice Lane, the school nurse who is the advisor of the school's GSA. Lindsey views Janice as a trusted adult ally with whom she can talk openly and honestly:

The person I trust most in my school to talk to as, like, an adult would be Janice, and she's a nurse. And um, I talk to her about anything, you know, because I'm just—she's a GSA leader, and, um, she just listens, and she's been there, and, you know, I can just talk to her.

In describing the relationship she shares with Janice, Lindsey uses similar language to that she uses when describing her relationship with her mother. ("I can talk to her about anything. . . . She just listens. . . . I can just talk to her.") It is also important to Lindsey that, because Janice is lesbian, she has "been there" and can understand Lindsey's experience on that level.

In addition to Janice, Lindsey mentions her English teacher, Mr. Martin, as someone with whom she feels supported in her LGBTQ identity:

Mr. Martin, my English teacher, he—he lets us write a lot of essays about things like sexual orientation and gender and things. And he just lets us, like, go wherever we want with them. I wrote one essay on gender. It was, like, twelve pages long. So that was pretty cool. He's one—he's the best teacher ever. . . . And we were sitting there talking about my essay, because he goes over the essay, and he goes, like, "I don't know anyone that's transgender." I was like—I was like, I know a couple people. . . . He just gets really into it.

For Lindsey, the interest that Mr. Martin shows in her paper on transgender identity seems to be a powerful motivator. Whereas some teachers might steer students away from LGBTQ issues for fear that they are too controversial for classroom discourse, Lindsey says Mr. Martin "just gets really into it." He shows a strong interest in the topic and encourages Lindsey to pursue it, thus broadening her own knowledge about LGBTQ issues and receiving school credit for studying a subject she is eager to know more about. Here, Lindsey gets another opportunity to develop her voice, this time through writing, about issues that clearly are important to her.

Overall, Lindsey has a positive attitude about school and describes herself as "good in academics," except for math. As one might predict from the degree to which communication is important to Lindsey in her relationships, she adds, "I like English. I like poetry. I like Shakespeare. I like to read." Another reason why Lindsey enjoys her high school experience is that she feels accepted and supported in transgressing the traditional boundaries of gender and sexuality. In the following interview excerpt, Lindsey even goes so far as to say, "I love school," and she articulates how her ability to choose a carpentry shop has contributed to her viewing school as a place where she feels she can express her true self:

School's awesome. I love school. Um, I'm going to a tech school. I'm in carpentry, which is a guy's shop. . . . So, I took that step; I didn't go into like an all-girls' shop like cosmo [cosmetology] or office tech or something to try and make myself feel better or anything. I, yeah, I—I don't know. I feel a lot better that I did that than—I chose a shop that I really wanted instead of choosing a shop that I would fit in. And the guys, they love me; they call me one of the guys, and, you know, it's great. Um, my grades are pretty good, except math, but other than that, I'm good. The teachers love me, and I'm in GSA and stuff.

Lindsey is also out as bisexual at school, another factor that seems to contribute to her comfort in and enjoyment of her school environment. At the end of the previous passage, she cites being "in GSA" as one of the things that contributes to her enjoyment of school, as well as the fact that "the teachers love me," a set of relationships that does not seem to have been damaged by Lindsey's disclosure of her sexual orientation. At the time of our initial interview Lindsey has been in a four-month relationship with another female student, Alana. Lindsey says that she and Alana are "totally out" at school and often hold hands in the hallways. Instead of making them subject to ridicule, however, Lindsey says that her relationship with Alana has resulted in their being a sort of "class couple" that many of her peers look up to:

> People at school think it's so cute that we're together. Like, the freshmen and stuff, they'll come to us and be like—the last day of school we must have got, like, twenty people taking our picture. "We want to remember you guys." Click! . . . Like the freshmen are really open to that, I guess. Like, a lot of them are my friends, and they just, like, respect me, and it's really cool. I appreciate that a lot.

In contrast to her middle school environment, Lindsey sees Clay Tech as a place where she can be who she is without negative consequences—and even be respected and liked *because* she is an LGBTQ student.

Connections in the Community

When I ask Lindsey to identify other supportive relationships, one of the first things she mentions is YouthWest (the LGBTQ youth group from which she was recruited for the study) and its umbrella social service organization, Middle Counties Advocacy (MCA). As in Lindsey's descriptions of other relationships she finds important in her life, she stresses the value of open communication, which she says makes her experiences at MCA and YouthWest especially beneficial: "The things that helped me most are, like, coming here to MCA. Like, everybody here is so understanding and just like—I can tell these people anything in, um, YouthWest."

As another venue in which Lindsey feels she is able to talk to people "about anything," she associates MCA and YouthWest with the recent turnaround in her life, before which she "never talked to anybody" and after which she feels "so much more open and so much more free now." In addition, Lindsey says YouthWest (along with her school's GSA) is a source of close, supportive friendships based on a level of mutual respect and honesty she had not experienced before. She believes this relatively newfound capacity to be "close to people" also carries over into other aspects of her life:

> I have a lot more friends that I keep in touch with, you know? I get really close to people, closer than I ever have. I talk about things, you know? When I develop a relationship, it becomes very strong. I'm close with my parents, my sisters, even though, you know, we fight a lot. And now we have kind of a strong bond, and I respect everybody now as long as they respect me.

Lindsey also contrasts her "before" and "after" periods by explaining that she hasn't experienced depression since shortly after her release from the mental hospital. Even when one of her best friends, Jake, died as the result of an asthma attack at age fifteen, Lindsey was able to cope with her grief without its plunging her into a prolonged depression: "I don't know what changed, really. I think that I just got stronger and that I just learned to live with who I was." In addition, Lindsey says that in the past two years she has turned away from violence as a solution to her problems. Whereas before Lindsey would often resort to fighting as a way to resolve conflicts at school (including incidents in which she was victimized with antigay harassment), her newfound respect for herself and for others has encouraged her to work toward ending violence in a variety of ways. Lindsey now has a job with a conflict resolution group through MCA:

> I changed a lot, you know. I'm not—I haven't gotten in a fight in like two years. Um, I work at a violence prevention group now. I respect people. I respect myself. I teach other people, you know, about what I've been through. I talk to other people who are going through the same thing, and I think that makes the difference in people's lives, and I've just, you know, grown to—to really respect myself first before I respect anybody else, and I think that was a big part of my life, was learning how to respect myself. And I think that's what changed, was I started respecting myself, and then I started respecting other people. I think it was, like, after I got out of the hospital I learned that I needed to change, and I never wanted to go back to a place like that again.

Finally, when I ask Lindsey what she is hopeful about for the future, she returns to the themes of self-respect, service to others, and the power of her own voice that resonated throughout our Phase I interviews: "Just knowing that there's a future. . . . Just knowing that it's going to change and knowing that I can make a difference and knowing that my voice counts."

A Glimpse at Lindsey's Future: Catching Up at Age Twenty-One

When I began recontacting study participants for Phase II of the research, I was pleased to see that Lindsey's openness and eagerness to communicate had not been diminished by the potential stresses of adulthood. I contacted Lindsey by e-mail, reminding her of who I was and what the research was all about (as I felt I needed to do with all respondents after six or seven years), and received an immediate response: "Hey, buddy!" And, yes, she would be happy to meet again and talk about how her life and relationships had changed since we had last met.

In keeping with Lindsey's socially oriented style, we agreed to meet for an early dinner at a burrito and taco restaurant near Lindsey's home, in the same town where our initial interviews had taken place. Having already told her friend Sam, who dropped her off at the restaurant, all about the research project on the ride over, Lindsey seemed eager to start the interview. Except for the fact that she had cut her waist-length hair to her neckline (five years before, as I was to learn later), Lindsey seemed in many ways simply a more mature version of the candid, easygoing adolescent I had met at age fifteen.

Since our first interviews had taken place at the end of Lindsey's freshman year, we began our conversation by catching up on her later years of high school. She reiterated that the difficult experiences she had had with harassment during her first months at Clay Tech were followed by a dramatic turnaround, prompted largely by support from friends in the gay-straight alliance and an openly LGBTQ adult mentor. When I remind Lindsey that she was a freshman in high school when we last spoke, she remembers:

> When I was a freshman, yep. In school—school for me was really hard. I mean, I had, like, long hair, and I always dressed in like baggy pants, a hoodie. Like, I didn't care, you know? I still don't care. I just dress how I'm comfortable. They used to call me like—one of my [harassers'] favorite nicknames was President Butch. That was probably the most unique, and I used to get picked on by other guys.
>
> But I linked up with this kid named Sam. He was actually trans at the end [of high school], and we were like best friends. He was a

senior, and I was a freshman. . . . He made everybody stop hassling me, like stop, you know, picking on me and said, "That's my friend." You know? And he introduced me to, like, GSA, and I got really into that.

So I was, like, planning events and, like, talking with the nurse [also the school's GSA advisor]. The nurse—our school nurse—amazing woman. Amazing. She'd been married to her partner for like thirty-something years, and her partner loves me. We hang out sometimes now that I graduated, and we're like—she was, like, a really big support for me. She, um, she really, like, was there through everything.

Lindsey then goes on to describe how, after her freshman year, she took on a "career" as an activist and educator at the school, one she would have until graduation. During her sophomore year Lindsey went to a dean at Clay Tech and asked if she could conduct classroom visits to educate freshmen about anti-LGBTQ language and harassment:

I brought that to my dean, and I was like, "This is what I want to do." And at first he was like, "Oh, I don't really think that's a good idea." Like, "People's parents are going to get mad." I was like, "By this time, they're freshmen in high school. They're exposed to all sorts of things." I was like, "I could be sitting there exposing them to drugs and alcohol and all that. But I'm trying to let them know what things are out there."

Once the school administrators agreed, Lindsey, along with several other members of the GSA, facilitated education sessions about homophobia for freshman classes:

A lot of times I opened up with like, "Who knows who Matthew Shepard is?" Nobody. Nobody knew, you know? And I'd be like, "Let me tell you the story about Matthew Shepard." And I would go on, and I'd tell the story, like, "All because he was gay." And then, like, you could see the faces, like people's faces just completely changed. . . .

I love talking to people because I love people's reactions. I love how they're like—you can see them thinking. You can see them like—they'd be really mad. I just love to, like, be out there and talking to people and educating people because a lot of people don't know. I mean, it's—it's not like everyone has the knowledge I have. It's not like everyone grew up getting spit on and beat up because they were gay. They don't, you know—some people just say, "Oh, that's gay." Or, you know, "That's retarded." Well, listen, think about what you're saying. I love to be that. I love people to go, "Wow."

In another aspect of her mission to make Clay Tech a safer school for LGBTQ youth, Lindsey says that when she was in the upper grades she took on the project of documenting fellow students' use of anti-LGBTQ language in the hallways and brought a report to the attention of faculty and administrators:

I walked in [to a meeting of faculty members], and I was like, "This is what's going on. The hallway is like—it's not that I'm scared because I'm strong and, like, I don't care. But there's freshmen here, there's sophomores here, there's kids that haven't established them-selves as being gay. They don't know, and they're scared to come out. Like, this is supposed to be a safe place." And I, like, had tears in my eyes, and I was like, "I'm begging for your help. Like, I can't do this by myself." And then, like, the faculty was asking questions: "What can we do? How can we help?" And I'm like, "Listen, this is what you need to do. This is what you need."

Lindsey's work teaching others about homophobia and other LGBTQ issues extended beyond her own high school, through an education and out-reach group she participated in as part of her work at MCA. Like her high school interventions, visiting other schools and colleges as a guest speaker about LGBTQ issues seems to have given Lindsey a strong sense of agency and purpose, and it helped her realize the difference she can make in other people's lives. While out celebrating her eighteenth birthday, Lindsey recalls:

This guy grabbed my hand and was like, "Lindsey!" I was like, I have no idea—I still don't know his name. I don't know who he is. He's like, "You changed my life!" And I was like, "Who are you?" He was like, "You spoke in Grayville [a nearby college town]." And I was like, "I did?" He's like, "You changed my life. You made me de-cide to come out of the closet." And he gave me the biggest hug I've ever received in my entire life, and I was like, "I changed somebody's life!" Because all the people I've talked to, even if I just changed that

one kid's life, like, that makes me feel good. It makes me feel like
I can do anything. . . .

I feel like my high school career, quote-unquote, made a difference. I talked to people—I talked to probably five thousand kids in
my life . . . but I had to have—I had to have changed some of those
people, you know?

Concurrently with Lindsey's work educating others about sexual orientation and gender identity, she seems to have also developed a different relationship to herself during her later years in high school, including a greater
acceptance of her own unique sexuality and a rejection of gender-bound expectations about her appearance:

I got to this point where I was, like, so comfortable in my own skin
that like it was—it's unbelievable how much I changed since freshman year, when I was kind of like, "Yeah, I'm bisexual. I'm not really
gay," and this and this. And then I was like, "Why am I even trying
to fool myself? I can't fool these people." I'm like, "I like girls. I don't
like guys. I only like girls. Like, this is me. . . ."

And sophomore year I cut my hair off, which was really, really
hard for people to get used to. I used to get yelled at for going in
the girls' bathroom a lot. . . . I always wanted to be like GI Jane and
shave it. So I did. My mom was not impressed. But, um, shortly
after junior year I joined the Army National Guard.

Lindsey's adoption of a "GI Jane" identity through service in the Army
National Guard seems connected to her choice to express gender in her own
unique way, but it also echoes other themes that run throughout her story.
Like her efforts to educate her high school peers, teachers, and others about
LGBTQ issues, Lindsey's National Guard service was a way in which she
expressed her deep connection to other people through service:

I feel like the National Guard is there to—to be there when things
happen in your state. Like that's what the Guard is for. When Hur-
ricane Katrina happened, they deployed the Guard, Guards from
all over the United States, to go help. And like with this thing in
Haiti,[2] the Guard units are everywhere over there, you know? It's

---

2. The 2010 Haiti earthquake took place shortly before our interview.

not the active-duty army that's doing everything. It's the National Guard. That's what I thought I needed to do to keep the people in my country safe.

After serving in the Army National Guard for several years (attending trainings and participating in service projects mostly on weekends), Lindsey suffered a fractured spine in a car accident, an event that ultimately led to her resignation from the Guard when the training exercises became too physically demanding. Yet she even discusses her departure from the Guard in service-oriented terms: "I was just [thinking], 'You know what? I'm wasting your money. I'm wasting my time. I'm going to get out and let a soldier in who can do the job, be there for people.'" If her injuries heal sufficiently, Lindsey says she'd consider reentering national service at a later date, "but I'd go active into the army, just because they really take care of you."

Current Close Relationships in Lindsey's Life

At the time of our Phase II interview, Lindsey was working as a prep cook at a local chain restaurant, a job she discusses with great enthusiasm. She enjoys the food preparation work and the relatively low stress of working in the restaurant's kitchen (instead of out front waiting tables), but Lindsey's favorite aspect of her job is clearly her relationship with her male coworkers, a group she says is "like a family" in which she is a "little brother." Three coworkers in particular are central to Lindsey's current support system: "They're like family. And they just—they build me up—nothing but build me up. If I'm ever having a bad day, 'Lindsey, smile. You're beautiful.' You know, like anything to make me feel better."

Another mainstay of Lindsey's current support system is her girlfriend, Robin, who is twenty-nine and lives about an hour away in another state. Despite the distance, Lindsey says Robin will drop anything (and has) when Lindsey needs support. For example, when Lindsey found out that a close friend had died:

Robin drove over and came and got me. I spent the night at her house, and, you know, for the funeral and stuff she was like, "Do you want me to take some time off work to go?" And I was like, "No, I'm going to go with my friends." Like I said, she's my support for anything. I just call her up and go, "Listen, I need you right now." And she'll put everything aside and drop anything to be there for me.

At the time of our Phase II interview, Lindsey had recently moved back in with her mother, sisters, and stepfather after finding out that a young man with whom she had been sharing an apartment "was into drugs and stuff, and I was like, 'I can't be around this guy.'" As in our first interview, Lindsey describes her family relationships as close and supportive despite a period in her early teens during which she was emotionally abused by her stepfather and older sister. As is perhaps typical of young adult children who "return to the nest," however, Lindsey says she is finding it difficult to live under her mother's rules again: "It's a hard adjustment to make, because once you have your freedom and you do whatever you want whenever you want, it's like—it's hard."

Lindsey says that she and her older sister, Kelly, "still fight a lot," but she has a close relationship with her younger sister, Chloe, who is fourteen years old. Lindsey even has Chloe's name tattooed on her arm: "She's wise beyond her years. . . . She doesn't always understand, but she can put her hand on my shoulder and say, 'It's okay, Lindsey. Don't worry about it.'" Perhaps most surprising, Lindsey's relationship with her previously abusive stepfather has become one of the most important in her life since our last interview:

> My stepdad and I are, like, very, very close now. We weren't before. He really didn't like me. He didn't like me being gay. He didn't like a lot of things. And I think he kind of just like got to know me aside from everything else. . . . And like we'd go out and work on cars together. He's a tow truck driver, so we'd go and pick up cars. You know, he'd be like, "Let's look under the hood, and let's see what's wrong with this thing." And we'd, like, figure it out together. He really became like a role model for me. I looked up to him more. He's a great guy. That's a lot different from what I thought about him before.

Most strikingly, Lindsey's relationship with her stepfather seems to have grown closer through activities that cross traditional gender boundaries. Like Lindsey's participation in carpentry shop in high school, Lindsey's interest in auto repair runs counter to what is normally considered the typical range of women's interests. In embracing this side of Lindsey and using it as a point of connection, her stepfather now seems able to grow closer to her and play a much more supportive role in her life.

Lindsey's rejection of gender-bound notions about interests and activities was evident in her interviews at age fifteen but seems even more pronounced in her young adulthood as she discusses her Army National Guard service and her relationships with her coworkers and stepfather. Similarly, Lindsey's ideas about gender reflect a rejection of rigid norms of behavior and a desire to have people focus on who she is as an individual, not a "label":

> I just feel like gender plays too much of a role in, like, the way you talk to somebody or the way you are around somebody. I don't—you know people say in public, "Act like a lady." Come on. You know, act like you have some respect, not act like a lady. . . .
>
> I mean, like I feel like everyone wants a label, and I don't. I'm just happy. That's who I am, you know? . . . People call me "sir" all the time, and everybody's like, "Why don't you get mad?" I'm like, because that's how they see me. Gender is just—it's basically, you know, it's what people see.

Looking Ahead

Looking into the future, Lindsey sees a number of possibilities at her still-young age of twenty-one, all of which are connected to themes that have come up earlier in our interviews. In addition to staying in the restaurant business and enjoying the family-like atmosphere of her job, Lindsey says she is interested in perhaps becoming a police officer in the future. As a police officer, Lindsey believes she can "be there" for others (as she was in the Army National Guard) and serve as an LGBTQ role model:

> I like protecting people. I know people think of police officers and think of getting pulled over on the highway or this or this, but they don't think of, "Well, this guy is breaking into your house, and you're calling the police." Like who is going to come there and be there for you? Like that's what I want to do. I want to be a friend in the community. I want to be like the, "Look at this girl. She's a cop. She's a lesbian." I can be a role model at the same time as I am protecting people.

Alternatively, having not attended college yet, Lindsey is considering going back to school to study public speaking and/or communications so that she can expand on her previous work educating others about homophobia and "be there" in a different capacity: "That's, like, my goal in life—to educate people and be there with them. Let me speak for you. Let me speak for those people that can't speak. Let me be your protection. I'll be there. That's like—that's what I do. That's what I would love to do on a regular basis."

Listening to Lindsey: A Journey from Silence to Service

The two related themes running through all three of my interviews with Lindsey (two at age fifteen and one at age twenty-one) are relationships and communication. In cliché terms, Lindsey might be called the ultimate people person: She feels deeply connected to the family and friends who make up her immediate sphere, and she feels a responsibility to educate and "be there" for others whom she does not know personally but who nevertheless may need her help. In discussing both her immediate and community relationships, Lindsey returns again and again to the importance of talk, whether it is in a one-on-one conversation with a friend or an address in a high school auditorium. This is in direct contrast to the person Lindsey says she was in her early teens, who "couldn't talk to people." Certainly Lindsey's maturation over time has played a role in her learning how to communicate more effectively with others, but additional factors also seem to have contributed greatly to Lindsey's belief that she has a voice worth listening to, one that she does not have to silence or modify in her relationships and that can serve as a force for good in the world.

The findings of psychologist Lisa Machoian, a coinvestigator for Phase I of this project who has conducted extensive research on depression among adolescent girls, provides a useful lens through which to view the theme of communication and how it evolves in Lindsey's story. Machoian notes that suicidal and self-harming behaviors peak for girls between ages thirteen and fifteen (Machoian 2001; Gilligan and Machoian 2002; Machoian 2005); Lindsey was thirteen when she says her wrist cutting led to a suicide attempt and her mother had her admitted to a mental hospital. As Carol Gilligan and Lisa Machoian explain, girls' violent acts of self-mutilation and self-harm are often motivated by a desire not to annihilate themselves but instead to communicate thoughts and feelings they are unable to articulate in other ways:

> When their speaking voices are not heard or when they have no
> words to say what they feel and think, children and adolescents will
> often speak in the indirect discourse of symptoms, enacting or say-
> ing indirectly what they want and know. Running away, stealing,
> cutting, starving, bingeing, and suicidal behavior can all be seen as
> forms of communication. (2002, 322)

Lindsey describes the motivations behind her wrist cutting in her early teens as complex—in one sense suicidal but in another motivated by a seemingly opposite impulse to find a lifeline to relationships in which she felt unable to speak. ("I was trying to get the pain of what I was feeling inside on the outside.") Lindsey's description of her motivation for cutting is strikingly similar to one offered by Skyla, a participant in one of Machoian's studies: "It was a way to get out the pain that was inside of me. If I'm watching my blood leave me, it was as if that would be some of the pain leaving too" (Machoian 2005, 83).

However one might interpret the severe wrist-cutting event that led to Lindsey's being admitted to a mental hospital, it was after this incident that Lindsey's family finally seems to have heard her voice. Whereas Lindsey had previously felt isolated and unsafe because of the extreme verbal abuse perpetrated by her stepfather and older sister, this critical moment seems to have led to an abrupt shift. Lindsey's mother suddenly became aware of the distress she was in, and the two forged a new relationship in which Lindsey could be who she really was and could "tell her [mother] anything." Lindsey's mother's ultimatum to her husband ("Either you're gonna appreciate my daughter and love her or you can leave") also helped catalyze a new relationship between Lindsey and her stepfather that continues to grow stronger to this day. As Lindsey experienced, and as Gilligan and Machoian observe:

> Violence is a language that people understand and take seriously.
> When girls threaten to harm or kill themselves or place themselves
> in dangerous situations, for example, by running away, people do
> take notice. Thus girls learn that people respond to threats of danger
> and self-directed violence. (2002, 322)

As Machoian, Gilligan, and others also note, however, it is important not to dismiss adolescents' suicidal acts and other self-harming behaviors as mere "cries for help." In addition to their inherent danger, these behaviors often represent an extreme expression of a young person's need for relational connection, a need that, if unmet, can lead to additional serious consequences.[3] Survey research has shown consistently that LGBTQ youth have suicide attempt rates four to five times higher than their heterosexual peers (Massachusetts Department of Elementary and Secondary Education 2010), and in far too many cases they succeed at killing themselves. Lindsey was fortunate enough to have had her need for open communication fulfilled, and her family relationships—once severely damaged by verbal and

---

3. Machoian (2001) and others also note that the etiology of self-mutilating behaviors is complex and can include a variety of factors not discussed here.

emotional abuse—ultimately provided her with an important foundation through her high school years and later into young adulthood.

As Lindsey's family relationships improved, so did those at school, fueled largely by her involvement in the GSA. An emerging body of research is beginning to show associations between the presence of GSAs and highly positive outcomes for LGBTQ youth, including perceptions related to safety and a sense of belonging in school (Heck, Flentje, and Cochran 2011; Lee 2002; Szalacha 2003; Walls, Kane, and Wisneski 2010), lower rates of school-based victimization (Goodenow, Szalacha, and Westheimer 2006; Heck, Flentje, and Cochran 2011), lower rates of depression and psychological distress (Goodenow, Szalacha, and Westheimer 2006; Heck, Flentje, and Cochran 2011), lower incidence of suicide attempts (Goodenow, Szalacha, and Westheimer 2006), and feelings of self-efficacy and empowerment (Russell et al. 2009). Moreover, GSA adult advisors often serve as mentors to LGBTQ youth who belong to these organizations, filling an important relational void for youth who may otherwise lack fully accepting, supportive relationships with adults (Macgillivray 2008). Lindsey seems to have benefited from her GSA involvement in all these respects. The friends Lindsey made in the GSA helped her feel accepted at school and took active steps to create a safer school environment for her. Lindsey's newfound sense of safety and belonging at school in turn paved the way for what she calls her high school "career" as a peer and teacher educator about LGBTQ issues. Moreover, Lindsey had access to an openly lesbian GSA advisor in Janice, who became a trusted mentor to whom Lindsey felt she could "talk about anything."

It is obviously difficult, especially in retrospect, to determine precisely how Lindsey's ability to communicate in positive (rather than self-destructive) ways was nurtured by these relationships—and, conversely, how much her increasing maturity and developing communication skills enabled her to engage in more supportive, honest relationships with others. What is clear from Lindsey's story, however, is that the GSA, along with other aspects of her high school environment, provided her with multiple opportunities to form supportive relationships and to achieve a strong sense of self-efficacy, which in turn helped her develop a unique personal voice as an LGBTQ student and student leader.

As a former high school teacher, I find Lindsey's statement "I love school" especially striking following her depiction of middle school and the first five months of high school as "horrible." While there may well be many reasons why Lindsey enjoyed school, at least some of these seem to be connected to opportunities she had at Clay Tech to express her queer voice. In her English class with Mr. Martin, Lindsey was able to research and write about issues related to sexuality and gender and receive affirmation from a teacher for her exploration of these issues. As a student in carpentry shop, she had an opportunity to express a genuine creative interest free from the constraints of expected gender roles and a community (mostly male) in which that expression was welcomed. In her work as a peer educator, she had the opportunity to see the impact of her voice on younger students, and in her meetings with the faculty and administration she saw how speaking out and educating others about her observations and experiences could lead to change.

The development of Lindsey's voice seems to have been supported in similar ways by her involvement in YouthWest. When Lindsey talks about herself in this context (see the italicized "I" statements that follow), it is clear that she believes the open communication in which she learned to engage there contributed in an important way to the positive turnaround in her life:

> *I can tell these people anything* in, um, YouthWest. There's so many, like, support groups and things that *I never knew about before*, and just like, *I can talk to people now*. Like, *I never used to be able to talk to people. I just—I didn't care. I never talked to anybody*, and that was hard. *I feel so much more open* and so much more free now.

In addition, Lindsey's queer voice was developed in a different way through the education and advocacy initiatives she took part in through YouthWest's parent organization, MCA. When Lindsey relates the story of the young man who told her, "You changed my life," after she spoke at an event near his college, she exudes a strong sense of pride that she can, by sharing her knowledge and experiences, make the lives of other LGBTQ youth better.

Now that Lindsey is an adult, her connection to others and her commitment to helping those in need continue even though she has been forced to end her military service because of injury. Her friendships with her coworkers and her status as a "little brother" among the restaurant staff are clearly important to her, and her ambitions of being a police officer or pursuing additional work in communications are logical extensions of her earlier pursuits. For Lindsey, who in her early teens "couldn't talk to people," connection to others is not only something she enjoys on a social level; it is central to how she views the world and her place in it.

Perhaps the way in which Lindsey's voice best exemplifies a queer sensibility is her insistence on being accepted as she is, on her own terms. Whether as a female student in carpentry shop, "GI Jane" in the Army National

Guard, or a daughter who now fixes cars with the stepfather who once verbally abused her for being gay, Lindsey lives gender and sexuality in her own way and has learned, through significant support from others, that her voice is valuable just as it is and can be used in many ways that matter deeply to others.[4]

---

4. A case study of Lindsey's Phase I interview appears in Sadowski, Chow, and Scanlon 2009.

3

Ruth: A Person to Trust and a Place to Belong

> "[I] knew that I had like a responsibility if I was going to make it and not fall through the cracks, like so many LGBT youths do . . . to be a safe person for LGBT youth to go to."

Standing in a hilltop field on the small campus where Ruth attends graduate school, I cannot help being struck by the idyllic feel of the surroundings: the bright sun of an early fall day, the pair of Frisbee-playing dogs on the lawn, the inspiring vista of the city skyline in the distance. With the typically idealized perspective of an outsider, this strikes me as a perfect environment in which to attend graduate school, and I am happy for Ruth that she has made such a place her home. I meet Ruth in the vestibule of one of the campus's well-ordered libraries, and her status as a fully integrated member of the academic community is immediately apparent. Library staff smile with recognition as Ruth guides me through the front lobby and book stacks toward a conference room she has reserved, in which we are able to conduct our interview undisturbed for well over an hour.

Ruth was nineteen and less than two years out of high school when she first entered the study;[1] now, six years later, she has a master's degree in divinity and has begun work toward her Ph.D. at Morgan Divinity School, part of a larger theological institute on the West Coast. In addition to her own studies, which are related to bioethics and the ethics of the health-care industry, Ruth serves as a teaching assistant in courses on ethics and anti-oppressive education and teaches a course in youth development to master's degree students preparing to enter the ministry. Ruth's comments about her

---

1. Ruth's Phase I interview was conducted and analyzed by Constance P. Scanlon. Sections of this chapter, based on Phase I of the research, are adapted from Sadowski, Chow, and Scanlon 2009.

work at Morgan Divinity suggest that, after a period of professional soul-searching, she has comfortably come into her own:

> I thought I had a call to Unitarian Universalist ministry, like, upon graduating from college, and I knew that I wanted to go for a Ph.D. eventually. . . . [But] I ended up taking my first bioethics class with my advisor here and fell—just fell in love with health-care ethics. . . . And I was also already interested in the antiracism work. I'd done a lot of antiracism training back east and then with the UUA [Unitarian Universalist Association]. So I got to fuse both of those by doing ethics. And then I was just really suddenly happy. My grades improved. I was interested in what I was doing. So that's kind of what drew me to it.
>
> And I think I have always had a latent desire to be a teacher. My mother was a fourth-grade teacher, and I don't know whether I inherited it or what, but certainly it was kind of—I kind of became more open to following in her footsteps, but not in fourth grade, you know. No elementary school for me! But—so teaching and ethics, a combination that really just now feels really natural.

In addition to Ruth's obvious passion about the subject matter of her work, being a teacher and mentor—sharing her knowledge and experience with younger or less experienced people in various ways—is a central component of her professional life that comes up repeatedly in our interview. When I ask Ruth to describe herself, she uses a telling variety of adjectives that focus typically on physical and personality traits but also on her role as a mentor to others in the divinity school community: *friendly, mentoring, funny, redhead.*

Beyond Ruth's youth ministry course and teaching assistantships, she started an antiracism group at the divinity school three years ago and facilitates sessions "for white students to work on issues of racism related to our community, and then our own internalized biases." She also had recently served as a youth coordinator at a local YMCA, helping first-generation college applicants understand the process. In this capacity, she recalls mentoring a young woman who came out to her as lesbian and whom she referred to the local LGBTQ youth support group. In addition, Ruth says her youth ministry course includes a strong LGBTQ component, and she makes a specific point in this work of reaching out to students who may be LGBTQ themselves or may face difficulties addressing LGBTQ issues in their future ministry work:

I mean, they're Lutheran or Presbyterian or Episcopal and Method-
ist. They're really having a lot of barriers to being [out as LGBT], or
to reaching out to LGBT youth. . . . People who are here, who are
being trained here, and then they're going to go back to either, like,
the Bible Belt or to the Midwest.

When Ruth talks about her current work, her voice is imbued with confidence, purpose, and a passion for helping others. She also feels a strong
sense of belonging and being "wanted" at Morgan that she says began the
day she arrived:

I came to the campus and—of Morgan and just really fell in love
with it and just loved it, and the curriculum seemed like something
that I really wanted. And they seemed like they wanted me, and that
was, like, a real big pull. I also got into [names of other graduate
schools], but . . . something about them wanting me here felt really
good.

Ruth's story illustrates how the support and embrace of institutions can
provide a crucial sense of belonging and play an important role in the development of a powerful young queer voice. For Ruth, institutions—especially
those related to the church—and the people associated with them have filled
important gaps in her life when relationships with family members and others have been damaged by disconnection, alienation, and even abuse.

Violations and Disconnections within the Family

In Ruth's Phase I interview six years earlier, she reveals that her stepfather (to
whom she usually refers simply as "my father") is severely mentally ill and had
been physically, emotionally, and at times even sexually abusive toward her
in various ways since early childhood: "I was abused by him since I was an
infant. So until I was fifteen, that went on, and then when I was fifteen, my
mother and I received a restraining order against him. And right now . . . he's
kind of not with it [mentally], can't really maintain conversation."

Although her father's abuse was four years in the past by the time of
her Phase I interview, Ruth was clearly still disturbed by it at that time,
and she discusses it again in her Phase II interview another six years
later. As a graduate student, Ruth was initially misdiagnosed with attention deficit disorder because she had difficulty concentrating. When

therapists and doctors learned more about the abuse she had endured during childhood and adolescence, however, they concluded that her symptoms were more aligned with a post-traumatic stress or anxiety disorder: "I've had it diagnosed both ways."

In addition to the physical and sexual nature of the abuse, Ruth says one of the most painful aspects of her relationship with her father during her childhood was that when he was not actively abusing her, he exuded a general feeling of contempt for her and at times even a lack of tolerance for her very presence. He often blatantly ignored her, she recalls, sometimes for weeks at a time: "Our relationship was so determined by whether he was speaking to me or not or, you know, how I held the remote." She describes this painful aspect of the father-daughter relationship in more detail in the context of a film she saw recently, *The Secret Life of Bees*, in which a scene resonated with her own childhood experiences:

> There was, like, periods of time where I was ignored for weeks and weeks and weeks and weeks. Actually, I just saw last night *The Secret Life of Bees*, that movie. . . . Well, there is this part where—where the daughter is being ignored completely, and it was like—it resonated with me so much because it was really—that was a—I mean, that was life. I didn't really understand that other people had these tight relationships with their parents because I was being ignored for so—for weeks.

Ruth then goes on to explain that her brother's death from AIDS, which resulted from an HIV-tainted blood transfusion when Ruth was a high school sophomore, was a trigger for her father's mental illness and seems to have exacerbated his mistreatment of her:

> After my brother passed away, it got—my dad's kind of anger and kind of removing himself from the world got stronger, so then it was just—well, the silence was like most of the day, every day for—it's like years. And then the—kind of the straw that broke the camel's back is that my dad ended up . . . he eventually said something sexual to me in front of my mother. And it happened like two or three times, and after the third time, I told my mom that, you know, we need to—he just needs to be out tomorrow or I'm moving.
>
> And I had a plan. I was moving in with my youth group advisor, who was like my primary mentor then in high school. And,

you know, I know that they'll take me no questions asked, and so, you know—and the next morning she threw him out and got a restraining order. So she made the right decision, but that—that was kind of the end of it.

This is one of several scenarios from Ruth's adolescence that foreshadow the importance she later places on mentoring as an adult. When she feels unsafe in her home environment as a teenager, her backup plan is to move in with her mentor from church. Although Ruth's mother ultimately took action and the move was not necessary (Ruth's father was later institutionalized), this incident is one of several in which Ruth places her trust in a nonparent mentor when her family relationships fail to meet her needs, or at least when she fears they might do so.

In Ruth's first interview, she describes her relationship with her mother in generally positive terms, explaining that she has always been supportive of Ruth's lesbian identity and has helped facilitate Ruth's coming out to extended family members. In our Phase II interview, however, the sense of alienation Ruth feels from her mother is more apparent, and she believes that in her earlier interview she had perhaps depicted the mother-daughter relationship through an idealized lens: "I think I also was at a point [at the time of my first interview] where I was idealizing my relationship with my mom." Although Ruth reiterates at age twenty-five that her mother is and always has been accepting of her lesbian identity, other aspects of their relationship have been strained, and Ruth is especially critical of her mother for not having protected her more effectively from her father's abuse:

We [my mother and I] had a really big falling out and didn't talk for about six months. I had, like, just a lot of anger towards her from the—from, like, her allowing the abuse to continue when I was in high school, so—or you know, for not even just high school but for all of childhood. And then—so I was really angry, expressed that anger, and she—you know, it upset her. She didn't want me to talk to her until I went to therapy.

Ruth's current alienation from her mother also stems from the fact that her mother has remarried, this time to a man who Ruth says "has a lot of mental health issues as well." Although Ruth says her new stepfather is "not abusive from what I can tell," the fact that her mother has married another man with mental illness frustrates her and makes her too uncomfortable to go back east and stay with her family for holidays or other visits.

In addition, Ruth says she feels estranged from much of her extended family because they do not understand or support her pursuit of advanced graduate study, and because they are "sort of not so GLBT-friendly on my mom's side." She relates one incident in which she was invited to bring a guest to a cousin's wedding. She was planning to bring Cheryl, the woman who was her partner at the time, but the couple was then disinvited from the wedding because the bride's mother (Ruth's aunt) "didn't want us to make a statement." Ruth ultimately complied with her aunt's request by attending the wedding ceremony alone while Cheryl waited in the car. (Neither Ruth nor Cheryl attended the reception.) Incidents such as these, however, combined with Ruth's challenging relationship with her parents, seem to contribute to a general sense of estrangement from her family of origin—a feeling that is amplified by the fact that Ruth has built a new life more than three thousand miles from most of her relatives:

> And so I don't go home. . . . It's very complicated, but it's also very—
> like, in my day-to-day it's not present with me. I think the most I
> talk about it is probably in therapy, and then if I talk to my mom,
> it's every other week. And she didn't come out to see me graduate,
> so certainly she hasn't really shown up for significant things. So that
> further, I guess, makes me deprioritize those relationships, which is
> unfortunate.

The language Ruth uses in discussing her relationships with her family of origin—particularly her statement that her mother "hasn't shown up" for significant things like her graduation and her choices of words such as *complicated* and *unfortunate*—suggests a complex set of feelings. While on the one hand Ruth's physical and emotional separation from her family reflect choices she has deliberately made to build her life around a different set of relationships, her voice when talking about her family is also tinged with ambivalence and perhaps even a wish that things could be different.

Limited Support in Middle and High School

In contrast to Morgan Divinity, where Ruth feels supported as an LGBTQ scholar and in making this an important aspect of her faith and work, Ruth had only limited emotional support in dealing with her sexual identity in middle and high school. In her first interview, in which Ruth identified as "bisexual" and "questioning," she reveals that she realized she was "not straight" as early as middle school, but she chose to dissociate from this aspect of herself in order to be accepted by, or at least not further rejected by, her peers: "I was definitely the fat girl, picked on in middle school. So it was not a time to add another adversity."

When Ruth got to high school, there was a gay-straight alliance, and Ruth was an active member of it, but she still felt the need to conceal her LGBTQ identity and participate as a "straight ally." While Ruth does not believe that her school was severely homophobic, or that there was a significant problem with hate language against sexual minorities, she experienced a dilemma that many young, closeted sexual-minority youth face:

> [There were] two girls who were the year ahead of me who were out. And they, I guess, were pretty accepted. Um, we didn't have much of a problem. But I didn't really see that it *wouldn't* be a problem. But I think that I didn't have that many connections in school with people, that it was too much to afford to—I would rather have been, like, kind of just like—like, I was kind of a floater among my peers. But I felt like that was probably easier than actually putting it against myself that—I would have been the only one in my class.

Ruth's equivocal voice here shows a conflict between thinking that she might have been "pretty accepted," just as the two older girls seem to have been, and fearing that she might face rejection. Her ultimate choice was one of survival, but it required disconnection from close relationships: "I was kind of a floater among my peers. . . . That was probably easier."

Another factor that Ruth believes kept her in the closet in high school was the fact that her guidance counselor and closest mentor at school, to whom she turned for support when her brother died during her sophomore year, was also lesbian but never came out at school:

> She wasn't out. So it was kind of hard to understand, like—and that was probably one of the reasons that kept me in the closet throughout high school. Like, I didn't tell anyone that I was gay. I just kind of didn't say, or would say I was straight. I mean, I also dated—senior year, I dated a couple boys, so—or, was—or like, yeah, was, like, involved with straight boys, too. So it was kind of, like, reemphasizing the fact that I was straight. . . . But I think one of the reasons I didn't come out was the fact that she, my guidance counselor, didn't either.

Turning to Church and Community

Ruth's church provided a contrast to her high school in terms of the support she felt there to be open about her sexual identity during adolescence, and this institutional support seems to have laid the groundwork for the further integration of her LGBTQ identity and her faith at Morgan Divinity. The Unitarian Universalist (UU) church has formally adopted a policy of open acceptance of and respect for LGBTQ people, and this institutional affirmation seems to have held special significance for Ruth. She relates one incident in which she participated in a panel presentation at an area UU church. This event was especially important to her because her high school guidance counselor, to whom she had turned for support when her brother died, also served on the panel:

> The guidance counselor and I, the one that I became really close [to] after—because I needed a lot of help, um, like, talking to my teachers after my brother died. . . . She thought I was just a straight ally, too. And then eventually, um, we both ended up being on a panel together for a UU church in [a local community]. And so it was, like, she told her story, and then I told mine. It was like, whoa! Like, we had already become really close, but then, now, one more thing we knew about each other.

Like Ruth, her guidance counselor did not feel safe enough to be out within the institution of the school, but for both, the church seemed a safer community in which to be open about their sexuality.

In addition to the church, Ruth found a sense of institutional and personal acceptance in community-based advocacy and support groups during her adolescence. While a freshman in high school, Ruth became a peer educator about HIV prevention (an interest perhaps related to her brother's illness) through a local organization, Health Central. She also began attending meetings of CityYouth, the urban LGBTQ youth group from which young people were recruited for this study, and, through connections she made there, became immersed in LGBTQ youth culture for the first time. Ruth began to go into the state capital for Gay Pride and Youth Pride parades, as well as an annual dance, an alternative prom for LGBTQ students who do not feel safe or welcome at their own school's prom. She attended this prom in her sophomore, junior, and senior years of high school. In her Phase I interview, Ruth is enthusiastic about the impact these experiences have had on her life and contrasts them with the lack of connection she felt to her LGBTQ identity at her high school:

> Now that I feel like I'm in queer youth culture—like, I'm pretty im-
> mersed in it. Like, all my activities have to do with that. My connec-
> tions come from that. So I think that—and I feel so comfortable in
> it that I really can see why I wasn't comfortable in the mainstream,
> like, social structure. I didn't get it. I didn't understand. I didn't
> know how to, like, function.

Ruth also mentions CityYouth in her Phase II interview and tells me she has made plans to return to the East Coast and serve as a chaperone for the group's dance later that year as a way of "giving back" to the organization that helped her connect to her LGBTQ identity. She says that her work as a teacher and mentor at Morgan Divinity has been inspired by the mentoring she received from adult advisors at CityYouth and by a desire to continue their legacy:

> When I teach dynamic youth ministry, we definitely have a focus on
> LGBT youth and queer youth, I think. And I'm even always kind of
> conscious of wanting to contribute in some way to, you know, con-
> tinuing on the path of the mentors that I had when I was younger, or
> when I was involved with CityYouth. . . . I always have in the back
> of my mind when I would be at CityYouth and there were the adult
> advisors and the staff, like [names of advisors], where I wanted to—
> not *be* like them but knew that I had like a responsibility if I was go-
> ing to make it and not fall through the cracks, like so many LGBT
> youths do, that I would want to be fulfilling that role in some way
> and just kind of be able to be a safe person for LGBT youth to go to.

Developing an Integrated Voice

At Morgan Divinity School, Ruth is able to integrate the most salient aspects of her earlier life as a scholar, a teacher, a mentor, a person of faith, and a woman who now identifies as both queer and lesbian. Although the theologi- cal institute of which Morgan is a part encompasses faiths often associated with less respectful attitudes about LGBTQ rights and identities (such as Catholicism, Islam, and several of the more conservative Protestant denomi- nations), Ruth explains that all of the various faith communities within the institute take a "left of center" approach to LGBTQ and other issues. She also notes that a large proportion of her classmates are LGBTQ:

> [I'm] in a seminary community that is to the left of their faith tradition, that incorporates an antihomophobic lens to the work that they contribute. Not necessarily all the time but definitely bringing in sources from women, which is rare—is kind of rare in the Catholic tradition—but there's kind of a lot more celebration of diversity than at maybe seminaries of the same denomination in the East or in the South or Midwest. It's kind of a feeder school for gay religious people. I would say most of my school is GLBT, like 75 percent.

Given Ruth's strong Unitarian faith and the large proportion of LGBTQ people at Ruth's school, one might expect the focus of her studies to be on LGBTQ issues and to have a strong Unitarian strand, but Ruth focuses instead on black feminist ethics from a secular perspective. The secular aspect of her work, she notes, is a part of the institution's effort to prepare graduates for a broad range of jobs in academia as well as the clergy (a flexibility she says is especially important to her as a scholar who plans to be out as LGBTQ in her career). Ruth says she is attracted to black feminist theory (e.g., the work of Audre Lorde, bell hooks, and others) because it allows her to "queer" the study of ethics in a way that goes beyond traditional, white-dominated gay and lesbian political issues:

> With my work, it's interesting because I don't do queer ethics. I do more black feminist ethics, which happens to—happens to have a queer element to it, for the most part. So—but it's very much centered in, like, more antiracist politics than in queer or gay— mainstream gay—politics or ethics. So I would say I probably queer things as a verb. But I don't necessarily do queer theory or gender theory necessarily in the more kind of—I don't know, monolithic sense. But it's more integrated into the black feminist ethics that I follow, which I think is queering ethics in and of itself.

Still, Ruth considers herself a "Christian ethicist," and many of the significant relationships in her life are centered on her communities of faith, whether through the UUA (in which she is still active) or the seminary itself. One of her key mentors as an adult is the youth group advisor from her UU church when she was an adolescent:

I have a small network of really good friends that are Unitarian Universalists that have been—so my best friend from since like fifth grade, we still keep in touch. So he's kind of my—we're still best friends. We still will be best friends forever. . . . And then a couple of the friends I have in seminary are pretty significant, the ones that have been here since the beginning. . . . Also my youth group advisor [from church] continues to be really significant—the same one from high school. So he flew out for my graduation. He actually left his wife when I was in high school—maybe a year after—and came out of the closet, so he's kind of like my "gay dad," I would say.

Ruth adds that, although it isn't a central aspect of her studies, her identity as lesbian and queer is fundamental to her relationships and her ability to form strong bonds with others. When Ruth first came west to attend the seminary, she says her partner at the time (Cheryl) came with her. Ruth notes that they are no longer together as a couple but adds, "My ex is definitely one of my best friends." Ruth's current partner, Leslie, lives with her part time at the seminary and is also someone Ruth says is "certainly significant" in her life, though they recently have had "rocky spots about trust."

Also, several mentoring relationships that have been important at various points in Ruth's life have been closely connected to her LGBTQ identity, including those she formed at church, in CityYouth, and (now with her serving in the mentoring role) at Morgan Divinity. Echoing David in Chapter 1, who feels "lucky" to be queer because of the many supportive people he's met in LGBTQ circles, Ruth says she's not sure she could have formed such supportive relationships had she been "straight," and she believes that peer and mentoring relationships through queer communities have served as a lifeline for her going at least as far back as high school:

Straight friendships and priorities just didn't work for me in high school. . . . The queer community kind of provided an outlet for me to even have a social life, be able to have friendships in the same way. I don't have—I mean, I have a couple of straight friends that I have close relationships with, but they are people who either identify as queer and have heterosexual relationships or, you know, might as well. They're not—they're outside of sort of the heterosexual culture.

In addition to influencing *which* relationships are most important and supportive in her life, Ruth believes that her queer identity gives her a unique perspective on the nature of relationships that she would not otherwise have.

It allows her to question the traditional notions of family with which she grew up and her own sense of values and personal priorities as both an ethicist and a person capable of loving in her own way:

> I think it [being queer] changes my value system. I also think that—and this kind of relates to the love part—that it can look in different ways than I may have grown up thinking was possible. Identifying as queer or being in a queer community, that love and friendship take on—it doesn't have to mean marriage, and it doesn't have to mean a specific parenting style, and it doesn't necessarily have to mean that I'm in a relationship with a woman who was born a woman all the time. So there is both—there is a lot more freedom for love to take many forms, as opposed to fitting a very narrow box, either in parent love or in a relationship, love in the heterosexual context.

In light of the dysfunction and abuse Ruth experienced within her own family of origin, the act of forming her own "queered" notions about love and family has played an adaptive role in Ruth's life and has helped her build resilience to weather the challenges of her adolescence and young adulthood. Through access to queer relationships and the queer community, Ruth has learned new ways of loving beyond what she "may have grown up thinking was possible," which she now is able to express articulately as a young adult using the language of an ethical scholar.

Coming to a Place of Healing, Efficacy, and Hope

Although Ruth has seen little of her father in recent years, because he lives in a residential mental health facility far from her current residence, her abusive relationship with him continues to be a source of considerable anxiety for her, one she deals with by going to psychotherapy twice a week. Ruth says the therapy gives her a sense of "equilibrium" to cope with the residual trauma of that experience. She also believes that her current life circumstances, in which she feels a sense of agency and the ability to make her own choices about her life and relationships, serve as an important source of healing:

> I need to be in therapy. That's part of the—the process. It's because I don't want to be on medication. In my experience, there is clinical depression on both sides of my family, but I've been really lucky that I don't have the classical depression, which, given my life circumstances, is pretty—I feel pretty remarkable in that way. Like, "Okay,

I was able to get through a month." So this daily life now, which is such an improvement on my childhood; the way I get to choose to be in a relationship with people or how I do things is just so radically different from how I grew up that I think in some way it kept me from being depressed, having depression, or needing to take medication to kind of maintain a—um, some sort of equilibrium.

When I ask Ruth to estimate on a scale of one to ten how happy she is with her life now, she says, "Probably eight—I'm doing good. Yeah, an eight." In addition, Ruth's telling responses to several of my standard final interview questions (in italics) echo themes heard throughout her story: the role of her scholarship and her work as central components of her life, the value of relationships (especially those founded on love and not abuse), and the importance of teaching and mentoring in supporting the growth of others and in providing Ruth with a sense of her own efficacy:

> *What do you think is your best quality as a person?*
> Um, ah, probably my conscientiousness, I would say. Either in a relationship or in work, that I will do what I say I will do, and if I—and if I'm not going to or I'm not able to, I will tell you. And we'll, you know, have a conversation about that. I think that's probably—I would say that's—I mean, when I get jobs, that's why I get the jobs. When I have good friendships, that's something that they say about me.

> *What things would you say are most important to you?*
> Hmm. Hmm. [*Laughs*] My cat—yeah, my cat. I mean, it's such a stable, primary relationship. . . . I really do think love is important. I think I do really value that, I would say, when it comes down to it. I don't think that's something I talk about all the time. It's probably one of the more difficult areas. It's very related to, I mean, my childhood, but it's—I would say when push comes to shove, that's what I really want.

> *And what gives you hope when you look ahead?*
> Probably the students that I come in contact with, the ones that I get to teach or mentor, and peer relationships. I mean, part of the work I do and didn't talk a lot about is with antiracism work and working with mostly other white folks on dismantling racism. And so some of that, I think, is where I get a lot of hope for being able

to see people organize and figure stuff out and kind of understand their own biases in relationships. It's really where I think, "Okay. Yeah, I have—you know, I have gifts to give, and they work." And I get to see the results of that. . . . And it's really like, "I'm okay." There is real stuff I can do and be useful in probably either a movement sense or in—you know, in just helping ministers be the ministers that they really want to be in the culture. So that's kind of—I think that's what gives me hope, that, "Okay, I can do this. I can get this done."

Listening to Ruth: Making Connections with Mentors and Institutions

In a widely cited and frequently corroborated finding in child development, psychiatrist Michael Rutter (1987) noted that having a mutual, caring relationship with a nonparent adult can have protective effects for children who are at risk for negative outcomes, particularly if there is stress in the child's home environment. Rutter based this conclusion in part on his work with children of divorced or separated parents and those from low-income families and found that even one relationship with an additional adult was associated with lower dropout rates among these youth.[2] Similarly, Emmy E. Werner and Ruth S. Smith (1982), in another classic longitudinal study of children and adolescents in Hawaii, found resilience to be associated with strong relationships between youth and nonparent adults.

Jean E. Rhodes, author of much of the more recent research literature on mentoring and the 2002 book *Stand by Me: The Risks and Rewards of Mentoring Today's Youth*, found in her research that even one positive mentoring experience, provided that it is of sufficient duration and consistency and there is an empathic connection between the mentor and mentee, can help build resilience in and confer positive outcomes to youth who face a variety of psychosocial risks. Although the primary focus of Rhodes's work has been on formally organized mentoring relationships (e.g., those organized through groups such as Big Brothers/Big Sisters), she notes that "naturally occurring mentoring relationships" (Rhodes 2002, 4) such as those youth can have with teachers or clergy can provide similar benefits to youth at risk provided that conditions such as consistency, emotional closeness, and

---

2. In later writing, Rutter notes that resilience is best promoted through "a range of good relationships and therefore the protection that comes from multiplicity, rather than reliance on one or two" (2006, 39).

empathy are met. Moreover, psychologist Norman Garmezy, based on a review of the research about protective factors for youth who have faced adversity, adds that the "external support" provided by nonparent adults can also come from "an institutional structure, such as a caring agency, a church, etc." (1993, 132).

Certainly in Ruth's case, factors in her childhood and adolescence placed her at considerable risk, especially her abusive relationship with her father. The fact that Ruth did not feel safe coming out as lesbian at school also seems to have contributed to her distress during adolescence. And although Ruth says her mother was always accepting of the fact that she was lesbian, several people in her extended family were not. Given this context, nonfamily relationships and institutions other than school have made a crucial difference in Ruth's life, providing her with a sense of safety and belonging and with relationships in which she feels she can communicate honestly and be accepted for who she is.

The UU church was a key asset for Ruth throughout her adolescence, and the fact that she has chosen an academic and career path centered on her UU faith speaks to the strong, positive influence this institution had on her early life. She belonged to a church-affiliated youth group and spoke on a panel about LGBTQ issues in her late teens, and Ruth's church youth group advisor has served as an important mentor to her through much of her adolescence and young adulthood.

According to Rhodes and her colleagues, mentoring "works" through three interrelated processes, all of which seem to have been occurring in Ruth's long-standing relationship with her church youth group advisor: "1) by enhancing youth's social relationships and emotional well-being; 2) by improving [youths'] cognitive skills through instruction and conversation; and 3) by promoting positive identity development through [mentors'] serving as role models and advocates" (Rhodes et al. 2006, 692). Ruth's church youth group advisor, to whom she refers as her "gay dad," had a strong influence on her academic planning and choices, helping Ruth develop positive images of what psychologists Hazel Markus and Paula Nurius (1986) have called "possible selves." This mentor also filled an important relational void in Ruth's life at critical points when she believed her relationships with her parents were failing her. Ruth says he offered to take her in "no questions asked" if her mother did not take steps to end her father's abuse, and many years later (unlike Ruth's parents), he attended her graduation from her master's degree program. Although it is impossible to know all the relational dynamics between Ruth and her parents, it is clear that from her perspective, this mentor has been a consistently supportive presence in her life in ways that her family has not.

Another key nonschool institution for Ruth was CityYouth, where Ruth made friends, became heavily involved in aspects of "queer youth culture" such as the city's pride parades and the LGBTQ prom, and learned how to engage in relationships as a young lesbian woman. The contributions of CityYouth's adult advisors made a strong impression on Ruth and seem to have influenced the priorities she has today as a teacher and scholar, particularly her desire to pass on the benefits of this support to her students and to others with whom she comes into contact at Morgan Divinity. Ruth's plans to travel across the country and return as an adult chaperone to CityYouth's LGBTQ prom provide further evidence that her involvement in CityYouth was one of the high points of her late adolescence.

In Chapter 2, Lindsey speaks to the potential for gay-straight alliances to turn around (in her case quite dramatically) the school experiences of LGBTQ youth, yet Ruth describes her experiences in her high school's GSA with considerably less enthusiasm. Although Ruth's school had an active GSA and she was a member, she did not feel safe being out as lesbian at school—not even in the GSA. Although all the reasons for this perceived lack of safety are not clear, one relevant factor seems to be that Ruth saw few examples of other openly LGBTQ students and therefore had little sense of how her disclosure would be received. Moreover, the fact that Ruth's guidance counselor was lesbian but remained closeted at school may have confirmed her fear that if she came out, her safety could not be guaranteed.

CityYouth, on the other hand, was an organization made up largely of openly LGBTQ youth and adult advisors in which the culture was decidedly queer. Ruth's UU church was presumably more mixed in terms of gender and sexuality than CityYouth, but she nonetheless seems to have similarly perceived the church to be a culture of acceptance in a way that school was not. The national UU church's pro-LGBTQ stance, widely known among people in the church and many others, may have strongly influenced Ruth's perception of safety within that institution, whereas at school mixed messages made Ruth feel considerably less safe.

Because they provided Ruth safety and acceptance, the UU church and CityYouth were institutions in which Ruth developed close relationships, unlike her high school, in which she characterizes herself as a social "floater" whose relationships were based on the false maintenance of a "straight" identity. It was on a church panel, not in a school assembly, where Ruth came out publicly. The UU church also clearly influenced Ruth's choice of scholarly pursuits and her voice as a scholar, teacher, and mentor at Morgan Divinity, another institution in which she feels accepted and, as she puts it, "wanted."

At Morgan Divinity School, Ruth is a valued and important member of the academic and spiritual community, and her queer voice is a central aspect of the unique contributions she makes there. By including LGBTQ issues in her youth development course and mentoring other seminarians concerned about how their being LGBTQ or LGBTQ-friendly will be received in their home congregations, Ruth's sexuality, instead of the "adversity" she feared it might be if she came out in middle or high school, is an asset. In her scholarship and teaching, Ruth also takes the idea of "queer" beyond sexuality and gender, challenging oppressive social conventions in other ways as an antiracist, anti-oppressive educator and ethicist.

Finally, Ruth's story illustrates how teaching and mentoring can be expressions of one's unique voice in and of themselves, especially if they stem from one's own experiences with the value of being mentored. Clearly, Ruth's family relationships and other aspects of her life continue to cause her some emotional distress, but this has not prevented her from having a strong sense of her own agency. As Ruth explains at the end of her final interview, "I have gifts to give, and they work," and her queer voice is one of the most important gifts she has to offer.

4

Travis: Twenty-First-Century Everyman

"I'd like a nice, calm, kind of mundane existence."

I n comparison to David, the activist (Chapter 1); Lindsey, the peer educator and aspiring speaker (Chapter 2); and Ruth, the teacher, mentor, and academic (Chapter 3), Travis's focus and ambitions are much more personal. Patching together income from two jobs at the time we meet for our Phase II interview, Travis, twenty-seven, was working late-evening shifts as a customer service leader at a big-box discount department store and as a baker and manager for a wholesale baking business, the Bakery Commons, of which he is part owner. Although Travis at first appears groggy and bleary-eyed on the morning we reconnect at a coffeehouse in the small college town where he lives, he soon opens up and updates me on the details of his daily life: "I work two pretty much full-time jobs. I live here in town. I have three roommates. I live with my boyfriend of three years. We have a dog, too, and that's pretty much it. I work and walk the dog, and when I have time to hang out, I go out."

While Travis says the department store job sometimes feels like "shoveling sand against the tide," he finds the baking work "creative and appealing" and would someday like to buy out the other bakers and be full owner of the business. When I ask him to describe himself early in our interview, his responses illustrate how hard he feels he must work to make ends meet but also how a strong work ethic forms a central aspect of his identity (my questions in italics):

How would you describe yourself today, at this moment?

Today? At this moment? Exhausted yet driven. It is a pretty big deal in my life that all I do is work. That's for some reason my niche that I've walked into. Um, if I'm not working or I'm not being productive, I don't feel like I've accomplished anything at that point.

I was going to just ask you to talk a little bit more about being driven and what that means to you.

Um, always trying to do something, persevere, make yourself better somehow, even if it's like learning one new thing in a day. Just keep moving, keep going, get things accomplished, get things done. By the end of the day, you look back on your list, and have you accomplished anything?

So is that something you feel good about, or is that something you feel is a burden?

Um, both. It's kind of ingrained. It was the way I was raised. Everybody worked. Everybody pulled their weight. Everybody did what they needed to get done.

For Travis, work is not merely what he does to pay the bills; it is connected to a sense of personal accomplishment and improvement, a way to make himself "better somehow." It is also something that connects him to his family of origin, where Travis says "everybody worked" and "everybody pulled their weight." From Travis's resigned yet also prideful tone here, it seems as though it would be hard for him to imagine living any other way.

A Stable Relationship

In addition to work, Travis's relationship with his boyfriend, Mark, is another highly significant aspect of his daily life. Travis describes Mark, who is from the South and whom he met online three years earlier, as "very calm, very relaxed, very laid-back about things," and he explains how their relationship is different from those he's had with other men in the past:

What makes it different is that it's an actual relationship. It's an equal partnership. It's love, not just what I equated it to be: physical, lusty feelings. It's—I'd say that it's similar to—if something were to happen to him, then my life would be in shambles. I go to bed every night looking at him, and I wake up every morning looking at him, and I'm not sick of him after three years.

I tended to, in my past relationships, get very bored because I dated one very specific type of people, and I liked them broken. Like, if he had some form of personality disorder or social anxiety problem, I was all about it. Um, and it's a great relationship because Mark is not codependent, that we are two very different, functioning people. But at the same time we are a couple, and we do things together. But we can also be apart from one another and not have anxiety about it.

In addition to Mark's being a different kind of man than those with whom Travis has had relationships in the past, I ask Travis if he believes the relationship has changed him in any significant way. He responds, "Before, my only responsibility was me and the dog, and if anything went south, I grab the dog, I get in the car, I go. And it's now us. Before, it was just me against the world. Now it's us together and the adventure of life, and we're planning on getting married."

Since Travis lives in a state in which same-sex marriage is legal, he and Mark had already set a wedding date for a year before we spoke, but, he explains, "we got to that point, and we just looked at our financial situation, and it just—it didn't make sense." They still plan to get married in the future, however, and Travis says he would like to adopt children. He currently has an eleven-year-old son from a relationship (or, in his terms, a "really bad decision of a one-night stand") with a young woman when he was sixteen, but he sees his son infrequently because the boy and his mother live on the West Coast. Travis says he would like to have children with Mark when they are financially able to do so.

As Travis describes it, his relationship with Mark represents a loving, centered, and healthy change from his past intimate relationships, which he says were based on "physical, lusty feelings" and often "codependent" behaviors. The fact that the couple is planning to get married in the future suggests that Travis is now interested in a stable, long-term commitment. In many ways, Travis's emphasis on work and family, and his ambitions for the future, read like the classic American dream, or at least a twenty-first-century version of it. While Travis self-identifies as gay, and this is clearly a significant factor that influences his everyday life, he does not view his sexuality as a significant aspect of his identity.

How do you identify yourself [in terms of LGBTQ identifiers]?
Um, I still identify as a gay man. Um, pretty straightforward there, and I'm attracted to men, and that's it.

What do you like about being gay?

You know, I've never really thought about it because it's not—to me it's not a label that I like or dislike; it just *is*. That there's not anything I'd change about being gay, I—just you are, or you aren't. I don't really have a—something I like about being gay. I just am.

Do you identify with the word queer at all?

No. It's another word. And, you know, I did all the queer studies and queer literature, queer psychology in the university. It just—it's not a huge aspect of my life. It doesn't make my identity. It's part of my identity.

Although Travis clearly expresses his gayness frankly and without shame or equivocation ("I'm attracted to men and that's it"), a gay identity is neither a political nor an academic issue for him. As he explains simply, "It's not a label that I like or dislike; it just is."

Relationships in Travis's Adolescence

As an adult, Travis seems to have integrated being gay into his life in such a way that he does not experience it as central to his sense of self. Reflecting on his life as a teenager, however, Travis says his sexuality was something he "had to come to terms with and widely accept that this is who I am, and that's it." When I ask him how he got to this point, Travis simply says he eventually "stopped listening to everyone around me and just listened to myself."

At age twenty-one, Travis was one of the oldest participants in the original research study and was recruited from YouthWest, the rural LGBTQ youth group site. Significant in Travis's discussion of his sexual identity at the time were his family relationships, which he says were characterized by a "don't ask, don't tell" approach to the fact that he was gay. Travis's mother had died three years before our first interview from a pulmonary embolism, and his father had died less than a year before the interview from liver disease. Travis's brother, Jack, who is five years older, was thus the only surviving member of Travis's immediate family when we first met. In his Phase I interview, Travis describes Jack, who is heterosexual and married, as "the stereotypical, vinyl-wearing, gun-toting Republican" and says that upon Travis's initial coming out, Jack "didn't take it well." Travis says his brother has been more accepting in recent years, but he adds:

Most of my family has been—it's kind of "don't ask, don't tell," you know? If we don't talk about it, it's better. It's not that he [my brother] doesn't care, and it's not that he overly cares. It's just that it's not talked about. He asks the occasional awkward question, so—but that's about it.

Travis adds that his mother also had difficulty accepting his homosexuality when he first came out to her several years before, but she later "eased into it." Travis's father, like his brother, Jack, seemed uninterested in discussing Travis's homosexuality at all:

With Mom it was very hard for her to accept that I was gay at first. Then she just kind of eased into it. Um, Dad, again, was "don't ask, don't tell." He didn't ask any questions, and I didn't volunteer any information. Um, collectively I'd say that he was probably on the same level [as my brother]. You know, we don't talk about it, and I don't volunteer any information.

Travis's statements here illustrate, at least to some degree, his own complicity in the family silence around his homosexuality: "We don't talk about it, and I don't volunteer any information." In asserting somewhat matter-of-factly that "if we [my brother and I] don't talk about it [my being gay], it's better," Travis suggests that he finds the silence between him and Jack preferable to any conversations they might have about the topic. At another point in the Phase I interview, Travis expresses beliefs he would echo six years later:

I'm a firm believer in that my sexuality doesn't define who I am. So, it's not a huge topic for me to talk about with any member of my family. Yeah, they all know I'm gay, but it's not something I talk about at the dinner table or we sit down and have long conversations about.

Reflecting back on high school, Travis says it, too, was characterized by "don't ask, don't tell" attitudes about homosexuality, but he still managed to carve out his own locus of self-expression there. When he was in tenth grade, he founded a gay-straight alliance of which he was the only gay male member and served as its president: "I became kind of lost that year, and just—it was one of those things that gave me a purpose, kind of." Travis says that his school's administration, however, attempted to keep the GSA "on the down low" with the community and that teachers' and administrators' general attitude about LGBTQ students was one of apathy: "To the school it [the GSA] was absolutely unimportant. They could have cared less whether we had one or not."

Still, despite the fact that Travis felt he was something of an "outcast," both as a gay student and as part of the goth social group, he "enjoyed most of [his] teachers" and felt especially accepted in the GSA and the music program. He also had a confiding relationship with the theater program's technical director, an openly gay man with whom he "talked about everything": "He always knew exactly what I was about and always knew just by looking at me how I was feeling and knew where I was coming from, because he'd grown up in the same town and the same high school."

Travis says that community-based LGBTQ youth groups also played an important role in his youth because they provided connections that even his school GSA could not. For example, he says the community-based group he joined while in high school was different from the school's gay-straight alliance in that "it had gay people—there was more than just me and the straight girls." When he was recruited for Phase I of this research study, he was an active member of YouthWest.

Travis also shared in his Phase I interview that during his teens he had been a "hard-core drug addict" who used cocaine and LSD, plus "meth, uppers, downers, Ecstasy—just about anything." He says he does not necessarily see a connection between his drug use and stress he experienced as a gay youth, so it is difficult to determine if these things might have been related in ways outside his awareness. In his Phase I interview, Travis reports, "I don't do drugs, I don't drink, and I don't smoke." When we reconnect six years later, he reiterates that these addictions are a part of his past.

"The Poor, Nine-to-Five Everyday Guy"

Although Travis has relatively little to say when I ask him what he likes about being gay, he offers a quick response when I ask him if there's anything he dislikes about it: "the gay community." Upon further probing, it seems clear that Travis sees himself as an "everyday guy," someone he believes is not represented in the larger gay culture or in media depictions of it:

> I find it ridiculous that in a subculture that's denied rights, we
> have to create more subcultures to it, that we have to be catty, that
> we have to look a certain way or dress a certain way, or you're not
> accepted. You know, we have shows like *Queer as Folk* that portray
> one side of the gay community and not, you know, the poor, nine-
> to-five everyday guy who just wants to get along in life.

While Travis seems to integrate being gay easily with his current day-to-day life, he seems to find being a "poor, nine-to-five everyday guy" within the gay community more difficult, since that may mean "you're not accepted."

The salience of social class to Travis is evident at another point in our interview, when he describes his decision to give up a professional-track career for what he views as a simpler, more satisfying existence. Having completed a bachelor's degree in social counseling from a university in Canada, Travis originally worked as a youth counselor after graduating from college. But he says he became "emotionally detached" from this field while working for an organization based in Jerome, a wealthy northeastern suburb:

> I worked in Jerome for a little while, which was kind of like on the upper side of "middle white class" America. And that just got really irritating because you would look at the family history, and Mommy's on Prozac because she burned the family turkey two years ago at Thanksgiving and has never gotten over it. Another one of those very calming, silent moments in life where I was like, "Wow, there are real issues in the world and people who have real problems. And then there are people that just make their problems and choose to be the victim." So I just decided that that's when I couldn't physically and emotionally deal with the people who had real problems, and then the people who created their own problems just angered me. So I just decided that it was at that point just to get out of the field. So I went into baking, and, you know, bread doesn't talk back, and it doesn't have an issue.

Given Travis's difficult family history, particularly the deaths of both his parents during his late adolescence, his frustration with what he perceives as "people who just make their problems and choose to be the victim" is not surprising. This attitude seems to follow even more logically from Travis's experiences when he relates a health challenge he faced in the period between our Phase I and Phase II interviews, when Travis was in his early twenties:

> I was working with teenagers with emotional difficulties at that point, and I went in [to the doctor] one day because I had this really bad, raspy cough. That turned out to be just seasonal allergies, but they did an X-ray of my lungs, and they found a shadow, and then we went through the whole CT scans and biopsies, and they caught it [a cancerous tumor in one of his lungs] in time. I did have to do chemo and radiation. And after they shrunk the tumor enough, they actually zapped me with a laser.

Travis describes his experience with cancer as "one of the very few times in my life that I felt completely helpless," but he adds that he relied on people with whom he had close relationships to help him deal with both the physical and emotional challenges of the disease and its treatment: "You know, it's one of those times that I've had to rely on my friends and my family."

> *And did they come through for you?*
> Yeah. Actually, my best friend from high school—I did chemo once a week on Fridays, and she would come up—I'd drive myself to chemo and radiation and get home, and then I would be sick at that point. But she would come up every Friday and stay with me, and we'd watch movies and just try to make it better.

> *And then coming out of that whole experience, what was that like?*
> I think it's one of the major things that has actually made me more comfortable in life. I've been more accepting of limits, knowing that I just have to radically accept that there are things that I cannot do and things that I cannot control.

Travis seems to speak in both his interviews with a degree of stoicism and emotional impenetrability. In discussing his gay identity, for example, he emphasizes its lack of importance in his life ("I'm a firm believer in that my sexuality doesn't define who I am") and its insignificance in his family relationships ("If we don't talk about it, it's better"). Moreover, he accepts his current circumstances working two jobs without complaint and views it as necessary and even self-defining. In talking about his bout with cancer, however, a more vulnerable voice emerges. While Travis says he has been cancer-free for more than three years, he readily acknowledges the extent to which he was dependent on friends and family to get him through the experience. He also recognizes that as difficult as it was, having cancer and relying on others helped him give up believing that he needed to be completely independent and in control of his life: "I've been more accepting of limits, knowing that I just have to radically accept that there are things that I cannot do and things that I cannot control."

A Nuanced View of the Self

When I ask Travis toward the end of our Phase II interview to tell me what he believes is his best quality as a person, his stoic voice reemerges for a moment: "Being the rock. I tend to be that anchor, that stable person that everybody needs in their life." Still, Travis's experiences between his Phase I and Phase II interviews, particularly his bout with cancer, also seem to have changed him somewhat from the person he was when he was younger. When I ask him how he thinks he is different from the person he was when we spoke last, he replies:

> I'm a lot calmer. I am—I'm not as spazzy. I don't have the hair-trigger temper that I used to. Um, it's just life has changed from that person to who I've become today. Um, people are—my friends and family definitely contributed to who I am. Events, you know, having cancer was a huge one that just—once you survive cancer, you can pretty much kick anything's ass. But at the same time you're like, "Wow, I survived." There are a lot of things that you used to freak out about that just really there's no point to.

Although Travis's self-perception as a "rock" is still evident in the sense of imperviousness he seems to have developed out of his successful battle with cancer ("once you survive cancer, you can pretty much kick anything's ass"), he also seems to believe he has mellowed from the "angry young man" he used to be and no longer feels the need to control every aspect of his world. Moreover, he credits his close relationships with having played a central role in making him the person he is today.

Foremost among these is Travis's relationship with Mark, which he sees as central to his future as he looks ahead: "We've gotten to the point where I don't want to say we're comfortable, but we're locked in. We know where we're going. We know that it's going to be us." Given the fact that Travis's parents are both dead, his relationship with his grandmother is also extremely significant in his life:

> She's the last kind of true family connection that I keep. Like, I have a brother, and he has a family. But that's his family, and, you know, I feel awkward at times being there. My nana is my shining star. And it's always been myself and, you know, Nana against the world. So—and I understand that she's getting older and all that.

When I ask how his grandmother supports him, he replies, "Oh, she's always been very supportive, always very emotionally supportive, always calls. If I don't call her every couple days, she'll call and want to make sure that I'm okay. And it just—it's always been that way." As was also evident in Travis's Phase I interview, Travis's relationship with his grandmother fills an emotional void left by his parents' absence and a need for open and frequent emotional connection that, even when Travis's parents were alive, seems to have been lacking.

In Travis's Phase II interview, I remind him of the fact that he characterized his relationship with Jack as "don't ask, don't tell" with regard to his homosexuality, and I ask if that term still rings true when he thinks about his relationship with his brother today:

> It is and it isn't. We don't discuss what goes on. It's—it is what it is. He has a family, and I do try to be a part of the family as much as I possibly can. But we do live about two and a half hours away from each other, so major holidays are when I get down to see the family, but that's about it. It's about the same.

When Travis discusses his current relationship with Jack, which he characterizes as "about the same" since we spoke six years earlier, it is perhaps not surprising that his stoic voice reemerges. Using phrases such as "we don't discuss what goes on" and "it is what it is," Travis seems resigned to this level of interaction in his relationship with his last surviving immediate family member, thus making his other close, supportive relationships that much more important.

Travis does not have as close a relationship as he would like with his eleven-year-old son, since the child moved to California with his mother about three months before our interview. Travis says he sees his son on some major holidays, and "we e-mail and text, and I talk to him two or three times a week." In addition, Travis says he has "two very weird pockets of friends," one from high school and one from college, with whom he stays in touch. In general, though, Travis says, "I'm not a huge social crowd kind of person. There's a lot of acquaintances but very few inner-circle friends."

Looking Ahead

When I ask Travis to look ahead at his future goals, concerns, and hopes, he outlines his "five-year plan" to buy out the other owners of the Bakery Commons using life insurance money he received after his father's death. In envisioning his future, Travis echoes the "everyman" voice that I heard throughout our interview:

> I'm still wanting a family and, you know, the 2.3 kids, white picket fence, the house, you know, the minivan. Um, but I see myself at the Bakery Commons, running it with Mark and just, you know. I

don't want to use the word *normal*, but just having a life that's not crazy or hectic or jet-setting. I don't need any of that. Just calm. I'd like a nice, calm, kind of mundane existence.

I ask if he thinks this kind of life would make him happy; he responds pensively, "Yeah."

In addition to his hopes, Travis's worries about the future are also expressed from an "everyman" perspective, one that reflects the economic concerns of the twenty-first century. He discusses the fear of losing his job, particularly at the big-box retail store; the financial feasibility of his "five-year plan" to buy out the bakery; and his plan to get a degree in small-business management in order to prepare himself for the future:

> Well, I'm always nervous about the economy, but everybody's nervous about that. You know, am I going to walk in one day and [name of the discount store in which he works] is going to be closed? Um, you know, is the bakery—well, yeah, the five-year plan of buying out—am I going to be able to run a business and make sure everything is going? And I have, you know, ten plans—plans within plans. I'm going to be starting a small-business degree at the community college next year. And, you know, I read *Consumer Reports*, and I try to go with the consumer trends, and we're always trying to develop new, better—find bigger contracts, find steady income.

While concerned about the economy and how it might affect his life, Travis also makes clear that he plans to play an active role in his future rather than just let it happen to him. Consistent with his earlier statements that he is "always trying to do something, persevere, make [him]self better somehow," Travis already has concrete ideas for ways he can make his goals as an entrepreneur a reality: obtaining a small-business degree and following consumer trends so that he can make the best decisions possible. While Travis's attitudes and plans may obviously change in the years to come, his commitment to hard work, at least at this point, clearly defines not only his current life circumstances but his imagined future.

Finally, I ask Travis to talk about the topic with which I ended many of my interviews: the things that give him hope.[1] Here again, Travis's goal

---

1. The interview question "What gives you hope when you look ahead?" is inspired by the work of Lisa Machoian, who has used versions of it in her interview studies with adolescent girls suffering from depression.

orientation and personal drive are clearly wellsprings of optimism for him, but he also recognizes that trust in the key relationships in his life give him reason to hope as he looks ahead:

> Um, knowing that I do have the support system that I have, and they're very close coworkers or friends, and the fact that I have a plan. I know that always having a plan doesn't mean the plan's going to come to fruition. But having a plan, having obtainable goals set, just gives me some sense of hope and knowing that there will be a good future. . . . I just—I kind of come across as that I'm just looking for a plain, mundane, ordinary life and—you know? And not a lot of things change. But the whole—I remember doing the first interview, and I was, "Gay is A-okay," and that's who I was. That was my identity. And I think in the past couple years I just realized that it's not who you love; it's how you love.

In this final statement of our interview, several strands of Travis's story come together—his work ethic, his attitude about his gayness (and the fact that it does not define who he is), the important role of relationships in his life, and his desire for a simple life. In the end, it seems that for Travis—an "everyday guy" who is also gay—hard work, commitment, and the creation of a simple, satisfying life with a partner are expressions of "how you love" and are ultimately what matter most.

Listening to Travis: "Queering" Conventions of Sexuality, Class, and Gender

In trying to decide on the name of this book, I struggled when I thought about participants like Travis, who do not identify themselves as queer, and wondered whether *In a Queer Voice* was inclusive of their experiences and self-perceptions. When I ask Travis whether he has any personal associations with this term, his response is short and unequivocal: "No. It's another word." Although Travis cannot therefore be considered queer (since self-perception is essential to the concept), his voice nonetheless expresses a queer sensibility. That is, his words and actions imply a rejection of societal conventions associated with gender and sexuality (and, in his case, social class) in ways that are unique among this group of research participants.[2]

---

2. I do not suggest in this chapter that Travis is by life circumstances or choice part of a particular "social class," since I find this kind of attribution to individuals artificial. Rather, I suggest that

Most apparently, simply in living his life as a gay man and being in a committed same-sex intimate relationship—and in talking about this relationship proudly, affectionately, and unapologetically—Travis has queered the culture of his immediate sphere and of the larger culture, both of which are predominantly heterosexual. But Travis also queers the culture around him by rejecting culturally reinforced notions of what it means to be gay and living his life on his own terms. Despite the fact that he is aware of the political and academic discourses around LGBTQ identity, he has little interest in making these important aspects of his life and claims his right to live a "nice, calm, kind of mundane existence" (a choice that he might not even feel compelled to articulate if he were heterosexual). Moreover, although Travis has a college education and was on track toward a professional career in social work earlier in his life, he has rejected what he views as the cultural stereotype of the well-dressed, upper-middle-class professional white gay man (reinforced by television shows such as *Modern Family* and the earlier *Will and Grace*) in favor of what he views as a simpler, more satisfying life.

Travis's voice is thus fiercely independent, a quality that seems to have been cultivated at least in part by his life experiences. Losing both of his parents before age twenty-one obviously contributed to Travis's sense of independence, but there are other ways in which Travis in his earlier life seems to have been largely on his own in dealing with challenges, particularly coming to terms with being gay. In Travis's family, an unspoken "don't ask, don't tell" policy about his homosexuality was in force, and although he was allowed to start a gay-straight alliance at his high school, the fact that it was kept "on the down low" by administration and was populated primarily by "straight girls" suggests there was little visibility of LGBTQ issues at school beyond the GSA. Travis did have a supportive relationship with the high school theater program's technical director, a gay man with whom Travis says he "talked about everything." Consistent with other youth in this study such as Lindsey (Chapter 2) and Jordan (Chapter 5), who found that having confiding relationships with openly LGBTQ adults helped them feel comfortable talking openly at school (see also Mayo 2008), Travis explains: "He always knew exactly what I was about and always knew just by looking at me how I was feeling and knew where I was coming from, because he'd grown up in the same town and the same high school."

---

social class is an issue with special meaning in the LGBTQ community, something to which Travis seems especially attuned, and that he actively resists what he perceives to be the social-class implications of being gay. Susan Raffo's (1997) edited volume *Queerly Classed* is a collection of writings that explore the issue of social class in the LGBTQ community.

By his account, however, Travis has taken a "me against the world" approach to many challenges in his life and even dealt with the coming-out process mostly on his own: "I stopped listening to everyone around me and just listened to myself." In many ways, Travis's independent streak is representative of the ways in which boys are socialized in our culture, and many of his comments, particularly when talking about his adolescence, reflect a stoicism that is in keeping with what psychologist William Pollack (drawing on prior work by Deborah David and Robert Brannon) has called the "Boy Code." In his widely read book about boys' development, *Real Boys* (1998), Pollack notes that boys are socialized in our culture to be "sturdy oaks" in the face of significant life challenges, to manage their feelings stoically and project a sense of impenetrability and control.

In accepting his family's "don't ask, don't tell" culture, which seems to continue even today in his relationship with his brother, Jack, Travis chooses not to care about the silence that affects this relationship and even seems somewhat complicit in maintaining it: "If we don't talk about it, it's better." Travis's stoicism about his family relationships was also evident at another point in our interview in which he discussed how his parents were somewhat emotionally unavailable to him while he was growing up, in part because they were "both very busy" and because, from his perspective, Jack was their favorite son:

My mom and dad were both very busy. I'm the youngest of two.
Probably at the last interview, my brother was the prodigal child,
so everything he did was absolutely amazing, and I kind of feel like
I got ignored. But, you know, again, then you just radically accept
your emotions, identify them, and move past them.

After a brief moment of vulnerability in discussing how he felt "ignored," Travis checks his emotions and explains (interestingly, shifting to the second person) how he learned to adapt: "You just radically accept your emotions, identify them, and move past them."

In some ways, Travis's stoic voice in the face of unsatisfying relationships echoes those heard in the research of psychologist Niobe Way, whose studies challenge the conventional notion that friendships and other close relationships matter only to girls in adolescence. In her 2011 book *Deep Secrets: Boys' Friendships and the Crisis of Connection*, based on longitudinal studies with more than a hundred boys, Way notes that intimate, communicative friendships matter deeply to boys during adolescence, but many boys give up closeness in these relationships and keep their desire for intimacy with friends concealed in the face of culturally enforced expectations of masculine behavior. Publicly, they project an air of emotional invulnerability because they fear that having intimate connections with male friends will result in their being viewed by their peers and society as unmanly or even, in what is many boys' worst fear, gay:

> In the midst of boys' discussion of shared secrets and feelings, the mocking voice of masculine conventions was ever present. Sometimes this voice was direct, as when Omar said that the reason he wouldn't tell his best friend about his hurt feelings is because "that's gay." Other times it was subtler, as when boys talked about their desire to have friends who knew when "something was not a joking matter." When asked in his freshman year if the teasing between his male peers results in hurt feelings, Justin says: "I really wouldn't know 'cause they never really say, oh you hurt my feelings, 'cause guys don't share things like that." (Way 2011, 111)

In drawing this analogy to Way's research, I am not suggesting that Travis's independence and stoicism are inauthentic or even necessarily maladaptive. (It would be far beyond the scope and capability of this research to analyze Travis's narrative in this way.) To the contrary, there are points in Travis's story at which his independence seems to serve him extremely well. He took the initiative to start (and become president of) a GSA in his high school, where none had previously existed. He also faced cancer and, with the help of friends, emerged from that experience with a new sense of his own capabilities and perspective on life. Moreover, Travis's refusal to be defined by his gayness, instead of reflecting emotional distance from this aspect of himself, can alternatively be viewed as a healthy example of identity synthesis, an advanced stage of sexual identity development whereby a person comes to incorporate being gay or lesbian with other aspects of a complex, multifaceted identity (Cass 1979). (See Chapter 6 for a more detailed discussion of stage theories of LGBTQ identity development.)

Travis's story raises questions, however, about how the socialization of boys in our culture may put gay, bisexual, transgender, or queer-identifying boys at particular risk if they do not have the outlets or the encouragement to express their feelings about coming out, harassment, or other issues they are facing. Especially in school cultures where calling a boy gay is viewed as the most humiliating attack on his manhood imaginable, many boys choose silence over expressing their thoughts and feelings to another person, and the consequences at their most extreme can include violence directed at others or self-destruction (Kimmel 2008). As Pollack and others have noted (Pollack 1998; Pollack and Shuster 2000), boys often turn to alcohol and drug use to cope with feelings they are unable to express in other ways, and although Travis does not associate his serious drug problem during high school with any stressors related to his sexuality or gender, these behaviors clearly put him at risk for serious consequences.

Having now reached adulthood, Travis seems to have developed the skills and the will to manage his life challenges—with the past support of friends, his high school mentor, and organizations such as YouthWest—and has emerged with his own unique queer voice. In expressing his own version of what it means to be gay, Travis expands traditional notions about the future lives to which some advocates may encourage LGBTQ youth to aspire—beyond activism or traditional upper-middle-class success—to include, if they wish, being "the poor, nine-to-five everyday guy" who also happens to be gay.

5

Jordan: Across the Gender Border—and Back Again

"It really makes me happy when I realize that I finally found, you know, the one thing that identifies me the most."

T he story of Jordan begins as the story of Matt, a female-to-male transgender youth I met at YouthWest in 2004.[1] Although still biologically female, Matt presented himself at the time as a young man, with his brown hair cut short, the use of a typically male name, and the oversized flannel shirt and carpenter jeans typical of late adolescent boys in the rural community in which YouthWest is located. During our initial interview, Matt shares with me his plans to start taking male hormones within the next several months and to work toward a biological sex reassignment in the near future, although he still has many questions about how he will pay for the treatments and procedures involved. He seems to view adopting a male identity as a sort of "coming home to himself," a release from a prior state of confusion and discontentment: "I do like being so in tune, you know, with myself and who I am. It really makes me happy when I realize that I finally found, you know, the one thing that identifies me the most."

---

1. Definitions of the term *transgender* differ. One used by the U.S. Department of Health and Human Services (HHS) Leadership Campaign on AIDS offers a useful starting point: "Individuals whose gender identity, expression, or behavior is not traditionally associated with their birth sex. Some transgender individuals experience gender identity as incongruent with their anatomical sex and may seek some degree of sex reassignment surgery, take hormones, or undergo other cosmetic procedures. Others may pursue gender expression (masculine or feminine) through external self-presentation and behavior" (U.S. Department of Health and Human Services 2005). This definition presumes, however, that gender expression can be only masculine or feminine, whereas many transgender individuals argue that transgender identity need not be defined in terms of one or the other binary gender category (e.g., Bornstein 1994).

For Matt, the sense of feeling "different" in some way went back as far as he could remember. Before identifying as transgender, Matt used his traditionally female given name and identified as lesbian; later, he wondered if the way he felt and the way others responded to him meant something else:

> I have always known my whole life I have been attracted to women. It's just something that has always been there, so, you know, when I was old enough to understand it and I started to, you know, realize that there were other people out there like me, I was less afraid of it. . . .
>
> You know, but now it's just nice to have people call you "sir" and stuff because that's how you want to identify. But before, it was more like funny to me. Like, I didn't realize the significance of it. You know, I was kind of like, "Well, I do have really androgynous features," and I started to realize more and more, the more I got mistaken for a guy, that I actually really felt like I was a guy and wanted to be a guy.

Two aspects of "being a guy" that became particularly important to Matt once he realized his transgender identity were having the physical attributes of a man and having a man's name. Matt mentions his desire to have chest surgery at several points in the interview. ("I would love to get chest surgery, but it's expensive.") He also explains his decision to adopt what is typically considered a man's name as preparation for his eventual transition to being biologically male: "Once the hormones start kicking in, you know, you can't go around with a girl name."

Although Matt exudes an easy sense of pride about his sexuality and gender identity during his Phase I interview, which took place shortly after his twentieth birthday, a story he shares illustrates that his early adolescence was marked by significant emotional turmoil around these same issues. When Matt was in sixth grade, he had a physical and emotional breakdown that he believes was in some way related to a growing realization:

> When I was younger I used to get that way [deeply depressed], because I was very sick when I was younger. In sixth grade I was sick for at least six months straight, and I got so depressed to the point where I called my mom and I was—I couldn't breathe, you know, I was so upset. And I told her she needed to come home, and when she got there, she said I was sitting on the stairs, and I didn't even really acknowledge her presence. When she finally spoke, I asked

her what she was doing there. She said, "You called me, and you couldn't even breathe. I thought you were going to die." Then I told her I wished I did die. That's at the point where she brought me to therapy, and that was around when I was at least twelve or thirteen. That was around the time when I started to realize my sexuality more. I haven't been that depressed since then.

Matt is unable to pinpoint the exact nature or origin of his illness here, but he describes it as a sort of "depression" that had physical manifestations, including—at least at one point—the inability to breathe. Matt also connects his suicidal thinking at the time to unspoken issues related to his gender and sexuality that, at the time, he did not understand. Thankfully, Matt says he no longer feels the same level of depression and connects this change temporally to the time he began seeing a therapist and when he "started to realize my sexuality more."

Family Tensions Related to Matt's Gender Identity

Another troubling issue Matt discusses at length during our first interview is the difficulty he is having reconciling his gender identity with the key relationships in his life, especially those with his family. He even expresses fear that he might "lose" his parents altogether if he follows through on his plans to begin taking hormones and, ultimately, to have chest surgery and other surgical procedures for sex reassignment.

Matt's relationship with his mother is especially strained, and he returns several times during the interview to the topic of his mother's negative reaction to his being transgender, which he had disclosed to her five or six months earlier:

My mom and I used to be close. Ever since I said, you know, I was trans, we haven't been that close. We just argue about it and stuff. . . . At first she was kind of angry, you know? Well, she was sort of sad at first, and now she's in the angry part. So I think it's better to just not mention it to her.

I ask how her anger comes out. He replies, "She yells, and she gets upset, and she gets really sad after we argue, and she just gets really depressed, I guess."

Matt's statement that "it's better not to mention it to her" reflects a significant break in this relationship, at least in terms of mother-child communication; Matt chooses to silence his voice rather than provoke an emotional reaction from his mother. In a relationship that, by Matt's account, "used to be close," now communication about what Matt considers a core aspect of his identity is off limits. Later in the interview, Matt discusses at length his mother's especially strong objections to his decision to begin taking hormones in the next few months. He explains that his mother has serious concerns for his health and believes he should wait several more years before making a final decision, since there will be "no turning back" once the treatment begins.

Despite Matt's apparent comfort with his gender identity and sexuality, he seems badly torn between his desire for self-fulfillment and his wish to spare his mother emotional suffering. At one point in our interview, Matt finds a dramatic metaphor for the dilemma in which this places him and describes the tension several times as a sort of internal "war":

> I think I war between that [being true to myself and pleasing my family]. You know, like a part of me wants to be, you know, the person that my mom wants me to be, but then I realize that I'm a greater person when I'm not the person she wants me to be. So it's kind of like a war between myself. 'Cause I know if I don't go through with the hormones and the surgery, I know I would just be miserable. And—but my mom and my family would be happy. You know, it's just kind of like a war.

Before coming out to his mother as transgender, Matt had come out to her as lesbian while in high school. He explains that this disclosure, at least as he recalls it now, was much easier because his mother had a greater familiarity with lesbian women than she did with transgender people:

> I first came out as a lesbian to my mother. And she seemed kind of upset at first, but she wasn't really verbal like she was with the whole transgender thing. Because, um, I think it's because she's met lesbians, and she's interacted with them, and she hasn't really known any transgendered people. If she has, she doesn't realize it. So when I came out as lesbian, it wasn't as big of a deal. And then when I came out as trans, it's just the whole concept of her losing her only daughter.

Matt's last statement here about his mother's fear of "losing her only daughter" is illustrative of the unique issues transgender youth and their parents face in negotiating family relationships. Whereas the parents of gay and lesbian youth face adjustments in their expectations for their children if they presumed they would grow up to be heterosexual (Saltzburg 2004), parents of transgender youth must reframe their fundamental notions of who their children are, and they may see a change in a child's gender identity not just as a change in expectations but, as Matt's experience illustrates, the "loss" of a son or daughter (Wren 2002).

Although not as extreme as those of his mother, Matt's father's reactions to his being transgender lead him to silence this aspect of himself in order to keep peace in this relationship as well: "He gets upset when I mention it but not to the point where he is screaming and yelling like my mom. He's more sad. And so, I don't like seeing anyone sad, and so it's hard for me to talk to him about it."

Matt's relationship with his only sibling, a twenty-two-year-old older brother named Curtis, seems affected in a different way by issues associated with Matt's transgender identity. Whereas Matt expresses distress at both his parents' pain, he speaks in a more disdainful voice about the way Curtis abuses his knowledge of Matt's sexuality and gender expression:

> He's kind of an ignorant person. Like, uh, he's very strong set in his values, um, and like one second he'll be fine with everything, and then the next he'll turn around and have a bad mood and just take it out on you and use, you know, whatever he can against you. Obviously, sexuality and transgenderism is something that can be used against you, and he knows that. He knows, you know, it hits really hard when he mentions those things. . . .
>
> [One] instance recently was I went downstairs to talk with him because I work with him—and he works downstairs, and I work upstairs—and he said, "You're not a guy; you just dress like one." And that really hurt my feelings, and I told him I didn't want to talk about that with him and just kind of walked away before it got, you know, worse. So he says things really derogatory like that, and it just makes me think of him as an asshole, which is really sad because he's my brother, but what am I supposed to do?

Although Matt is able to distance himself from his brother's attitude and adopts a judgmental tone when describing it, Curtis's emotionally abusive behavior clearly causes Matt considerable distress. Like many of Matt's statements about his mother, his last statement in this passage ("which is really sad because he's my brother, but what am I supposed to do?") reflects his recognition that family relationships are deeply important to him. Matt clearly wants to have close, supportive relationships with the members of his family and seems hurt and regretful when such closeness and support are lacking, but issues associated with Matt's sexuality and gender identity block these relational connections from happening in the ways Matt would like.

Matt also seems especially wounded in this instance by Curtis's negation of his transgender identity. Curtis's assertion that Matt is "not a guy" but just dresses like one is one that Matt says really hurt his feelings. Matt's inner self-assurance about his gender identity is once again in conflict with his family relationships, and where people close in his relational circle question or threaten his inner sense of self, the conflict seems to be a source of especially acute emotional distress.

The Emergence of Matt's Voice at School

At the time of our Phase I interview, Matt was roughly two years out of high school and working full-time in a local box-making factory. When I ask him how he feels about the job, he somewhat ambiguously says, "It's all right. It can be pretty stressful, but it's enjoyable. . . . I don't have any loathing for it." Matt's eventual goal is to go to school "for either writing or drawing or both" and, ultimately, to live in New York City fully transitioned as a man.

Reflecting on his high school experiences, Matt describes himself as a student who "didn't mind doing the academics" and who earned "mostly Bs and As, sometimes Cs once in a while." The first high school Matt attended, Smith County Regional High School, is a comprehensive school that two of our other research participants also attended. Of these three students, one dropped out of school altogether and one left because of repeated harassment based on his sexual orientation and transferred to the local technical high school. Matt also left Smith County Regional and cites the harassment he experienced there as one of the main reasons for his transfer:

> I went to Smith County for about two, three years. And a lot of people were accepting there, but then there were people who weren't.
>
> I lost a lot of friends when I told, you know, them about my sexuality, and they were very derogatory, very, very—they would laugh at me behind my back and say stupid shit. It just was so bad that I just didn't want to be there anymore. Like, I didn't really feel comfortable being there. I mean, I had four or five friends who stood up for me and accepted me, but to me, that wasn't really enough.
>
> I actually used to get harassed, too, for looking like a guy. People used to come up to me and say, "Are you a guy or a girl?"

you know, and that really pissed me off at the time because I don't think it was [about] how I felt about my gender; it was more that I knew they were just doing it to be an asshole.

Matt eventually left Smith County Regional and transferred to Clay Technical High School, where he says he noticed a palpable difference in the school climate with regard to LGBTQ issues. (Lindsey, profiled in Chapter 2, also attended Clay Tech after attending middle school in the Smith County district.) Matt's voice changes immediately when our conversation shifts from Smith County to Clay Tech, a school where, much to Matt's surprise, LGBTQ students had a support group, anti-LGBTQ harassment was addressed effectively by staff, teachers were "very accepting" of LGBTQ students, and he had a considerably easier time forming supportive peer relationships: "It was a lot better. People were a lot more accepting of me, and I had a lot of friends actually. You know, like I was kind of the neutral person who could talk to basically anybody, you know? I was pretty well acknowledged there."

In addition to the dramatic differences in Matt's overall descriptions of the two school environments, which are compared in the following table, his use of two words in particular, *friends* and *support* (italicized in the table), further illustrates how Matt experienced a level of peer support at Clay Tech that was largely absent at Smith County.

Matt's experiences at Smith County	Matt's experiences at Clay Tech
I went to Smith County for about two [or] three years. And a lot of people were accepting there, but then there were people who weren't.	Clay Tech was a lot better. People were a lot more accepting of me, and I had a lot of *friends*, actually. You know, like I was kind of the neutral person who could talk to basically anybody, you know? I was pretty well acknowledged there.
I lost a lot of *friends* when I told, you know, them about my sexuality, and they were very derogatory, very, very—they would laugh at me behind my back and say stupid shit. It just was so bad that I just didn't want to be there anymore. Like I didn't really feel comfortable being there. I mean, I had four or five *friends* who stood up for me and accepted me, but to me, that wasn't really enough.	It was very nice. It made me feel even more, you know, accepted, because Smith County didn't really have any *support* as far as if you were gay, lesbian, bisexual, whatever. You know, they didn't really have that. When I found out that Tech was—that they did have that *support*—I was just shocked. I mean, I was just—I didn't even think there would be anything like that, any kind of groups or anything.
I actually used to get harassed, too, for looking like a guy. People used to come up to me and say, "Are you a guy or a girl?" you know, and that really pissed me off at the time because I don't think it was [about] how I felt about my gender; it was more that I knew they were just doing it to be an asshole.	And so I was very grateful. And the atmosphere was very fun-loving. You know, they were—it was a lot like YouthWest, except for it was smaller. But a lot of my *friends* went to it, the people that I associated with, and people that I didn't even know went to it, and I became *friends* with them. And it just—it was awesome.

Much of the relationship building Matt was able to do at Clay Tech was facilitated by the presence of a gay-straight alliance, a form of support that was lacking at Smith County Regional and that, as indicated in previous chapters, researchers have found to be strongly associated with a variety of positive outcomes for LGBTQ youth, including greater feelings of belonging at school (Heck, Flentje, and Cochran 2011; Walls, Kane, and Wisneski 2010).

In addition to the important relational connections Matt formed with students in the GSA and through other peer networks at Clay Tech, he cites close, supportive relationships with several significant adults there as having made a positive difference in his experience of high school. These include his English teachers, who encouraged him to continue to develop his writing, and, perhaps most significantly, Janice Lane, the school's nurse and GSA advisor (also cited as a mentor by Lindsey in Chapter 2):

> I mean, I could talk to her about anything, and I did. She was just very—just a very brave woman, you know? And you could tell her anything, and it just stayed there. Um, I got a lot of support from my English teachers, too, because I'm very good at English, and, um, they loved my stories. They were always telling me, you know, "You've got to show me your stories. I want to read them." They were very supportive. They told me that, if I wanted to, I should go to college for writing and, you know, actually think of it as a career. So once they told me that, I really started feeling better about my self-confidence and my ability to get out in the world.

From his English teachers, Matt received strong encouragement to develop his voice as a writer, which he explains gave him a more general sense of self-confidence and an "ability to get out in the world." With Janice, the benefit was open communication; she was someone to whom Matt could talk "about anything," including his feelings about his sexuality and gender identity. Matt's description of this important mentor and GSA advisor at Clay Tech is strikingly consistent with Lindsey's description of Janice in Chapter 2 ("I talk to her about anything. . . . She just listens, and she's been there"), underscoring how an adult school staff member who listens to LGBTQ youth in an open and accepting way can be a key asset in multiple young people's lives.

Immediately after discussing these supportive relationships with adults and peers at Clay Tech, a strong, assertive voice emerges in Matt's interview. When I ask if he ever talked to adults at school about either gender identity issues or sexuality issues, he speaks with a sense of pride about being able to be himself at Clay Tech, as is especially evident in his first-person statements, italicized here:

> Yeah, *I did actually*. You know, mostly Janice, but *I was out to everybody*; you know, teachers, whoever. You know, like, *I was very proud* of saying that *I was in GSA*. *I was just a proud individual*. You know, *I was very independent*. *I knew if somebody was going to like me* for who *I am*, and *I just had to be as outspoken as possible* about everything. And *I never had any harassment there*.

Still, Matt did not identify as transgender, even to himself, while in high school. He attributes his nonidentification to a lack of knowledge among those in his school community, himself included, about transgender identity:

> Well, at school no one really knew about, like, transgenders, and it wasn't really anything I learned about, so I didn't really think of myself as transgender at that time.
>   I mean, thinking back on it now, if I knew about it, I probably would have. But if I did identify as trans, there are a few people from high school that I do know that are very accepting of it. I think even if I did, people would have been pretty supportive.

Matt assumes that, based on other aspects of the school community at Clay Tech, his peers and teachers would have been "pretty supportive" if he had been out as transgender at that time in his life. Yet his statements here also illustrate how, even in a school community that is relatively supportive of sexual-minority students, there can be a lack of understanding about transgender identity and the specific issues associated with it among faculty, students, and staff.

Other Key Supportive Relationships

When I ask Matt in our Phase I interview which relationships in his life are the most important and supportive, he once again cites friends, especially insofar as these relationships support him in his transgender identity in ways that those with his family do not: "You know, I mean, when I'm down and whatever, you know, I always go to my friends because I can't really talk to my parents about—or my brother about—that kind of stuff anymore."

Matt says his two best friends are also transgender. Cam, Matt's boyfriend, is another female-to-male transgender youth who, like Matt, has not undergone surgical sex reassignment:

> Cam is, you know, like, basically the most important person in my life right now. We talk a lot about transitioning, you know, our transitions, and, um, he's just—he's wonderful, you know. Like, he really cares about me, and he's doing everything he can to make our relationship work. It's just incredible, you know—an incredible experience to have someone that actually, you know, cares so much about me. Like, I've had pretty bad relationships in the past, so it's just kind of mind-blowing, you know, for him to be there for me that much.

The other relationship Matt cites as very important at this time in his life is the friendship he shares with Jarrett (who Matt says is about twenty-three), a transgender man who is one of the adult facilitators at YouthWest:

> Jarrett works here [at YouthWest], so it's not like we can hang out outside of here or whatever, but we are like very good friends as far as that's concerned, you know. . . . I see him like every week, pretty much. So we just talk basically a lot about the trans stuff and anything. You know, he's open to talking to me about anything, so he's one of the main supports, too. You know, I know that even if, um, you know, I'm bumming out or something, I can just call him, and he'd be there, you know, at the drop of a hat because he's just—he's awesome.

These two relationships—and the strong, positive tone Matt adopts when talking about them—illustrate the importance Matt places on having close friends with whom he can be fully himself and who, based on their own experiences, understand "about the trans stuff." Matt's close relationship with his boyfriend, Cam, although he describes it as not strongly focused on physical intimacy and sexual contact, seems strengthened by the mutual understanding both participants in the relationship have as transgender youth. Jarrett's transgender identity also seems to be a key element in his ability to support Matt as a sort of "big brother," a mentor with whom Matt can share his experiences and his stresses and who is there for Matt "at the drop of a hat."

Another key relationship for Matt is the one he shares with his therapist, Diane. Matt sees Diane as an especially strong source of support because of her knowledge of transgender issues: "Therapy has helped me a lot because Diane knows so much about transitioning. She's worked with so many trans people that she can definitely identify with what I'm going through."

Finally, like several of the other youth in this study, Matt highly values the friends he has made online through LGBTQ chat rooms and over e-mail: "I see my online trans guys and women and stuff, and you know, I love talking to them and catching up with them." Thus the Internet provides another opportunity for Matt to develop his voice, even if only in a virtual way, and connect with other transgender young people who may otherwise have few people in their lives who can "hear them" for who they are.

The Battles of a "Superhero"

One of the most illuminating and poignant parts of my first conversation with Matt was his discussion of the film *Spider-Man 2*, which had been released in the cinemas shortly before the time of our interview. Matt feels as though the tension he experiences trying to negotiate his own personal wishes with those of the people close to him, especially his mother, is analogous to the difficulty Spider-Man has in the film having to choose between using his superheroic powers and living a "normal" life:

> Well, it was a very emotional movie for me. You know, I found myself crying through it because in the movie he gives up being Spider-Man to make himself happy. And when he does, he realizes that he's not happy at all. And that's how I felt when I told my mom I would wait three years [before starting to take male hormones]. I mean, I was going along with that for at least a good two weeks. When I talked to Diane [Matt's therapist] about it, I realized how ever since I made that decision, I had gotten more and more depressed. And it just totally—I related to it more than I've related with anything because I gave up being transgender in a way. You know, I put a halt—a very big halt—on my transition, and I wasn't happy at all. And I realized that if I did wait three years, that would be three years of being untrue to myself, and that's one thing I just can't do.

Despite the obvious emotional pull Matt feels from his mother's concerns, it is again clear in this passage that Matt's core as a transgender person is solid, and he believes that not honoring his transgender identity would be equivalent to "being untrue to [him]self." In addition, Matt focuses on more than the difficulty of his situation in this comparison to Spider-Man. He also sees something heroic about his own, as well as others', decision to live as transgender despite the tremendous pressures against doing so:

> It's almost like being transgender is being a hero to me because, you know, there are so many people that just won't come to the realization, and they don't advance on their transition because of the pain and suffering it causes. But I just realized it's something I had to do. . . .
>
> A lot of people would call it selfish, but I think we're brave, and I think it takes a lot of emotional stress out of us to do these kinds of things. And people don't realize these things. They don't realize the emotional circumstances. They think you're this selfish asshole, you know? And it's not that at all. You know, you're just doing it to be happy, and it takes a lot of guts to do that, to go against everyone you know, and be like, "This is what's going to make me happy, so I'm going to do it." People don't understand the grief and depression you go through when you're doing that.[2]

Becoming Jordan: Following Up Six Years Later

When I began in 2009 trying to contact youth who had participated in Phase I of the study, following up with Matt presented several challenges. Both his e-mail address and phone number had changed, and because of the sensitivity of the issue of his transgender identity with his parents, I was reluctant to call them and ask if they knew where he was. (I also was unsure which name I would use if I called. Would I ask for Matt or use the traditionally female name he told me he was given at birth but with which he no longer identified?) Calling any telephone number except for the one he gave me on his survey, or asking any other former YouthWest members, would breach his anonymity as a study participant. I eventually found Matt through means I do not disclose here in order to protect his privacy, and when I recontacted him he was immediately receptive to the idea of a second interview in which he would share the next chapter of his story.

---

2. For extended excerpts of my Phase I interview with Matt, see "The Story of Matt: 'Transgender Superhero'" in the second edition of my edited book *Adolescents at School: Perspectives on Youth, Identity, and Education* (Sadowski 2008c).

In the fall of 2010, I flew to the midsized southern U.S. city in which the study participant I had come to know as Matt was now living. No longer using the name Matt or Jessica (Matt's female birth name), Jordan—a name chosen specifically for its androgyny and for other reasons discussed later in our interview—welcomed me to the apartment where Jordan's partner, Mary, and two friendly ferrets also lived. Since our last interview, Jordan had readopted an identity as a woman for reasons we discussed at length in our conversation, and I therefore refer to Jordan using female pronouns for the remainder of this chapter.

Since I began most Phase II interviews by asking participants to talk about how their lives had changed since we had last met, the story of Jordan's efforts toward sex reassignment were among the first things we discussed. As planned at the time of our Phase I interview, and despite the objections of family members (particularly Jordan's mother), Jordan began taking testosterone about a year later as a first step toward a surgical sex reassignment. Jordan was happy with the results of the early treatments, both in terms of how it made her feel and how others related to her. After beginning the treatments, which came in the form of a gel absorbed through the use of a patch on Jordan's abdomen, her voice became lower, she developed "peach fuzz" on her face, and, as she explains it, "People thought I was a guy when they first met me, which was nice."

At several points in our interview, Jordan describes the initial efforts toward a female-to-male transition as "right for me" and describes some of the nearly euphoric feelings she felt during this period. These feelings were dampened, however, by her family's continued objections:

> It was pretty amazing. There were like highs and lows. You know, there were times where I was so happy, you know, I felt like I could cry from joy. And there were other times when I was fighting with my family and everything where it was sad. And, you know, there was no doubt that I questioned myself and if what I was doing was right, but at the end of the day, I knew it was right for me.

Although Jordan says her family eventually accepted her decision to begin treatment and that her parents "would likely have accepted me as their son" (something that seemed in doubt during our Phase I interview), the initial transition period was marked by significant stress within the family:

> My mom had a hard time with it. Um, she just didn't understand. Like, she loves me so much that she didn't understand why I wanted

to change myself because she loved me the way I was. But her biggest concern was not that I was doing it; it was my health that she was most concerned about, and that was her main argument: "It's just not natural to change your body and expect that complications aren't going to happen." And my brother was really harsh; like, he's kind of, like, a blunt person. You know, he calls it as it is. So he's not afraid to get in your face and tell you how he feels, which is awesome because he's honest. But it can also be hurtful. "Why are you doing this? You're not a boy, and blah, blah, blah." And so I got all of that from him.

Even though family members' objections were clearly a source of emotional distress for Jordan as she was attempting to make a major life change, her discussion of it as an adult reflects a more generous assessment of her family's motivations than she expressed in the Phase I interview. In stating that her mother's objections to her planned sex reassignment were based on the fact that "she just loves me so much," and in reassessing her brother's bluntness as "awesome" instead of just referring to him as an "asshole" (as she did in our prior interview), Jordan seems more aware as an adult of the close bond between her and her family members despite their differences. Jordan even refers to her father in our Phase II interview as "the hero of the story," since he was the only member of her family who agreed to accompany her to therapy sessions as she was planning to begin her transition:

My dad is really the hero of the story because I—you know, when I was going through therapy . . . where my therapist had to determine if it was right for me or not, the only one that came to a therapy session was my dad. And my mom just absolutely refused to go; like, she said she would just—she could not listen to what the therapist was gonna say. Just, she would want to scream and argue, because she was frustrated with me, and no one can blame her for that. But my dad, you know—I was so upset, and he saw how upset I was. And he said he'd go. . . . I asked my brother, too, and he just said, "Hell no!"

Eventually, Jordan says all three of her immediate family members were "slowly accepting it" (her decision to have sex reassignment) when physical complications arose from her taking testosterone about half a year into the treatment:

I had been taking testosterone for about, like, six months, and she [my doctor] had increased my dosage and everything, because everything was going fine, and I felt fine. But then after about six months, I started having these spells where I would just get incredibly dizzy, and my heart would flutter, and I'd get hot flashes. And, um, you know, at first I was like, "It was just a reaction; it was normal," because I was told it was normal. [My doctor had told me,] "You're going to have some, you know, minor crazy reactions because your body and your hormones are going to be out of balance." So I thought it was normal. But, um, it started to escalate, and I started to get these spells like more and more, and then I started to have anxiety. And I got scared because I thought, you know, if I keep doing this, I could die. So I was pretty scared when it started happening.

After a period in which Jordan says she was increasingly tired and felt nervous going to work for fear she would pass out there or, worse, pass out while driving to work, she saw her doctor, who recommended changing the dosage. At that point, Jordan says, "I just wanted my health to go back to normal." Jordan made the difficult decision to stop the treatments completely, and she stopped seeing her doctor, who Jordan says "didn't even contact me" to follow up: "That was when I came to the realization that if they're going to play with my dosage, who the hell knows what that was gonna do to my health. Like, it just didn't feel that that would make it better. So it was rough, very rough."

As Jordan explains, the decision to stop taking hormones, and thus put a halt on her plans for sex reassignment, led to some complex and difficult emotions. Jordan became anxious and depressed and took antidepressants for a number of months to help her get through a sort of mourning period:

It was really hard when complications arose and I had to stop, because I truly believe I was doing what was right for me. . . . I cried. I cried a lot. You know, because, um, you know, I had pretty serious talks, like I said, with my family—my grandma, my mom and dad, my brother. They, of course, were accepting of everything at that point. . . . When all that [the physical complications] started happening, it was just a real letdown, so I felt very depressed, and I think that's why, you know, I had to go on antidepressants. I started to get anxiety and depression; even my blood pressure went up and stuff. I was depressed for quite a few months. It was really hard.[3]

3. Jordan makes no specific mention of anxiety in the initial months of her hormone treatment, so there is no evidence that it played a role in her physical symptoms.

When I ask Jordan to describe what helped her get through this difficult period in her life, she returns to family and her home community (she was still living in the Northeast at the time) as crucial sources of support:

> It took me a while to accept that it [the transition] wasn't going to happen, you know? For quite a few months I was just not—I was depressed and everything. But I still had my family, and I had a lot of support, and I guess that's what got me through. Lakeside is a very small place, so the neighbors knew what was going on, everybody knew what was going on, but that didn't stop them from being supportive. It was just nice after all that happened.

"Plugging On and Being Myself"

Two years after Jordan ended the testosterone treatments, she moved to the southeastern city in which she now lives to be with her partner, Mary, whom she met online and with whom she has been in a relationship for close to three years. The couple has shared an apartment for the past year, and Jordan says Mary is "pretty much my life." Jordan has a well-paying job as a technical support agent for a private company and, although she would love to move back to the Northeast to be closer to her family, she has been pleasantly surprised by the welcoming and accepting attitudes she has encountered in the South:

> The people here are great. Like, you know, I know my appearance, like, screams "butch lesbian," so I'm pretty sure that people can tell, like, right away that that's what I am. And, um, I've never had any issues here like I was scared that I might, because I know how—I'm not saying that the North is more, like, accepting or whatever, but I never had problems there, and I figured in the South they have more, like, problems. The people here are pretty nice—they call you "sweetie" and "honey." [*Laughs*] I had one lady even call me "baby."

Jordan's current self-identification as "butch lesbian" followed a long period of adjustment after her experience with testosterone treatments, but she says both it and the fact that she now thinks of herself as female feel right:

> I started identifying as a lesbian, you know, and everything. And I'm now just starting to be comfortable with that after a couple

years [since the treatment], so. But I've now totally accepted that I'm female; I just have to stay that way. I can't risk my health to be different. And I can't really feel like I could call myself transgendered because I'm not transitioning from female to male. . . .

It took me at least like a good two years to start accepting myself as a woman again, you know, um, and I still don't regret it. You know, I don't regret any second of it. But, um, it feels good actually, you know, now that I've, like, completely come to terms with it.

After a period of grief over the loss of her male and transgender self, Jordan seems to have found a new form of self-acceptance in living gender and sexuality in her own unique way. Although Jordan says her family of origin still uses her "born name" ("They just can't picture me as anything else"), she prefers the more androgynous "Jordan" and goes by that name in all other areas of her life, including with friends, with Mary and Mary's family, and online. Based on a character she created in an online chat room (the medium in which Jordan has continued to develop her writing), Jordan's name depicts her unique experiences across the boundaries of gender—and, in some respects, back again—a set of decisions she says she "would never take back."

When I ask Jordan how happy she is with her current life circumstances, she says:

I would say like a nine—pretty high up there. Um, the only reason I don't say ten is because of my family not being here, you know. But if my mom and dad up and moved here, I would say ten. But you know, um, all my family is back home, and I'm always gonna miss them. It makes me sad that I only see my parents twice a year, and my grandma, too. I see my grandma once a year, 'cause it's hard for her to make it out here.

Looking toward the future, I ask Jordan what gives her hope. Despite the family tensions around Jordan's transition, and her own difficulties making—and then being forced to abandon—a sex reassignment, Jordan's voice reflects hope, optimism, and an open-ended view of the future that challenges the boundaries of gender as they are traditionally drawn:

Just that I have so much support still and so many people in my life that love me, care for me, and I think that's the thing that gives me hope the most: that I'm accepted for who I am. I have a pretty good life, you know, looking at it. I mean, I don't, you know, earn enough money that I'd want to earn, and we don't have the greatest things here in the apartment, you know, but that's not to me what life is about. So looking ahead, I just—you know, plugging on and being myself, and, you know, it just gives me a lot of hope to know that no matter what happens, I've got support from both family and friends, and that gives me a lot of hope.

I—I still think about going back to transitioning, you know. Mary and I have even talked about it. And, um, but, you know, I just feel like I'm at the point in my life where I'm finally okay with just being myself.

Listening to Jordan: The Journey of a Gender Superhero

Jordan's experiences as Matt during adolescence illustrate the struggle that LGBTQ youth, and transgender youth in particular, can have trying to maintain positive and supportive relationships with their families. Researchers have identified that many transgender youth face verbal and physical abuse in their homes (Grossman, D'Augelli, and Frank 2011; Grossman, D'Augelli, and Salter 2006), depression and anxiety related to parental rejection (Grossman and D'Augelli 2006; Grossman, D'Augelli, and Frank 2011), and even forced homelessness (Lowrey 2010) for reasons associated with their gender and/or sexual identities.

As Bernadette Wren (2002) has noted, the parents of transgender youth often have difficulty reconciling their gendered images of their children with the new information that emerges when a child comes out as transgender. A young person's disclosure of transgender identity can thus result in a change in the parent-child relationship that both parties experience as a loss. At the time of his Phase I interview, Matt believes his relationship with his parents has changed significantly since he came out as transgender and says he fears he will "lose" his parents if he moves ahead with hormone treatment and sex reassignment surgery. He also explains that his mother views his being transgender as no less than "losing her only daughter." To avoid the loss of this relationship altogether, Matt silences himself, particularly the transgender aspect of his voice, in his family relationships because he concludes "it's better not to mention it." He even, for a time, agrees to halt his plans for sex reassignment in order to spare his mother emotional anguish. Yet the distress caused by this relational paradox (Miller and Stiver 1997)—whereby Matt keeps aspects of himself out of his relationship with his parents in order to keep at least a part of the relationship intact—is disturbing. He experiences this dilemma as a "war" between being true to himself and wanting to remain close to his family.

As Matt relates his experiences at his first high school, Smith County Regional, it appears that the climate there had a similarly silencing effect on his self-expression. Students at Smith County, Matt says, "would often laugh at me behind my back and say stupid shit" and harass him for "looking like a guy" even before he came out as transgender. (Although there is little information in Matt's interviews about his middle school experiences, he also connects the episode in which he had difficulty breathing and was deeply depressed in sixth grade to an emerging realization of issues related to his gender and/or sexuality.)

National surveys of LGBTQ youth have demonstrated that transgender students experience verbal and physical harassment in schools at even higher rates than lesbian, gay, and bisexual youth (Greytak, Kosciw, and Diaz 2009). Moreover, even in schools in which programs are in place to support lesbian, gay, and bisexual students, transgender students may not benefit in similar ways from these programs and may still perceive school as a hostile environment (McGuire et al. 2010). As a result of the harassment he experienced at Smith County, Matt says he just "didn't feel comfortable there" and transferred to Clay Tech. This "solution" to Matt's problem is unfortunately typical in cases where LGBTQ youth are harassed; it places the burden of correcting a hostile school situation on the victim of harassment rather than on the perpetrators or on the school that is failing to protect the student (Bochenek and Brown 2001; McGuire et al. 2010). As a result, the LGBTQ student is silenced altogether in the school environment by simply moving to another school, and the hostile school climate continues as before.

As in the case of Lindsey (Chapter 2), who also attended Clay Technical High School (Clay Tech), however, Matt's transfer there led to a welcome turnaround in his school experiences. One important asset that both Matt and Lindsey had at Clay Tech was the gay-straight alliance. As indicated in Chapter 2, numerous researchers have found the presence of GSAs in schools to be associated with a variety of positive outcomes for LGBTQ youth, the most relevant of which for Matt are a sense of belonging in school (Heck, Flentje, and Cochran 2011; Walls, Kane, and Wisneski 2010), which he clearly lacked at Smith County, and feelings of self-efficacy and empowerment (Russell et al. 2009), which are evident in Matt's ability to make many friends, do well academically, and live within the school community as a "proud individual." Matt's experiences at Clay Tech raise some questions about the extent to which the school was prepared to support transgender students—Matt says there was no discussion of transgender identity at all at the school, and it therefore did not occur to him to think about himself in these terms ("no one really knew about, like, transgenders"), but the general climate of acceptance at the school nonetheless led him to believe that if he had come out as transgender, "people would have been pretty supportive."

In addition to the peer relationships Matt formed at Clay Tech, he had relationships with several adults during his adolescence that supported him through the stresses of growing up lesbian and, subsequently, transgender. These relationships with informal mentors afforded Matt opportunities to communicate openly what he was thinking and feeling in a way he could not with his family. In this vein, he specifically cites Janice, his GSA advisor (to whom Lindsey in Chapter 2 also says she can "talk about anything"); Jarrett, the youth support group leader who is also transgender—and to whom Matt therefore feels he can talk openly "about the trans stuff"; and Diane, Matt's therapist, who Matt says is not transgender herself but has "worked with so many trans people that she can definitely identify with what I'm going through."

Drawing on these and other assets, and also benefiting from greater maturity than he had in early adolescence, by age twenty Matt talks about being transgender with a strong, independent, self-assured voice, despite the challenges he has had reconciling it with his family relationships. Even when talking about relationships in which his transgender identity is devalued (such as those with his brother and with abusive school peers), Matt is able to adopt a strong voice of disdainful resistance and retain his pride and self-assurance.

When we talk again six years later, Matt (now Jordan) appears in many ways to be the same person as before, despite the fact that she no longer considers herself either male or transgender. Although the health consequences of Jordan's hormone treatments have resulted in her decision to use differently gendered pronouns, LGBTQ descriptors (primarily "butch lesbian"), and even a different name in order to "start accepting myself as a woman again," she speaks with the same voice of self-acceptance she used when viewing and presenting herself as Matt, a transgender young man. While the decision to stop making the female-to-male transition was obviously a major disappointment to Jordan, she has come to a new level of acceptance of her gender identity based on neither the girl she was raised to be nor the man she wanted to become. Her gender identity reflects the unique combination of factors that make up who she is today, some that she views as beyond her control and others that reflect choices she has made about her own self-expression (such as adoption of the androgynous name Jordan). In this way, Jordan expresses her adult voice in a uniquely gendered tone that reflects a set of experiences only she can claim. Moreover, Jordan's current voice reflects the fluidity of her gender expression and a belief that, despite her acceptance of her current gender identity, she does not feel compelled to view anything as permanent: "I still think about going back to transitioning, you know. Mary and I have even talked about it."

Jordan's journey across the borders of gender has clearly been a difficult one at many junctures, including the relational conflicts she experienced when first coming out to her family as transgender and the disappointment associated with giving up what she once considered "the one thing that identifies me the most." Yet Jordan has come out of these experiences with a strong sense of self and describes her happiness, on a scale of one to ten, as "like a nine." Somewhat ironically, given the turmoil in Jordan's family relationships during adolescence, she says the one thing that would bring her happiness level to a ten as an adult would be having her parents live nearby. Jordan feels a strong foundation of support from her family, her partner, and past and present mentors and friends: "I have so much support still and so many people in my life that love me, care for me, and I think that's the thing that gives me hope the most: that I'm accepted for who I am. I have a pretty good life, you know, looking at it."

6

Eddie: Coming Out and Embracing the World

"As a white, privileged member of the world, you know, being a male and being American, I feel like I have—I have some ability . . . to kind of use that for good."

E ddie was one of the first people I met at CityYouth and was president of the organization when I paid my first visit to introduce the study to the steering committee. A friendly, outgoing young white man with wide eyes and the quick speech patterns of someone always ready to take on the next challenge, Eddie struck me immediately as a natural leader. He met me with an outstretched hand and a readiness to listen, and although there were also several advisors sitting at the table of about a dozen CityYouth decision makers, I knew that Eddie's support would be key to getting youth members to participate in the research.

After listening to the details of the study, and following some thoughtful questioning by Eddie and other steering committee members, the group agreed to allow our team to recruit participants at a subsequent CityYouth meeting. A few weeks later, colleagues and I explained the study to the roughly fifty members in attendance that night and asked if there were any questions. Eddie's hand shot up, and though we were not recording at the time (so I am not able to report his comments verbatim), he addressed the circle of his peers and said something like, "I just want you all to really think about volunteering for this. This is a really important thing these researchers are doing, and you have an opportunity to make a difference."

When Eddie first signed up to participate in the study, he was deeply involved in activism and in programs closely connected to his gay identity. In addition to his leadership role at CityYouth, he was part of a youth speakers' bureau that traveled around the state and educated teachers and students about LGBTQ issues, and he did volunteer work for an organization dedicated to the passage of same-sex marriage legislation. Constance P. (Connie) Scanlon, a member of our Harvard research team who conducted Eddie's Phase I interview, started by asking him why he felt it was important to speak to his peers as he did about participating in our research: "I was thinking about how all around that circle there's a different story, a different experience—exactly what you are saying. For someone else to read that—you think, 'Oh, somebody else knows how I feel, so maybe I'm not the only one.'"

Eddie also spoke about the need he believed younger adolescents had to hear a variety of coming-out stories so that they might feel less alone as they grapple with their own experience:

> Like when people are first coming out, people at first, like, learning about themselves, they need to learn that there are other people that have gone through the same thing. . . . Maybe someone who is fifteen or sixteen will read the book that you guys write based on the research, and the information that you get from us, and it will help them. . . . Coming out is a hardship, but it's just not the easiest thing to do, um, just because of the society that we live in, you know? Um, it's a heterosexual, like, society that we live in, whether you like it or not.

When I meet Eddie nearly seven years later for his Phase II interview at age twenty-six, he explains that the focus of his work has "pivot[ed] from LGBT activism to international activism." He now directs much of his effort and energy toward improving the lives of immigrant people and toward helping young people from economically disadvantaged backgrounds become "global citizens." Overall, Eddie's Phase I and Phase II interviews span eleven years of his life and in many ways chart the evolution of a "queer voice" through multiple stages. Eddie's story begins with a denial of his homosexuality and an inability to give voice to the strong feelings he was having as a teenager. It then evolves through a gradual (though not necessarily sequential) process: he comes out to family and friends; he proudly (and, as he describes it, somewhat loudly) begins to express his gay identity at school and among his peers; he speaks out about LGBTQ issues as a youth leader, educator, and activist; and he ultimately uses his voice to advocate for international causes while still maintaining a strong identity as a gay man.

Eddie's Journey toward Self-Awareness

After talking with Connie in his Phase I interview about the coming-out process and the difficulties he believes it poses for adolescents in general, Eddie shares his own experience coming to terms with the fact that he was gay. Although Eddie's family, as he explains it, turned out to be immediately supportive of his gay identity, he struggled with the initial disclosure to his parents for a long time and worried about how it would be received. He held the secret of his being gay and, as he explains, "ignored it" for a long time before he was even able to come out to himself:

> When I—when I came out, I first came out to myself. I had thought to myself, "Gee, um. I'm bisexual." Then I—I ignored it. I ignored everything. And one day [I met] this woman who actually [did] family counseling. . . . I told her all the things that were bothering me, and in the middle of the list of ten things, I said, "And there's one other thing that's driving me crazy, and I can't—I don't even want to think about it." And then I, um, I started thinking, telling her about other things. And she stopped me; she says, "Okay, now tell me." Now this is a tough girl from the city. She's like a tough city girl. She's like, "Cut the bull, all right? I want to ask you a question." I'm like, "Okay." We had a very special relationship, her and I.
>
> Uh, she's like, "You're having feelings for other men, aren't you?" And I was like, "Ah—oh—." I kind of made a face, and no noise came out. And I couldn't say no, but I didn't want to say yes. So I was like, "Maaayyybe," and we both started laughing.

Although Eddie ultimately laughed along with his counselor when she raised the possibility of his being gay (laughter that perhaps resulted from the release of long-silenced thoughts and feelings), he clearly was experiencing considerable internal conflict at this point in his life. On the one hand, he claims to have "ignored" his homosexuality, but he also refers to it as something that was "bothering me." He even told the counselor, "[It's] driving me crazy, and I can't—don't even want to think about it." When the counselor eventually, and somewhat bluntly, asks Eddie if he has feelings for other men, his voice literally disappears, and he is unable to speak: "And I was like, 'Ah—oh—.' I kind of made a face, and no noise came out."

Eddie seems to have been searching for a way to name feelings that he had previously found unspeakable, and the counselor gave him an opportunity—perhaps even a mandate—to do so. Although Eddie did not come out in this counseling session, it seems to have moved him toward a higher level of self-awareness. This led to his coming out to his family and friends, an experience that was emotionally charged and at times even frightening for him (Connie's questions in italics):

And what did that feel like when she [the counselor] . . . kind of named it, or said it?

I didn't know how to feel. I didn't feel anything. And so finally, like, I accepted it, and I was actually scared. I was scared, and the— um, the other person I told was my best friend, Dave, and I told—it was the first time I actually said it out loud. I told him that I was gay, and I started hysterically crying. It was just so overwhelming.

How old were you?

I was fifteen. And I didn't tell anyone else again until I was sixteen. And, um, the next person I told was my mother and my grandmother, simultaneously, in a seven-page, handwritten letter.

Coming Out to His Family

Eddie goes on to describe the experience of coming out as gay to his mother. Rather than speak to her directly (which apparently he was not ready to do), Eddie left his mother a letter to read while he was away for the weekend to visit friends out of town. On Sunday he went to his summer job, and at the end of the day he waited nervously for his mother to pick him up from work. Both Eddie's story and the halting speech pattern with which he relates parts of it capture the fear and anxiety he felt while anticipating his mother's reaction:

And she pulls up in the back. I'm like, "Oh, God! She's going to throw a suitcase out the window and drive away." And I walked out the back door, and she was sitting in the passenger seat, 'cause I would always drive home from work on my permit. And I got in, and I looked at her. . . . And I said, "Did you read the letter?" And she said, "Yeah." And I said, "What did you think?" And she's like, "I hope you know that I would always love you no matter what." She's like, "No matter what happens." She's like, "If you were in the electric chair waiting for the death penalty, I'd be holding your hand, and they'd have to drag me away." That's what she said.

Among the coming-out stories told by our research participants, we heard family members' reactions that fell on a continuum from anger and denial to unambiguous love and support. Yet even in this context Eddie's mother's reaction is extraordinary. The unconditional love and support she expresses here clearly mean a great deal to him ("'I'd be holding your hand,

and they'd have to drag me away.' That's what she said."), and it is hard to imagine this level of support not having helped Eddie feel safe and supported in his further coming-out process.

Even with the emotional boost that Eddie's mother's unexpected response might have given him at this point in his life, however, he says he was not ready to disclose his gayness to others for a long time. Rather than risk coming out, Eddie "waited for people to ask me," as his father did when his mother made a disclosure to him immediately after Eddie's grandmother's death:

> The last person [I came out to] was my father. . . . Tensions were running very high [when my grandmother died], and my mother and I had an argument. So she told my father that I was having a sexual identity crisis. So I picked my father up. We get half-way home—and I always think the car is the best place to have a talk because there's changing scenery, you can't get away, you have utmost privacy. And we're driving home, and he says, "Your mother says you're having a sexual identity crisis." I said, "Nope, no identity crisis." He was like, "Why would she say that? Aren't you confused?" I said, "No, no. I'm not confused. I know who I am." And he's like, "Oh, okay. Then why did she say that?" I'm like, "Well—um. It's 'cause I'm gay." And he's like, "Why are you so happy?"

It is difficult to tell in this scenario if Eddie's father, in asking Eddie why he is "so happy," truly does not understand that Eddie is gay or if his reaction suggests some combination of disingenuousness and denial. It is also unclear if Eddie's mother, in telling his father he was having a "sexual identity crisis," was perhaps less supportive of Eddie's gay identity than he originally believed. What is clear is that Eddie's gayness is not being discussed completely openly in the family despite his mother's previous expression of unconditional support. Nevertheless, Eddie's queer voice seems to emerge in an unprecedented way in this discussion with his father. He insists, for the first time, that his gayness—previously obscured in euphemism and silence—be spoken about candidly and explicitly among the family. Eddie goes on to talk about his father's reaction in a voice that reflects a complex set of emotions: "He quickly arrived at the point that he's still currently at after four years, which he'll stay at for the rest of his life, which is perfectly acceptable. But the fact that he arrived at it quickly was amazing to me." I ask where that point is, and he replies:

The point is that he doesn't understand it [my being gay], and he doesn't particularly like it, but he accepts it, and he still loves me. Like, I don't like that he smokes, but I accept it, you know? It's the same thing. Like, what more—I can't force him to like, love it, and I wouldn't expect him to. If he did, great. That's up to him. It's also up to him not to. . . . He sees me the same way he would see me if I were straight. That's just one aspect of my life that he doesn't particularly agree with, but he puts his own personal feelings about disagreeing with it aside because I'm his son. And he has treated my boyfriends and my gay friends—I mean, he gave my current boyfriend, actually, a set of keys to the house.

Clearly, Eddie's father's reaction to his homosexuality is mixed at best, and to a large degree Eddie seems to accept this state of affairs as normal. Even though Eddie's father gives his boyfriend keys to the house, Eddie's gayness remains an aspect of his life that his father "doesn't particularly agree with." Moreover, in comparing his own homosexuality to his father's smoking, and in saying "I wouldn't expect him to" like the fact that he is gay, Eddie seems resigned to, and perhaps even complicit in, his father's limited acceptance.

The acceptance of Eddie's two brothers, ages nineteen and thirty-one at the time of his Phase 1 interview, also seems ambiguous. Eddie reports that his brothers "act like gay guys to be funny" and "hold hands and pretend to be boyfriends." Instead of being offended by this humor, however, Eddie laughs along and says, "It's their way of accepting it." In this sense, Eddie is similar to other youth who participated in our study, whose expectations of family acceptance and respect, at least with regard to their LGBTQ identities, we found to be strikingly low. Like David, profiled in Chapter 1, a number of these youth indicated on their preliminary surveys that their families were "extremely supportive" of their sexual or gender identity, but the limits of this support became more apparent when they discussed the specific dynamics of their families in greater detail in their interviews.

Coming Out at School

Although Eddie grew up in a working-class community during his early childhood, through a school exchange program he attended high school in a wealthy northeastern suburb known regionally for its liberal attitudes, particularly about LGBTQ issues. The school has long had a large gay-straight alliance, of which Eddie was an active member, and a few years after Eddie's graduation, an openly lesbian woman became principal of the school. Even in this school environment, however, Eddie felt afraid to come out as gay to his peers for a long time. One reason he felt unsafe coming out at school, he says, was that there was a controversy while he was a student about a lesbian couple's public displays of affection in the hallways. Eddie saw a double standard in the furor over this couple's expressions of intimacy, and it made him feel as though the school community was not as LGBTQ-friendly as it was purported to be: "Guys and girls would make out in the hallway, and no one would say anything to them."

Ultimately, Eddie found the courage to come out at school, and he began this process with a furtive communication to an openly lesbian teacher who was also the school's GSA advisor. Eddie left a package of rainbow-colored candies in the teacher's mailbox with a note: "I bought a package of Skittles and left it in her mailbox. I was so careful that no one saw me putting it in there just in case, you know. . . . I said, 'Okay, um, I need to talk to you anonymously. Call this number.'"

Reluctant to talk with Eddie about his sexuality outside the school building, the teacher agreed to talk to Eddie at school. Eddie ultimately came out to her and attended his first GSA meeting, which he says was a major turning point in both his school experience and his own self-acceptance. He explains, "I'm like, 'I don't want you to tell anyone, but I'm gay, and I think I should come to a GSA meeting.' So I went to the GSA meeting, and I met all these great people."

Eddie became deeply involved in the GSA and took a major public step when he allowed a classmate to read (anonymously) the coming-out letter that he'd written to his mother at the school's annual LGBTQ awareness day:

> And they read my coming-out letter to my parents, to my mother,
> I mean, um, in front of people, and the people were crying. . . . I
> felt empowered. I felt that I had, like, an opportunity. I didn't feel
> uncomfortable. I did not feel weird. I felt empowered because I had
> a chance and opportunity to, like, become my true self.

From this point on, Eddie says, his gayness went from being a secret to being a central aspect of his identity at school. He says he even made a conscious decision to behave in a "stereotypical" gay manner among his peers: "I took it way overboard. Like, I went from one extreme to the other. . . . Stereotypical, I should say, gay. Um, with the glitter on the face and the 'Oh my Gawd!' Like loud, feminine lisping."

Thus, Eddie seems to have gone virtually overnight from silencing the gay aspects of his voice at school to projecting them loudly and even defiantly. Whereas some teachers or others might deride this kind of behavior as "flaunting it" or "in your face," for Eddie it seems to have been an important stage in his self-definition. Having dealt with the silencing of his gay identity for as long as he did, it is as if Eddie's "queer voice" made up for lost time, boldly staking its claim as legitimate in a school environment he had previously experienced as only marginally safe.

Community Connections

Having broken the ice at school in sharing his gay identity with people his own age, Eddie began attending meetings of CityYouth at age sixteen. Eddie describes himself when he first started attending CityYouth as an immature "hyper ball of energy" but says he later thought more seriously about the organization's purpose and chose to take on a leadership role. At the time of his first interview, Eddie was president of CityYouth and had served on the organization's board of directors as a youth representative. He also helped to plan the group's annual dance: "I was also the events coordinator for two years. . . . I was all kinds of things. I got to meet with the mayor a few times."

In addition to giving Eddie the opportunity to make friends and develop leadership skills, he credits CityYouth with providing him role models for responding to discrimination and adversity through positive action and helping others. In particular, he cites the example of Sheila, a CityYouth adult director, who he believes provides adolescents the kind of support to which people of her generation had less access growing up:

> She's, like, dedicated her life to enriching the lives of people who, you know, need what she needed but didn't have anyone to give it or to get it from when she was their age. And so you meet a lot of really amazing people, because through this type of adversity comes this type of strength.

Along with CityYouth, Eddie was active for three years in a youth speakers' bureau that traveled to middle and high schools, as well as some colleges, to educate teachers and students about LGBTQ issues:

> I loved doing the youth speaking engagements with [name of organization], where we would go into these like rural towns in the state and talk to the high school teachers. There was something like

four of us, and we would just sit in front of them and each take two minutes and tell our coming-out story in, like, two sentences. And we went through a whole training to know how to do this. And you would think it's so boring. Like, two sentences, what the heck are they going to get out of that? But that's all they needed.

And then we would have an hour for them to ask any question they want, and we got questions that you couldn't believe, across the spectrum. Some of the questions were just like, "Oh, how did your mother take it?" And some of them were, "Oh, well, have you ever had anal sex?" Every type of question you can imagine.

Eddie's work in the speakers' bureau illustrates how fully his queer voice had developed since he'd taken the courageous step in high school of having a classmate read the coming-out letter he had written to his mother. While a greater level of maturity likely accounts for at least some of Eddie's ability to articulate himself more openly, the support he received from his family, his school GSA, and CityYouth all seem to have played significant roles.

Transforming a Queer Voice into a Global One

After immersing himself in LGBTQ activities such as speaking engagements, activism, and leadership in CityYouth for several years, Eddie attended a conference with a wider focus, Building Bridges, that changed his perspective and ultimately led to the work and commitments he told me were central to his life when we met for his Phase II interview:

> [The conference] was amazing because it wasn't just about LGBT issues. It was also about, you know, race issues and, um, cultural and privilege issues in this country. And that was incredible. Actually, that's kind of what pivoted me. It started the process of pivoting me from LGBT activism to international activism.

After attending the Building Bridges conference, Eddie began to view LGBTQ issues within a larger context of subordination and domination, oppression and privilege. About eighteen months before we met in late 2009, Eddie had gone to the West Coast for a summer job with a nonprofit organization focused on international issues. He loved the work and hated the East Coast winters, and the combination led to his ultimate decision to make a life change and move west permanently to work in international programs:

"I loved it so much that when I got back east, and we had the snowiest winter on record, I was like, 'I'm out of here.'"

Having worked with several different organizations since moving west, at the time of our Phase II interview Eddie was working in a volunteer capacity for two groups, both of which have an international focus, and making ends meet as a barista in a local coffeehouse. One of Eddie's volunteer jobs was in a law firm that specializes in helping refugees seek asylum in the United States; the other was with an organization that prepares students from economically disadvantaged backgrounds for study-abroad programs, then places them in nine-month residencies in one of three countries:

> I switched gears from, like, gay activism to international activism. I've spent a lot of time in the last few years working at nonprofits that help construct curriculum for nine-month periods abroad for high school students and language immersion programs. I also worked at a few nonprofits for people who are seeking asylum and refuge from other countries, mostly from Cambodia and Iraq. And that has been really fascinating.
>
> Right now I am working on a program—working for two different programs, actually. I say work, but it's not paid. But I still work, and I still love it, whether or not I'm getting paid, helping create global citizens. So I'm trying to make more people like me, I should say. I met this amazing woman who runs a nonprofit that does that and basically takes marginalized and underprivileged youth—high school youth of the greater metro area—and puts them in . . . a very specific curriculum that they do after school and during the summers for language immersion in Arabic and Mandarin. And they do that for a year, and then they spend nine months—so basically an entire high school year—in either Morocco, Egypt, or China. And these are, like, kids who—who don't have parents that think very largely or worldly. Parents whose—and it's not their fault either. Their parents can barely pay the bills, so they're not worried about making sure their kids are doing this and that internationally.

Although Eddie's work in international programs is unpaid, he talks about it with the same passion and excitement he had for LGBTQ-focused projects several years earlier. When I ask Eddie why he made the transition from LGBTQ to internationally focused activism, he explains, "I guess I've always been drawn toward international people. You know, I speak a bunch of languages, which kind of opens the door to meeting international people and learning international things." He adds that although LGBTQ people face discrimination and homophobia in the United States, he believes he is relatively fortunate compared to many other people in the world and that his position as a "white, privileged, gay male" comes with certain obligations. Eddie uses the word *privilege* at three other times in our Phase II interview to talk about his life circumstances and expresses the belief that "as a white, privileged member of the world, you know, being a male and being American, I feel like I have—I have some ability . . . to kind of use that for good."

While Eddie says LGBTQ activism is still important to him, he believes his efforts are needed more urgently on the internationally oriented projects:

> There's, um, you know, a lot of people doing a lot of great work on the queer front in the United States, and I did a lot. And I'm not going to say that I wouldn't ever do any more—"Oh, I served my time." But I felt drawn toward that, to the other arena of helping international people.

A Committed Relationship

Although Eddie no longer works on a regular basis as an LGBTQ activist, being gay is still a central aspect of his personal life. He describes his relationship with Alan, his "boyfriend of about a year—hopefully for a lot longer than that," as one of the most important and supportive aspects of his current day-to-day life:

> [Our relationship] sustains me because it's stimulating, you know? It's—it's—like, it's, like, interesting. It makes me want to do things for him to see him smile. It makes me—we share ideas about what we want from life and how we might be able to both get those things together.

Eddie's supportive relationship with Alan is especially significant in light of a revelation he'd made in his Phase I interview: that he had been in a long-term intimate relationship with another man in his teens that was physically abusive. When Eddie talks about his future, he is hopeful that his relationship with Alan can evolve into something longer-term. Although they do not officially share a home, Eddie says they "practically" live together and plan to get an apartment in the near future.

Alan also supports Eddie by helping him cope with the frustration he feels in dealing with his family (his parents, siblings, aunts, and uncles), a set of relationships that Eddie says have undergone considerable shifts since his earlier interview, in part because of the ways Eddie's life priorities and commitments have changed. One downside to Eddie's relatively recent focus on international issues, he says, is that it has forced him to view some of his family members' attitudes in a somewhat negative light. For example, Eddie is particularly frustrated with the worldviews of his two brothers, whom he calls "small-minded" because he believes they are intolerant of non-Americans, especially people from Arab countries, and have little interest in learning about cultural differences:

> One of the reasons I chose to move [out west] was that my—the dynamic between my family and me was changing. And since I moved, it has changed even more because I moved. . . . I mean, I would love for my siblings to not be ignorant, you know? And not—and not hate everyone that's not American. . . . Basically, if you're not like them, then you're nothing. And I'm not like them, you know? I'm not a Christian. I'm not a Republican. I have been out of the country. It's just like—I'm not straight. I'm not—it's, like, I'm a vegetarian, and they think it's ridiculous. Why can't they respect the difference?

Eddie's Phase I and Phase II interviews were nearly seven years apart, and it is difficult to determine if the starkly different attitudes he has about his family in these two discussions reflect major changes in his own attitudes and priorities, in those of his family, or both. It is also difficult to know how his greater maturity at age twenty-six influences his views. What is clear, however, is that as an adult Eddie speaks with a strong voice of disdain for intolerance in its many forms, and his family—just by virtue of being his family—are not exempt from his social critique.

Reflecting on His Own Growth

When I ask Eddie toward the end of our Phase II interview to describe how he feels about himself, he responds, "I love me—in a healthy way." He then goes on to describe, with a sense of independence and pride, a set of beliefs and ethics that have become uniquely his own:

> I love it that I'm filled with a fire to learn more languages all the time and meet international people and go live abroad and go on road trips around America—and have values and stick to them

about not eating meat and treating people well and unconditionally loving someone if I'm going to bother loving them at all.

Looking toward the future, Eddie says he would like "maybe a few kids," perhaps with Alan if they are lucky enough to stay together long-term. Finally, Eddie would like to finish his bachelor's degree, since he left college in his late teens at a time in his life during which he says he was "very immature." Upon returning to school, Eddie would like to study anthropology and languages so that he can turn his passion for international issues into a long-term career. He is particularly interested in learning Arabic, he says, because of its special importance in resolving some of the most pressing conflicts around the globe: "There's so much work that could be done that needs to be done to try to bridge the gap between the Western world and the Middle Eastern world. I think 99 percent of the problems that exist are the result of lack of understanding, you know?"

Listening to Eddie: Hearing Gay Identity Development through an Evolving Voice

Eddie's gradual coming-out process is in many ways reflective of several models of LGBTQ (or, in earlier examples, gay and lesbian) identity development published over the last several decades. Perhaps the best known of these models, Vivienne Cass's (1979) theory of homosexual identity development, has been criticized by some researchers for its stage-oriented structure (which they say suggests an unrealistic degree of linearity in the identity development process) and for failing to take into account differences associated with race, gender, social class, and other factors. Nonetheless, the influence of the Cass theory on future models, which have addressed a variety of sociocultural issues and their intersection with sexual orientation, is undeniable.[1]

Most LGBTQ identity development models begin with a stage in which a young person uses one or more strategies to deny or negate the possibility that she or he may be homosexual and/or may have significant feelings or tendencies that are not in keeping with gender norms (Bilodeau and Renn 2005). This denial is evident in Eddie's account of the counseling session in which he refers to the homosexual feelings he was having as "one other thing that's driving me crazy, and I can't—I don't even want to think about it." From here, Eddie moves toward acknowledging his feelings as homosexual

---

1. For a review of these models, including a discussion of the rarely addressed issue of transgender identity development, see Bilodeau and Renn 2005.

in nature; gradually adopting a gay self-understanding; and coming out as gay to the people in his family, to his peer group, and ultimately to the world as a speaker about LGBTQ youth issues. Although the process is described differently in each of the various developmental theories, most models reflect movement in a similar way through a period of self-acceptance followed by coming out to an ever-widening relational circle (Cass 1979; Coleman 1981; Lipkin 1999; Troiden 1989).

Eddie's deep involvement with CityYouth and his work as a speaker about LGBTQ issues may be viewed through the lenses of several theoretical models as an immersion or identity pride experience (Cass 1979), whereby a young person becomes highly identified with her or his LGBTQ identity and a great deal of energy is devoted to involvement with LGBTQ culture, either socially, politically, or both. As Eddie begins to shift his focus toward broader issues of oppression and social justice (after his awareness is piqued by the Building Bridges conference), he moves toward what Cass (1979) called identity synthesis or, alternatively, what Arthur Lipkin (1999) has termed a "post-sexuality" stage of gay identity development. Eddie begins to view being gay as only one of many aspects of his identity that are important, and his activities and commitments reflect this more expansive view of his place in the world.

While developmental models can serve as useful lenses through which to view the experiences of some LGBTQ individuals (especially when conceived of nonlinearly, which I believe is usually the theorist's intent), a voice-centered listening to Eddie's coming-out story—and, in particular, the communication style he uses at various points in the process—is illustrative of how and where Eddie's queer voice was nurtured by the people and institutions around him, and where it was silenced.

Eddie begins his story of coming to terms with his gayness by stating that he simply "ignored it" for a long time. Then, at around age fifteen, when a counselor asks him bluntly if he is attracted to other men, Eddie—having dissociated from his feelings for so long—is literally unable to speak: "'Ah—oh—.' I kind of made a face, and no noise came out." Based on the research she and her colleagues have conducted with adolescent girls over several decades, Carol Gilligan notes an analogous self-silencing process as many girls move into their early teens: "At the crossroads of adolescence, girls may bury an honest voice inside themselves for safe keeping" (2011, 63). At this point in many girls' development, Gilligan says, their speech patterns begin to reflect dissociation, a "reluctance to know what one knows," particularly if such knowing threatens their place within the patriarchal structures that maintain gender norms. Girls who previously were astute and vocal about their feelings and their observations of the world begin to punctuate their statements with terms such as "I don't know" and other expressions that reflect self-doubt and docility. In Eddie's case, we see the burial of an honest voice in a more extreme form: With an emerging self-awareness that threatens Eddie's place in society's accepted gender order, he is rendered completely incapable of voicing what he knows, even to himself.

Although Eddie did not actually come out as gay in the counseling session he describes in his Phase I interview, it seems to have led him toward a gradual realization about his sexuality. He finds this realization extremely frightening at first, as a voice that has been buried for years slowly begins to emerge: "I accepted it, and I was actually scared." Not surprisingly, when Eddie tries at age fifteen to give voice to his feelings by coming out to his best friend, Dave, he finds the experience emotionally overwhelming: "It was the first time I actually said it out loud. I told him that I was gay, and I started hysterically crying. It was so overwhelming."

Eddie's disclosure to Dave is followed by a period of about a year in which his emerging queer voice goes underground again, and he does not come out to anyone else for some time. Eventually, Eddie makes somewhat furtive, unvoiced overtures in two contexts in which he seems to view the risks associated with coming out to be particularly high: at home and at school. Instead of telling his mother directly that he is gay, Eddie produces a "seven-page handwritten letter," which he leaves at home before going away for the weekend. At school, Eddie is at first unable to speak directly to anyone—not even the GSA advisor—about the fact that he is gay, so he leaves some rainbow-colored candies and a note in her mailbox and asks her to call him in confidence. Eddie later suggests that he and the teacher meet off school grounds, presumably outside the view of his peers, with whom Eddie does not feel safe despite the fact that his high school is generally viewed as among the most LGBTQ-friendly in its region.

As it does for youth in several other case studies (Lindsey in Chapter 2, Travis in Chapter 4, and Jordan in Chapter 5), involvement in the gay-straight alliance proves to be a turning point in Eddie's school experiences and leads to broader coming-out gestures in which he begins to experiment with the use of his voice as a young gay man. He has a friend read his coming-out letter to his mother, albeit anonymously, at the school's LGBTQ awareness day. After he decides to be out at school, he adopts what he views as a stereotypically gay speaking style—perhaps as a way of "trying on" a gay persona among his peers. Eventually, Eddie becomes involved in City-Youth, where he takes on a vocal leadership role and becomes president, and he gets involved in an LGBTQ youth speakers' bureau through which he tells his coming-out story—this time, not anonymously—to large groups of strangers.

Ultimately, Eddie's queer voice survives, builds, and reaches an ever-expanding audience as he moves from being unable to voice his feelings at all in his early teens to being a peer educator and leader of LGBTQ youth. Clearly, Eddie's mother's expression of unconditional love upon his disclosure and the acceptance he ultimately found at school (along with his developing maturity) provided a strong foundation for the development of his queer voice that followed. Yet there are also points in Eddie's coming-out story that suggest considerable risk, if not for Eddie himself, then for LGBTQ youth whose coming-out experiences might unfold in similar ways.

Underlying much of Eddie's coming-out narrative is a backstory in which he felt unable to communicate with others and thus was at risk for severe emotional isolation. Although there is little in either of Eddie's interviews to suggest that he became suicidal, used drugs or alcohol addictively, or engaged in other self-harming behaviors (as was the case for several other participants in this research during their teens), Eddie seems to have spent long periods of time alone in dealing with the turmoil he was feeling about coming out.

It is especially troubling in one sense that Eddie felt afraid to come out and thus isolated and silenced himself in family and school contexts that seemed ostensibly supportive, in some ways unusually so. Eddie's mother's statement of unconditional love is something all LGBTQ youth might hope to hear when they come out, yet other aspects of Eddie's family life—such as his brothers' homophobic humor and his father's qualified "support" and questions about a "sexual identity crisis"—illustrate the many ways in which family dynamics can silence LGBTQ youth despite outward appearances of support. As indicated previously, Eddie's high school is known around the region for its progressive approach to education about social justice issues and has a particularly strong and well established GSA. Yet Eddie still did not feel safe for a long time expressing himself as gay in this environment, thus illustrating how subtly homophobic messages within an otherwise accepting school community can have a silencing influence on LGBTQ youth and contribute to their feelings of isolation.

Eddie's shift in focus from LGBTQ to international activism after several years in queer youth leadership illustrates the breadth of the benefits that can accrue to society if we nurture young queer voices. Of course, we want all LGBTQ young people to feel safe coming out, to fully accept themselves as they are, to feel a sense of agency, and to play a role that helps move our society forward for future generations of LGBTQ youth—even if simply

by growing up and living their lives as visible LGBTQ people. Yet Eddie
is clearly interested in much more, and the development of his queer voice
seems to have equipped and inspired him to take on not only the injustices
that affect the LGBTQ community but also those that he sees as associated
with oppression in all its forms.[2]

---

2. As this book was going into production, I received an e-mail from Eddie in which he updated
me on recent changes in his life. After an emotionally difficult breakup with Alan, Eddie moved
to a large South American country and, in keeping with his international interests, was teaching
English as a second language at a school there.

7

The Quest for "One Good Relationship"

Connections and Disconnections in Adolescence

I don't necessarily think support is the word for it, but
[my parents] support me being a lesbian, I guess.

—Kate

I know this is for probably every kid—there is always
that one teacher in, like, high school or middle school that
they felt they could open up to. I think that's kind of
important. It makes you want to go to school.

—Jessie

The young adults profiled in Chapters 1 through 6 participated in both
Phase I and Phase II of this multipart research, but twenty-four additional youth completed questionnaires, fourteen of whom also participated in in-depth interviews during Phase I of the project. I interviewed
six of these additional participants myself and, when preparing to write this
book, recalled hearing a broad range of relational experiences, particularly in
school and family contexts, across their narratives.[1]

Despite my efforts to locate all the study participants whom I had personally interviewed and to invite them to participate in Phase II, I was not
able to reach these six young people, so I do not know how their queer voices
evolved as they took on the responsibilities of adulthood. Nevertheless, since
their stories as adolescents shed additional light on the way young queer
voices are both supported and suppressed at this crucial developmental stage,
I include mini-profiles of these six individuals, organized in sections by central themes, in this chapter. While in some respects these voices echo those
of the participants profiled in Chapters 1 through 6 (and are noteworthy in

---

1. Excerpts from these interviews also appear in Sadowski 2008b.

their reinforcement of patterns found across multiple interviews), others provide new insights into how young queer voices can be nurtured or silenced. In a few cases, they also highlight how sexuality and gender can intersect with issues related to race, religion, disability, and other factors in young people's lives.

Family Relationships: A Wide Spectrum of Communication

Many of the youth interviewed for Phase I of the study identified their families as being among the most important—if not *the* most important—set of relationships in their lives. Even in cases in which young people had difficult relationships with their parents or siblings (e.g., Ruth in Chapter 3 and Jordan in Chapter 5), their desire for closeness in these relationships was clear. None of the youth I interviewed reported a severe lack of support from their families. None said that they had been asked to leave home, and none were (as far as I am aware) physically abused by their parents for reasons associated with their sexual orientation and/or gender identity, although a number reported physical abuse from siblings, particularly during early adolescence. (Ruth, in Chapter 3, says she believes her father's abusive behavior was not related to her sexuality.)

As Sassafras Lowrey's 2010 edited volume *Kicked Out* poignantly illustrates, a disturbing number of LGBTQ young people are forced to leave home for reasons associated with their sexual orientation and/or gender identity and end up living in a variety of situations that put them at risk physically, economically, and in some cases even sexually. Thankfully, none of the participants I interviewed reported having experienced this level of family rejection. As the youths' narratives demonstrate, however, they received a wide range of responses from family members to their being LGBTQ and learned to voice or silence aspects of their identities in many different ways.

Clark: "It's Not Talked About at All"

Clark is an eighteen-year-old African American youth who identifies as gay and enrolled in the study at the urban LGBTQ youth group.[2] Friendly, polite, and buoyant in his initial self-presentation, Clark expresses a positive attitude

---

2. Although Phase I interviews took place a number of years ago, I describe and quote participants in the present tense to provide a sense of immediacy and to capture each youth's experience at the particular moment in time at which they were interviewed.

about many aspects of his life, as reflected in the complimentary statements he makes about his school, his friends, and other aspects of his relational world. When I ask him to describe the most supportive factors in his life, he cites "my friends, my family, and God." On one level, Clark's description of his parents and his relationship with them is similarly upbeat: "My parents, of course, are just always there for me, and they were always supportive of basically everything I did. And, I mean, they were good parents to me, so that's—I mean, I guess, like, everything they did, even the bad stuff, still helped me."

Clark, an only child, also reports, however, that there is tension between him and his parents that stems in large part from the fact that he is gay. He describes his parents as "hard-core religious" and reports that after he came out to them as gay at the end of his freshman year of high school, they sent him to a Christian counselor. Although Clark was not aware of the counselor's agenda when the sessions started, he says that after several meetings the counselor started to give him literature that suggested a conversion agenda, and Clark realized that the counseling was "about being gay." The counselor also revealed to Clark that he considered himself "ex-gay," and when Clark realized that the purpose of the counseling was to convert him from homosexuality, he refused to go to any further sessions. Although Clark's parents supported him in this decision, he believes that his parents still have not accepted his sexual orientation: "I still think they're in denial. I don't really know, but they don't really mention it. It's kind of like an unspoken thing in my family. So it's not—like, even though it's known, no one—it's like untalked—it's not talked about at all. It's not even brought up."

Clark's parents separated shortly before we met, and although both his mother and his father confided in him about the difficulties in their relationship, neither discussed his homosexuality with him after his initial disclosure. According to Clark, his father was particularly reticent about the topic: "My dad never really talked to me about any of that, like being gay."

Jessie: "The Fact That She Didn't Freak Out Was Enough Support for Me"

Jessie, a nineteen-year-old, white, biologically female youth from the urban group who identifies as gay and transgender, says she feels "support" from her mother, but she does not set the standards for that support very high: "I think just the fact that she didn't, like, you know, freak out [when I came out as transgender] was enough support for me." When Jessie came out as bisexual and subsequently as lesbian in high school, she says her mother tried to keep her away from her female friends and refused to meet a girl she dated for several months. Also, when Jessie got a short haircut while she was in eighth grade, she says her mother asked her why she wanted to look like a man and called her a "fucking dyke." But by the time Jessie came out as transgender, she says, "I think she [my mother] knew there was nothing she could do about it."

Jessie says her father has been much more accepting through her coming-out process because he's had gay friends. Yet even her description of his support seems to be tempered with the same low expectations: "My dad is just like—he's awesome. He's supported, like, everything that I have ever come in with. But just the fact that they didn't freak out about [my coming out] was very good."

Kate: "They Support Me Being a Lesbian, I Guess"

Clark and Jessie were among numerous youth in our study whose family support for their LGBTQ identities had clear limits; for others, parental support was much more unequivocal in ways that specifically included the youths' sexual orientation and/or gender identity. Kate, a nineteen-year-old white youth from the urban site who identifies as gay, lesbian, queer, and "dyke," says her relationships with her mother, father, and brother are the most important and supportive in her life, and that this includes support for her sexual orientation:

> My closest family are my mother and my father and my brother. I love—I love that they support me, and I love the interest that they have in my life. I've seen the way other families work. I've seen the way, you know, even their families growing up work, and I think that just the way that—just the way that they support me, I love that. Um, they support—I don't necessarily think *support* is the word for it, but they support me being a lesbian, I guess.

Before Kate came out at home, she mentioned gay issues from time to time with her parents, and at one point her mother asked her, without judgment, "You talk about gay people a lot. Do you think you're gay?" Kate then came out to her mother (when she was fourteen), but once the issue was in the open between them, Kate says she went back to avoiding the topic because she was uncomfortable discussing it with her parents:

> Um, because it's really hard for me to talk to my parents about sex or sexuality. It's just—it's hard for me to, like, watch movies with sex in them around anybody but incredibly hard with my parents. Like,

you know, two people making out is, like, emotionally uncomfortable for me with my parents. So, um, it was kind of hard to admit that to her. Um, and then we didn't talk about it for six months.

Unlike some of the other youth in the study whose parents did not want to talk about sexuality or gender issues, Kate says that in her case she was the one who kept the issue off the table. Her mother respected these boundaries, except to check in periodically, until Kate was ready to talk about it more comfortably and to include Kate's father in the discussion. Prior to her actually coming out, Kate says her father took a similar approach to that of her mother, bringing up the topic in subtle ways to let Kate know that if she was lesbian, he would support her:

> But around my junior year of high school—I mean, my father was a very smart man. He grew up in California and, you know, has had a variety of different gay friends. He started, um, bringing things up, like, he knew—he said, "Melissa Etheridge has a new album coming out." Or he said, "Ellen DeGeneres and Sharon Stone are in the new lesbian movie together. Did you know that?" Or, um, "Do you know that when I lived in San Francisco, I marched in the Gay Pride parade or the Dykes on Bikes parade? Did you know that when I lived in San Francisco, I lived in the basement of a lesbian's apartment?" You know, just things like that so it was obvious that I knew—you know, that I knew that he knew about it. He was kind of, you know, letting me know but still letting me bring it up.

Once Kate felt comfortable talking about her lesbian identity with her father, she says he was immediately accepting and willing to talk about it in whatever ways she wanted to. She particularly recalls a conversation she had with her father about a crush she had on a particular girl "and we talked about it as if it had been a boy."

Jason: Open Support from Three out of Four Parents

Jason, a seventeen-year-old white gay youth from the rural group, has had similar support from three of the four people he refers to as his parents: his mother, his biological father (who is also gay), and his father's partner. Jason says his closest relationship is with his mother: "My mom, she is the parent that I really relate to and open up to the most. I help her out. She's been needing a lot of help because we just got a house up in Vermont."

According to Jason, all of his parents play different roles that enrich his life in various ways. His biological father is more of a disciplinarian than the others. When Jason visits his father and his partner, which he does frequently, his father gives him long "lectures" and advice about performing well in school and other issues. At times Jason says he tires of these conversations, but he also realizes "they're for the better of me." His father's partner plays more of a confidant role. When Jason is visiting, they walk the couple's dogs together and talk about Jason's college and career plans, as well as "the current relationship scene": "His [my father's] partner is just like another dad. He may not be biological, but he's definitely a dad to me."

Jason's relationship with his legal stepfather (his mother's husband) is the most problematic, at least with regard to Jason's sexual orientation. Jason says he feels less close to his stepfather than to his other parents and senses a "weird tension" between them that stems, at least in part, from Jason's sexual orientation:

> With my stepdad, he's—like, he's not against it [my being gay], but he just—it's something that he just doesn't get. So he's just—that hasn't really gotten brought up very much with him at all. . . . So I'm just, like—he and I have always been—there's just sort of this weird tension there. Neither of us really know why, but it's just always sort of been there. So, it's kind of strange.

Kim: Different Levels of Support from Parents and Siblings

Kim is a seventeen-year-old white student from the rural site who identifies as lesbian, transgender, and gender queer, which she defines as "not identifying with the binary genders and not fitting into typical gender roles." Kim says her mother and father are "really cool" with her sexual orientation. When Kim came out as lesbian, she says, "My parents are very, very, very liberal, so they just kind of saw it as 'whatever.'" She says her mother and father once let an ex-girlfriend stay with her at their house and have promised her that they will go to her wedding someday.

While Kim is out as lesbian to her parents, however, she has not disclosed to them that she identifies as transgender or gender queer, and Kim has not come out as lesbian, gay, or transgender to her brother Dominic and his wife, whom she calls "very, very, very homophobic." Kim describes several recent family holidays during which, despite her openness with her parents, her sexual orientation was silenced:

My brother Dominic—I haven't actually come out to him and his family because I didn't grow up with him, and he's—he was raised Catholic, and they're very, very, very homophobic. . . . We had them over for Christmas dinner. I've had a shaved head since I was twelve years old, and my sister-in-law asked me at the dinner in front of my family and a bunch of my mom's friends and stuff when I was four-teen—yeah, fifteen—she asked if I liked boys at the Christmas din-ner table in front of everyone, and I had to say yes because I didn't know what else to say. Um, she always says things about how I don't wear skirts and about how I don't wear makeup and how I should grow my hair out and wear—look more girly. And she always makes jokes about how, like, if I keep my appearance up the way it is, then people are going to think I'm a big lesbian. . . . And I don't really want to come out to them only because I don't want them to not let me see my niece and nephew, because I'm really close to my niece.

In one way, Kim's story echoes those of some of the other youth in our study, who keep discussion of their sexual orientation or gender identity out of their relationships with parents or other family members because, as Kim says, they "just don't want to talk about it." In Kim's case, she seems willing to comply with the silence with her brother and sister-in-law primarily to maintain her relationships with her niece and nephew, whom she fears she will not be allowed to see again if her sexual orientation and gender identity are disclosed.

Phil: Abuse from His Twin Brother

Phil, one of the oldest participants in the Phase I research, is a twenty-one-year-old white gay youth who is a member of CityYouth and had attended a nearby suburban high school. Much of Phil's interview was dominated by the extreme emotional and physical abuse he suffered at the hands of his fraternal twin brother, Scott, which was still clearly a cause of considerable distress:

Well [sighs], before I came out, probably when we were in the third or fourth grade, he [Scott] decided to tell everybody I was gay. Everybody used the words gay, fag in school, but it was always directed toward me after he said that. . . . Oh, he would push me, he would throw me down stairs, he would [pauses] sit on me—you know, things like that, physically attack me when he felt he had to release some frustration. . . . How he specifically made me feel at any moment [*pauses*] was probably worthless; that's how much he made me [*pauses*] hurt emotionally, physically. I mean, it was like [*pauses*] constant battle.

In one incident, Phil, who is profoundly hard-of-hearing and communicates at CityYouth meetings through a sign language interpreter, relates that his brother kicked him in the head while he was recovering from ear surgery. Also, after Phil came out as gay at sixteen, he says Scott's emotional abuse took on a more sexual tone: "You know, uh, sexual jokes would come out of it, like, you know, 'butt pirate' and all that stuff. 'Surfin' the wrong wave.' Just, it got really brutal."

Although a number of participants (such as Lindsey in Chapter 2 and Jordan in Chapter 5) relate stories of abuse from siblings, one of the things that makes Phil's story different is the role of sexual orientation in it—not just his own but also his twin brother's. Two years after Phil came out, Scott also came out as gay and brought a boyfriend home to meet the family. While one might expect that having the same sexual orientation would help these twin brothers find common ground, Phil says that the rivalry and differences between them cross a wide variety of issues: "In a sense, um, he kind of despises me because he has all the academic problems; he has all the, uh, physical problems, whereas I didn't really have to struggle through anything, besides my—my handicap, which is my hearing."

Although Phil does not name it as such, the role of internalized homophobia also seems central to Phil's story. As Michael Kimmel (2008) and others have noted, homophobia and homophobic acts of harassment and violence can be associated with a fear that people will perceive the perpetrator as gay (and the harassment is thus an assertion of one's heterosexuality). As Phil describes his brother's particularly "brutal" attacks, it seems that Scott's fears of his own homosexuality may well have intensified his behavior toward Phil, who was out as gay at an earlier age and was therefore an easy target for Scott's homophobic words and actions.

Schools: From Hostile Climates to Supportive Environments

Despite some evidence that may suggest that American culture and particularly youth culture have become more accepting of LGBTQ people in recent years (see, for example, Savin-Williams 2005), the latest large-scale studies conducted with middle and high school students suggest that anti-LGBTQ language and the harassment of LGBTQ students are still pervasive in U.S. schools (Kosciw et al. 2010; McGuire et al. 2010). The stories of the youth profiled in this chapter—all but two of whom report having experienced anti-LGBTQ harassment in one form or another at school—help illustrate what these experiences can look, sound, and feel like to the students who are victimized. Nevertheless, there was wide variation, even among this relatively small sample, in the degrees to which these participants' schools provided them with relational and institutional support *as LGBTQ youth* and either supported or silenced their voices during their middle and high school years.

Kate: The Sexualized (and Gendered) Nature of School-Based Harassment

While home was an environment of open support for Kate, school was one of open hostility. Kate says that few of her peers at her suburban high school even noticed her before she came out at school, but after she came out as lesbian she was harassed frequently. Like David, profiled in Chapter 1, Kate says teachers "turned a blind eye" to the harassment she experienced, which had both verbal and physical manifestations and at times was disturbingly sexual in nature:

> People would push me into lockers or just mumble stuff at me under their breath. I once had pornography taped to my locker—like a girl giving a guy a blow job or something, and it said something on it like, "Learn how to do this," or something. I had a couple of the— the football players, like, corner me after school, you know, threaten-ing to make me like dick. And, um, a teacher walked out and kind of looked at them, and they dispersed, you know? And the teacher went back into his classroom, and nothing ever happened. I had *dyke* written on my locker. It was mostly verbal.

Kate says that other than a few close friends, she felt distant from most of her classmates in high school, who ostracized her for reasons associated with her sexual orientation: "I got out of high school not knowing most of the people in my class. . . . I went back for a party after I graduated, and, like, people knew who I was, but I had no idea who they were." Also like David, Kate feels that the teachers at her high school cared little about protecting or meeting the needs of LGBTQ students: "The school wasn't very—the school wasn't very supportive. I didn't really look to them [teachers and administra-tors] for support because I didn't expect it."

Kim: Giving Up on School

Several months before our interview, Kim had dropped out of Smith County Regional High School, the same school Jordan (profiled in Chapter 5) attended before switching to Clay Tech. Kim says she had few supportive relationships with either adults or peers at Smith County. She says there was a "large majority of kids" at the school who disliked her because of her sexual orientation and gender expression and that "most of the teachers really just didn't care, like, whatsoever if they were homophobic or not." In addition, Kim describes several teachers at Smith County who openly expressed negative attitudes about LGBTQ students.

Like Lindsey (profiled in Chapter 2), Kim organized a voluntary teacher training about LGBTQ issues for her school's faculty, but she says only four teachers reacted to it positively: "Um, a lot of the teachers said things like they—if they found homosexuality amoral, then how can they respect a student that's gay?" Kim also says many of the teachers at her school failed to address anti-LGBTQ harassment and that her chemistry teacher ignored—and even contributed to—her own victimization so much that she stopped attending his class:

> Like, if somebody walked by me, they could say, like, "faggot" to
> me, and he would—wouldn't even blink an eye to it. He didn't care
> if people called me things in class. Um, I actually went to the prin-
> cipal a few times about him and a few other teachers, too, and the
> principal would talk to them, and they still wouldn't stop, or—yeah,
> they wouldn't stop the abuse that people were putting me through.
> Uh, when he asked me what kind of car I had, because I was always
> late to school because it was my first-period class, and I told him I
> had a Subaru station wagon, and he said, "Oh, that's typical." Um,
> because I guess it's like a big stereotype that lesbians drive Subarus.

I follow up by asking Kim how it made her feel when her chemistry teacher or other people would say things like that. She says, "That was the only class I'd ever skipped. I didn't—I couldn't put up with it. I would get really upset. . . . I would do everything possible to avoid going to his class, um, because I didn't want to put up with it. It would make me really upset." Kim adds that the chemistry teacher's class was the only one she was failing when she decided to drop out of school:

> When I dropped out, I had all As and one F. So, I did well in the
> classes that I liked, um, and the subjects that I liked. I had an F in

chemistry when I dropped out, um, but I had an A in public speaking and an A in music, an A in art, and I think that those were the only classes I had when I dropped out.

Jason: Moving from a Hostile School Climate to a Supportive One

Jason also attended Smith County Regional and experienced it as a hostile environment. In our interview, he describes a set of experiences he had there that he believes ultimately led him to view suicide as his only option:

> I did a pill overdose of my medications I was on. Because, um, I was at a school that I just really didn't feel safe at, and there were kids who were always picking on me and stuff, and, I mean, it's the only, like, experience I had ever been in like that. So I wasn't sure if it was just always going to be like that. . . . [One student] was getting extremely hostile with me. He had—like between every class, before school, after school, if I was walking on the side of the road, or whatever, and he were driving by or something, he'd be, like, yelling out the window or he'd be calling, like, "Fag!" to me. Or like, "Flaming faggot!" or any possible word with any possible combination with "fag" in it. . . . So it was getting really hostile there, and I knew that if, like, I was going to stay around at Smith County, I'd probably end up, like, getting severely injured or whatever. And then, like, probably kids would make fun of me because I couldn't stand up for myself. And just, like, I don't know. At the time it [suicide] seemed like the only and best thing to do.

Jason goes on to explain that a few administrators at Smith County attempted to address the harassment he was experiencing regularly, but the climate among his peers was such that they believed there was little they could do. In an experience that closely echoes that of David in Chapter 1, Jason ultimately left Smith County Regional at the suggestion of his guidance counselors and transferred to a school they believed might be a safer environment for him. Although he did not expect his new school to be much different, Jason transferred to Clay Tech, a nearby technical high school:

> I had just started to say, like, "Well, it really can't be better than Smith." Or, "Because, I mean, every high school is the same, I may as well just stay at Smith and tough it out." And after my [suicide] attempt, we had talked with my guidance counselor, we talked with the guidance counselor of Tech, and, like, they just—they all

decided basically the best thing for me would be to get out of Smith, and it really was.

Along with a strong GSA—cited as a lifeline by both Lindsey and Jordan in Chapters 2 and 5, who also attended Clay Tech—the school has other attributes that Jason says made the environment much more welcoming to him than he expected it to be. In contrast to Smith County, Jason describes Clay Tech as "a school where you can't say things like 'fag' or you can't use, like, racial or sexuality slurs, or whatever." Also, Jason appreciates the fact that many of the teachers at Clay Tech have "LGB Safe Zone" stickers on their doors—a quiet way of indicating to students that their classrooms are spaces where sexual-minority students can feel safe and communicate openly about who they are. On a more personal level, Jason has come out as gay at Clay Tech, and he likes the way teachers sometimes subtly use this knowledge to make a positive example. An avid bicyclist, Jason says he felt particularly honored recently when his English teacher used him as an example to help expand other students' notions about masculinity during a unit on the play *Macbeth*:

> Like my English teacher is talking about—like, we're reading *Macbeth*, and we're talking about, like, what is masculinity? What is manliness and stuff. . . . He's like, "Well, what do you think is a man? This guy over here [*indicates teacher pointing at a male student*], who spends, like—who spends the day, like, sitting around on a tractor plowing the fields, or this kid over here"—and he was pointing at me, and he's like—"who just for the heck of it will hop on his bike and bike twenty miles to school and twenty miles back. . . ." And he's like—they're comparing those people to me. Because—and people are realizing this more and more and that—like, the typicalness of, like, being gay, is like, you're all femme, and you're really not—you can't be, like, manly; you can't be doing all these things. And then, like, he's sort of like trying to open up their horizons and stuff. And I've noticed that teachers do that periodically in other classes just because it's a good contrast and—I don't know. I think it's cool, because it sets me away from all the other kids in a way that they can't copy me.

Although Jason does not directly cite his transfer from Smith County to Clay Tech as a factor that helped him acquire a more positive sense of self, he describes his past suicidal thoughts and behaviors metaphorically as a "place" to which he can no longer imagine returning:

It's—I mean, like I said, I really don't know exactly what I was thinking at the time [that I attempted suicide]. Like for me to be at that point, it really just doesn't make sense for me anymore. And I don't feel like I would ever be back at that place because I've been there once, and I think I've been after, and I've seen that it can get better, and it is better. So I don't think I'd ever be down—back at that place anymore.

Clark: Positive Intersections of Race and Sexuality

In addition to the students who attended Clay Tech, another participant who describes his high school in mostly positive terms is Clark, who attended an urban fine and performing arts high school. Although the school did not have a GSA (an absence Clark attributes primarily to its relatively small size), Clark describes his school as "very community-like," a place where virtually everyone was accepting of him both as gay and as African American:

> [The school] wasn't that big, so everybody was cool with everybody, and no one, like, disliked you because you were gay or because—it was kind of a normal thing. So it wasn't like a big deal. Like, if you were gay, they're like, "Okay." [*Laughs*] And everybody—I mean, everyone liked each other, and like, the people—I mean, if you didn't like someone, it was because of something that they've done or said, not because of their sexuality or color or race or something like that. So, I mean, it was—it was a really good and open school, very diverse as well, so it wasn't—I mean, very few problems.

Clark adds that all of his teachers "were fine with who I am" and that he made many friends in high school with whom he continues to stay in touch during his freshman year in college: "And, I mean, everyone that was there—that all my friends, like, were just fabulous. I love them all, and, like, you know, we still keep in contact."

Recent research has begun to suggest that LGBTQ youth of color can face specific challenges related to racism in LGBTQ communities, homophobia in communities of color, and lack of representation in GSAs and community-based LGBTQ youth groups (Kosciw, Greytak, and Diaz 2009; McCready 2010). The intersection of race-, gender-, and sexuality-related issues (along with others such as social class and urban life) in the lives of LGBTQ youth of color is a crucially understudied issue and is the subject of a study I am currently planning with a colleague as a follow-up to the research profiled in this book. Feminist and other theorists have used the term "intersectionality" (Crenshaw 1991) to describe the ways in which systems of oppression related to race, gender, sexuality, and other issues operate together, rather than independently, in society and in people's lives. From Clark's perspective, however, the small culture in his school may be described as one of "positive intersectionality"—a place where he believes gay youth of color (and other students) are supported in an overall climate of inclusiveness and personal respect across differences.[3]

Jessie: "There Is Always That One Teacher"

In between the youth who attended schools with the most hostile climates for LGBTQ students and those who described their schools primarily in positive terms, other youth seemed to fall on a continuum with regard to the extent to which (1) their schools were supportive of LGBTQ students and (2) they were able to make positive relational connections with peers and adults at school.

Jessie says her relationships with peers improved dramatically from middle to high school, where she faced less harassment and had an easier time making friends. Although she does not believe that many teachers at her high school were supportive of her or of LGBTQ students in general, she cites her high school drama teacher as someone she "could always talk to" and says:

> Every school I have been to, there has always been one or two teachers that I really trusted. Like, my drama teacher in high school was like that, and, um, I knew I could always talk to her. So, I think there was usually—and I know this is for probably every kid—there is always that one teacher in, like, high school or middle school that they felt they could open up to. I think that's kind of important. It makes you want to go to school. It makes you want to—it just makes the experience better, I think.

Jessie also says that in middle school, where she faced harassment frequently, she had a highly supportive relationship with her seventh-grade

---

3. The school's lack of a gay-straight alliance, especially when considered in light of the tremendous benefits that researchers have found to be associated with GSAs, is cause for concern. Clark's description of his school's small size and overall climate of inclusiveness offer a plausible explanation for why there may have been a lack of urgency to start a GSA, but the school's location in a southern state where relatively few schools have GSAs may also be a factor.

health teacher. Jessie recalls an incident that precipitated the development of this relationship after a close friend of Jessie's had died of AIDS:

> I had a teacher in middle school. She was my health teacher. She's, like, this amazing woman. She is a lesbian, and, like, everybody kind of knew it. . . . I remember there was something up on the board in health class that said, "Write the facts that you know about HIV and AIDS down." Some of these kids had written this, like, heinous stuff up there that really, really upset me. It said like, you know, "Only queers get AIDS," and "Fags should die," and like stuff like that. I was like—I remember my health teacher was so upset about it, and she was, like, crying about it. I came up to her after class, and I was like, "I heard what those kids did, and I'm really sorry that they put you through that." I was like—I was just upset about that. She thought that was just amazing, that, like, somebody so young would be upset about something like that. We ended up talking. I told her I had just lost my friend. Then the more we talked, the more we got to the point, like, in—that was probably towards the middle of seventh grade. At the beginning of eighth grade, I came out to her. She was just very supportive, and, like, she got me through middle school.

In addition to being a rare student-teacher relationship in which Jessie felt she could talk openly about issues that were deeply important to her, this relationship had an added benefit. As a lesbian, Jessie's health teacher represented an important mentor and role model, someone who reinforced the idea that it was okay for Jessie to be who she was and who offered Jessie a safe relationship in which she could come out to an adult without fear of rejection (especially important given the homophobic slurs to which Jessie was subject at home). From Jessie's perspective, having access to this teacher made a life-changing difference: "She got me through middle school."

Navigating Challenging Intersections

In addition to their experiences in family and school contexts, these Phase I research participants described ways in which several other aspects of their identities intersected with their being lesbian, gay, bisexual, transgender, or queer (LGBTQ). The interaction of LGBTQ identity with other central components of who they are required these young people to navigate the challenges associated with being LGBTQ through a specific course, and the development of their queer voices seems to have been influenced in some unique ways by these experiences.

Phil: Experiencing Gayness with a Disability

Phil indicated on his preliminary questionnaire for the study that he was hard of hearing. Because I noticed that he used an American Sign Language (ASL) interpreter at CityYouth meetings, I asked if he would like to do so for our interview. He replied that he could lip-read well and would prefer to rely solely on lip reading for the interview.

When I ask Phil how he believes being hard of hearing has affected his life as a young gay man, he mentions only intimate relationships as having posed troubling challenges in this regard. Phil reports that he has thrived academically, has many friends (both LGBTQ and "straight," hearing and hard of hearing), and has begun a successful career in education. In describing his relationship with his "recent ex," Todd, however, Phil says that Todd "had a serious problem with the fact that I was hard of hearing." He goes on to explain:

> He would forget that I was hard of hearing, and he would just go on and on and on. He would get mad at me because I wasn't paying attention or I didn't understand what he was saying. And he didn't like the fact that I had deaf friends, because I would sign to them, and that really bugged him. He said, "It makes me really uncomfortable when you sign." I'm like, "I'm sorry."

Phil says he was willing to use sign language less often around Todd because "most of the people we interact with are hearing," but ultimately he believes it was Todd's homophobia that broke up the relationship. (Phil says Todd is still sexually involved with men but dates women because he wants a "normal" life.) It is nevertheless striking that Phil is willing to silence his voice, or at least his use of a preferred language, to accommodate a boyfriend in this instance, especially since in other aspects of his life he seems self-assured and confident in making his voice heard. Phil was extremely active in his gay-straight alliance and was its president for his junior and senior years of high school, has served as a meeting facilitator for CityYouth, and has extended his commitment to making schools safer for LGBTQ youth in his current work as a special-education teaching assistant in a high school: "Now [since Phil has been out as gay] there are students who feel more comfortable talking to me about issues in their life, especially the gay students."

The silencing Phil experienced in his relationship with Todd, however, suggests the potential for LGBTQ youth with disabilities to experience what Laura Rauscher and Mary McClintock (1996) have called "ableism"—discrimination and exclusion based on ability—in queer relationships and communities.

Clark: Reconciling Being Gay with His Faith

As indicated previously, after Clark came out as gay to his parents, they sent him to therapy sessions with an "ex-gay" Christian counselor. These sessions, along with other aspects of Clark's religious upbringing, resulted in his having considerable difficulty reconciling his gay identity with his religious faith:

> I believe in God and all that, and you, so, like—you get told that you're going to go to hell, and it was just—I just didn't—I was so—I was really uncomfortable with it [being gay] because I thought that I shouldn't be having these feelings and that they were wrong and that I should be straight.

Despite having had a set of experiences that might cause some young people to reject religion entirely, Clark continues to place his religion and his faith in God at the forefront of his life. When I ask Clark what he does when things get tough for him (one of my standard questions), he mentions talking with his friends, writing in his journal, and prayer as his three primary methods for coping with stress: "I pray and just kind of, like, talk to him [God] about whatever is happening and what I'm having to deal with."

Numerous young people interviewed for this research mentioned their connection to virtual communities as a way they combated the isolation they felt living as LGBTQ youth under a variety of circumstances. David, for example, as a rural gay youth, says that through the Internet he "found tons of gay people" and realized he "wasn't alone," and Jordan connected with transgender peers in chat rooms and over e-mail. For Clark, reading and meeting people online allowed him to feel less alone in his struggles as a gay person of faith and to begin to resolve his feelings about what had previously seemed like an irreconcilable conflict:

> I remember that I would go online and look up the whole—I remember, because like I said, like, religion was a thing, so I always looked that up. . . . And then with people I was talking to, there was this really—like, I would go to chat rooms and kind of, like, just

talk with people. Like, even just, like, friendly; it wasn't necessarily like, "Oh, I'm having trouble with it." I guess I was just trying to find, like, people that are, like, the same as me.

Before coming out to everyone in his nonvirtual world, the Internet afforded Clark a space to ask questions and connect with others in a realm of relative anonymity. And while Clark may still struggle in integrating some of the key aspects of his life with his gay identity (particularly in his relationship with his parents), he views friends, family, and religion all as key aspects of his support system: "I guess my friends, my family, and God are clearly things that I feel that really, like, support and strengthen me. . . . That's kind of like the foundation of things."

Listening to the Mini-Profiles: Finding "One Good Relationship"

A research, education, and intervention initiative that has emerged in the last decade, the Family Acceptance Project (FAP), places specific focus on the responses of parents and caregivers to having a child who is lesbian, gay, bisexual, or transgender. One recent study highlighting FAP research that appeared in the journal *Pediatrics* measured the experience and frequency of 51 parent/caregiver "rejecting behaviors" among a sample of 224 White and Latino lesbian, gay, and bisexual young adults (reporting retrospectively on their adolescence) and the associations among family rejection and various negative health and mental health outcomes. The researchers found that higher rates of family rejection during adolescence were associated with significantly higher rates of suicide attempts and of depression, use of illegal drugs, and unprotected sexual intercourse in young adulthood (Ryan et al. 2009).[4] Conversely, another FAP study found high levels of parent/caregiver acceptance during adolescence (measured by fifty-five "accepting behaviors" identified in prior research) to be associated with higher measures of self-esteem, general health, and social support. Moreover, the rates for suicide

---

4. Measures related to suicide that were examined in the study were suicidal ideation in the six months before the survey and lifetime suicide attempts (Ryan et al. 2009). According to an FAP publication, family behaviors that increase an LGBT child's risk include "verbal harassment or name-calling [based on a child's] LGBT identity," "blocking access to LGBT friends, events, and resources," "pressuring [a] child to be more masculine or feminine," and "telling [a] child that God will punish them because they are gay" (Ryan 2009, 5).

attempts and ideation were found to be significant lower for youth with higher levels of family acceptance (Ryan et al. 2010).[5]

The mini-profiles of the youth presented in this chapter, as well as the preceding case studies, provide examples of a range of both accepting and rejecting behaviors on the part of participants' parents. Parents who verbally abuse their LGBTQ children (Jessie), put religious pressure on them to change (Clark), or make deliberate efforts to open up the conversation about sexual orientation (Kate) or discuss a child's same-sex dating (Jason) play a wide variety of roles in the lives of even this relatively small number of LGBTQ youth. How a parent responds to the fact that a child is lesbian, gay, bisexual, transgender, or queer is only one aspect of the parent-child relationship, but as the FAP data suggest, parental responses to an LGBTQ youth's sexual orientation or gender identity can have a variety of health and mental health consequences that extend into young adulthood. Unfortunately, none of the study participants profiled in this chapter took part in a Phase II interview, so there is limited data here about the ways in which the development of their queer voices into adolescence was or was not supported by their family relationships over time. What is clear, however, is that— at least at the time they were interviewed—parental acceptance of their LGBTQ identities served as a self-affirming asset for some of these youth while rejecting behaviors caused others emotional distress. Moreover, it is worth noting (as I have elsewhere in this book) that some of the youth profiled in this chapter held low expectations for what they considered parental "support," including Clark, whose sexual orientation "wasn't discussed at all" at home, and Jessie, who in discussing when she came out as transgender says of her mother, "Just the fact that she didn't like, you know, freak out was enough support for me."

Several of these mini-profiles, like the longer case study of Lindsey in Chapter 2, also suggest that the sibling relationships of LGBTQ youth, studied even less frequently than those between LGBTQ children and their parents, warrant specific examination. Both Kim and Phil have highly abusive relationships with their brothers. In Phil's case the abuse is physical and at one point jeopardized his health following an ear operation, and the responses of Kim's brother and sister-in-law to her gender queer presentation

---

5. Among the accepting parent/caregiver behaviors measured in the study included talking openly about sexual orientation, inviting LGBT friends to participate in family activities, bringing youth to LGBT organizations or events, and "appreciating" a youth's clothing or hairstyle even if it is gender atypical (Ryan et al. 2010).

humiliate her at family events and force her to accept silence in order to maintain relationships with her young niece and nephew.

As in their family relationships, there is a wide continuum among the interview sample with regard to the degree to which they perceived their high schools as supportive of their identities as LGBTQ youth. All of the students who attended Smith County Regional High School (Jason and Kim in this chapter and Jordan in Chapter 5) experienced serious anti-LGBTQ harassment there and consistently reported that adults at the school did little or nothing to address it.[6] Jason even associates the suicide attempt he made while a student at Smith County with the harassment to which he was subjected there, and his experience along with those of David (Chapter 1) and Lindsey (Chapter 2) give voice to findings from other research that has associated suicide ideation and attempts with harassment and other victimization at school (Goodenow, Szalacha, and Westheimer 2006).

The findings of the Gay, Lesbian and Straight Education Network's latest National School Climate Survey (Kosciw et al. 2010), cited in this book's introduction, suggest that the kind of harassment experienced by Jason, Kim, and others is still pervasive in schools. In Kim's case, a teacher even contributed to the harassment, a problem also highlighted in the latest GLSEN survey. Moreover, Kate's account of her high school experiences illustrates how the harassment of LGBTQ youth can take on disturbing sexual overtones. As Joseph G. Kosciw and his GLSEN colleagues (2010) note, sexual harassment in schools affects many LGBTQ students, but female LGBTQ youth and those who identify as transgender are especially at risk.

At the other end of the spectrum, the students who attended Clay Technical High School (Jason in this chapter, along with Lindsey and Jordan, profiled previously) cited factors such as a "zero tolerance" policy with regard to anti-LGBTQ harassment, openly LGBTQ faculty members, a gay-straight alliance, and teachers who are open to discussing LGBTQ issues as those that contributed to their overall positive attitudes about school. Similarly, for Clark, the "very community-like" nature of his high school, where he says most students were accepted regardless of their race or sexual orientation, seems to have contributed to his overall positive attitude about his experiences there. (It is potentially troubling, however, that Clark's school lacked a GSA; see note 3 in this chapter.)

---

6. At the time Phase I of this research was completed, an adult advisor from YouthWest was working with officials at Smith County Regional High School to start a gay-straight alliance and improve the climate there for LGBTQ students.

Clark's experience going to an ex-gay Christian counselor may have been a serious risk factor for him. While there is no evidence that the counselor used any specific conversion therapies before Clark stopped attending the sessions, a recent American Psychological Association (APA) report notes that the available research evidence suggests that "attempts to change sexual orientation may cause or exacerbate distress and poor mental health in some individuals, including depression and suicidal thoughts" (APA Task Force on Appropriate Therapeutic Responses to Sexual Orientation 2009).[7] Moreover, in a position statement on conversion or reparative therapies, the American Psychiatric Association (1998) links them to "depression, anxiety, and self-destructive behavior," and "ex-gay" ministries have been associated in one qualitative study with exacerbated feelings of conflict about religion and sexual orientation among participants (Johnston and Jenkins 2006). Thankfully, given the space to reconcile his religious faith with his homosexuality in his own way (and by connecting online with others grappling with similar questions), Clark seems to have been able to turn his faith into an asset, one of the main things that he says "supports and strengthens" him.

Unfortunately, little research exists that specifically examines the experiences of LGBTQ youth with disabilities. In a recent synthesis of the findings of thirteen empirical studies related to the intersection of disability with LGBTQ identity in schooling, Thomas Scott Duke of the University of Alaska concluded, "LGBT youth with disabilities commonly experience prejudice and discrimination—based on sexuality, gender identity/expression, and disability—in a variety of social contexts, including at school . . . within the LGBT community, and in society" (Duke 2011, 37).[8] While Phil has clearly found an effective outlet for his queer voice as a teacher's assistant and mentor to LGBTQ students, his experiences also illustrate how attitudes of ableism can marginalize LGBTQ youth with disabilities even within queer culture and relationships.

Despite the various challenges that the youth profiled in this chapter have faced in family, school, and peer group contexts, their stories have one essential thing in common. Even those who endured severe harassment and isolation found ways to survive, and there is strong evidence to suggest that key relationships have made an important difference in this regard. Some of the young people in this small subsample had supportive parental relationships

---

7. The task force that prepared the report also acknowledged that the psychological effects of these therapies need to be studied further.
8. Duke's "meta-synthesis" was based on a total of twenty-four empirical and nonempirical writings, but the finding cited was based solely on the empirical sources.

that incorporated open acceptance of their LGBTQ identities (Jason, Kate, and Kim[9]), and others had supportive relationships at school with their peers (Clark and Phil), with adults (Jessie), or with both (Jason, after transferring to Clay Tech). Every youth profiled in this chapter seems to have found, at the very least, what researcher Jean E. Rhodes (2001)[10] has called that "one good relationship"—or set of relationships—that can help make a young person resilient in the face of risk and to progress on a positive developmental pathway. Ideally, of course, young people benefit from a multiplicity of relationships that interconnect across the ecology of their lives (Rutter 2006; Bronfenbrenner 1979), but these mini-profiles also highlight the compensatory power that one adult or peer can play within a social environment that a young person otherwise experiences as unwelcoming. As Jessie aptly puts it, "There is always that one teacher."

Since none of the youth profiled in this chapter completed Phase II interviews, we lack knowledge of how their queer voices evolved and whether they exhibited signs of long-term resilience into adulthood. But the expressions of self-acceptance and pride we hear in these young voices, even as they discuss considerable challenges they have faced or may still be facing, are cause for optimism.

---

9. Kim and I did not have the opportunity to discuss her parents' response to the homophobic words and actions of her brother and sister-in-law, but the fact that Kim remained silent in the face of this abuse suggests that her parents' support, though important to her, may not have been all it could be.
10. Citing Rutter and Giller 1983.

8

Foundations of Queer Voice

Silence and Support in Schools,
Communities, Families, and Society

The young adults and adolescents profiled in this book are survivors of trauma. Much of what took place in their homes, schools, and communities—including incessant harassment; attempts to convert them from homosexuality; and verbal, physical, and sexual abuse—can be considered nothing less. These are traumas specifically associated with growing up in a society that is homophobic and transphobic—that is, in which the fear-based marginalization of, discrimination against, and even contempt for LGBTQ people is in many ways still socially sanctioned.[1] Psychologist Annie G. Rogers (2006), drawing on her work with children and adolescents who have survived trauma, describes how the experience is often shrouded in silence and communicated "in code" through actions and other forms of communication that express "the unsayable." Expanding on Freud's theories related to the nature of trauma, Rogers writes:

> Experience becomes traumatic through a demand on us, which by its nature is in excess of what we can manage or bear . . . the excess that defines trauma is an inability to say what is happening at the time, and later to say what has happened in any fully accurate or complete way. (2006, 262)

---

1. The definitions of *homophobic* and *transphobic* suggested here represent my own understanding and synthesis of these terms based on my research, teaching, and advocacy work and may also apply to the less frequently used word *queerphobic*.

Participants in this research discussed a variety of "codes" through which they communicated to others (consciously or unconsciously) about the unsayable traumas they experienced—cutting, fighting, suicide attempts, disordered eating behaviors, dropping out of school. Even among those few who did not report having experienced excessive harassment or abuse, we hear accounts of isolation, dissociation from the self, and separation from relationships that can be viewed in and of themselves as traumatic. As Carol Gilligan (2002) has noted, voices particularly carry the mark of trauma when authentic feelings and experiences deemed culturally risky or unacceptable (in this case, those related to being lesbian, gay, bisexual, transgender, or queer) are kept out of a person's relationships and a more culturally sanctioned voice couched in silence and "code" comes to the foreground.[2]

As statistics and news stories periodically remind us, not all LGBTQ youth survive the traumas brought on by homophobia and transphobia, and the means through which they communicate their distress too often end in tragedy. We are therefore extremely fortunate that David, Lindsey, Ruth, Travis, Jordan, Eddie, Clark, Jason, Jessie, Kate, Kim, and Phil all found a language in which to tell their stories and places and relationships in which they could be heard. For the six participants whose stories we are able to follow into adulthood, we hear nascent queer voices—all silenced in various ways in adolescence—develop into voices distinguished by qualities such as progressive resistance (David), service (Lindsey), intellect (Ruth), contentment (Travis), self-acceptance (Jordan), and global citizenship (Eddie). Although there are clearly many more facets to these young people's lives than this list would suggest—including the stresses and challenges each of them continues to face—retracing their paths from silenced adolescence even to this limited set of qualities, to which all young adults might aspire, can teach us a great deal.

In the introduction to this book, I acknowledged, as all researchers are necessarily taught to do, the limitations of this study. The accounts of the relatively small number of people who took part in this research can in no way fully represent the myriad ways young queer voices are supported and silenced in schools, communities, families, and our society at large. Other important issues, including but certainly not limited to those facing many LGBTQ youth of color, immigrant LGBTQ youth, LGBTQ youth living

---

2. In *The Birth of Pleasure*, Carol Gilligan argues that boys' and girls' initiation into what it means to be men and women in a patriarchal culture results in an experience "that is akin to trauma in that a voice is seemingly lost or confused with another voice that finds more cultural resonance and thus carries more authority" (2002, 223).

in extreme poverty or extreme wealth, homeless LGBTQ youth, and others based on individual circumstances, have important influences on the development of queer voices within specific contexts. In a sense the participants in this research speak only for themselves, yet I believe that they do so both eloquently and urgently—and that the poignancy of their voices also speaks to an essential truth: if it matters to one young person, then it matters.

Much of the time, of course, it matters to many other young people as well, whether the "it" is going to a safe school, feeling close to one's parents, having a mentor to talk to, being able to express gender in one's own way, or many of the other themes heard repeatedly across these chapters. Where possible, I have attempted to set the individual voices heard in this book within a larger context of research and theory, demonstrating how they echo patterns of risk or resilience, deficits or assets found in prior work with LGBTQ youth or with different populations to whom useful analogies can be drawn.

I hope this book begins a new conversation about the tremendous potential LGBTQ youth possess, both as individuals and as a community, and how adults can best nurture it. With this purpose in mind, I offer the following cross-case synthesis of my own "lessons learned" from listening to these participants' stories and highlight what I believe they suggest as *foundations* for supporting the positive development of young queer voices in schools, communities, families, and society. In addition, I trust that readers will draw valuable insights of their own based on these interviews. As foundations, these are not the entire structure that needs to be in place to support LGBTQ youth in these relational domains. Rather, I offer them as a starting point—one on which I hope future research and practice will build as more voices enter the conversation.

Foundations at School: Getting Beyond the Basics

At the most basic level, to support the development of youths' queer voices schools need to be safe, yet for numerous participants in this research (David, Lindsey, Jason, Kate, and Kim, to name just a few) they were not. The lack of basic safety at school had a different silencing effect on each of them: David stopped raising his hand in class (and at one point came close to attempting suicide), Lindsey cut herself instead of talking about her feelings, Jason attempted suicide because he viewed it as his only way out, Kate did not bother to tell authorities that she was being harassed verbally and sexually because she believed they would take no action, and Kim simply dropped out. Although we might hope that school climates have improved since these people (now young adults in their twenties) attended high school, national studies such as the biennial surveys by the Gay, Lesbian and Straight Education Network, findings from which are summarized in the Introduction, suggest that little has changed. GLSEN's researchers have written urgently about the pervasiveness of anti-LGBTQ language and harassment in schools and the damaging effects these have on students' sense of safety, their attendance, and even their grades and future academic aspirations (Kosciw et al. 2010). Anti-LGBTQ language and harassment simply have no place in school, and all teachers, administrators, and school staff members have professional obligations to address it whenever it occurs, to try to prevent it from occurring in the first place, and to educate students and themselves about its damaging effects.

Although a basic level of safety is essential for young people to feel free to explore their authentic voices at school, however, building a foundation of safety involves more than attending to what is *not* happening in classrooms, hallways, and other spaces in and around a school building; it involves *creating* spaces where safety, and ultimately much more, can be fostered. To this end, the importance of gay-straight alliances cannot be overstated. GSAs have been shown in multiple studies to promote LGBTQ students' perceptions of safety and belonging in school (Heck, Flentje, and Cochran 2011; Szalacha 2003; Walls, Kane, and Wisneski 2010), and in other research they have been associated with lower rates of anti-LGBTQ victimization (Goodenow, Szalacha, and Westheimer 2006). Within this sample alone, participant after participant whose school had a GSA cited it as a key source of support that helped her or him get through high school:

> JASON: Like, our GSA is really supportive, and a lot of the people in there—like, if you're just getting, like, picked on . . . they'll actually, like, go and stand up to the people with you.

> JESSIE: Another good thing is my high school did have a gay-straight alliance . . . so there was a place for people to go if they needed support.

> PHIL: I think my GSA was probably the biggest step towards making high school bearable for me.

> TRAVIS: I became kind of lost that year [in tenth grade], and just— [the GSA] was one of those things that gave me a purpose, kind of.

For many students in this study, GSAs facilitated the kinds of open relational connections, both peer-to-peer and student-to-adult, through which young queer voices could develop simply by virtue of being heard. Jessie's description of her school's GSA as a "place for people to go" was typical of participants who viewed their GSAs as oases within school buildings in which they otherwise felt unable to speak freely. Another key benefit of the GSA for numerous participants was the support they received from the adult GSA advisor, that rare, safe adult to whom (as Jordan says of Clay Tech's Janice Lane) an LGBTQ student could talk confidentially "about anything." Particularly for youth who faced rejection in other relational domains, having the "ear" of the adult GSA advisor was critical in this regard, someone who explicitly and implicitly accepted them as they were and did not believe that they needed to change or silence themselves in any way.

A recent interview study by University of Arizona researcher Stephen T. Russell and his colleagues highlighted the potential for GSAs to go beyond the promotion of safety and support and to foster a sense of empowerment among LGBTQ youth. The researchers and their participants, leaders of high school GSAs, identified the empowerment built through GSAs as having multiple components, including access to the knowledge and tools needed to effect change in school and government policies, a sense of personal empowerment to be oneself at school (e.g., feeling safe holding a same-sex girlfriend or boyfriend's hand in the hallway and knowing that your GSA peers will support you), and the ability to pass on a positive legacy to younger students in the school community (Russell et al. 2009). As one of the study's participants explained, "Empowerment to me is when you feel like you have a voice and you feel like you make a difference" (897).

Numerous youth profiled in this book seem to have experienced their GSAs as sites of personal empowerment in similar ways. Lindsey, for example, worked with her GSA peers and advisors to educate the school community, extended her advocacy and education work beyond the school walls to high schools and colleges in the area (also through her involvement in Youth-West's parent organization, MCA), and felt supported by her GSA peers in breaking traditional barriers of sexuality and gender (e.g., taking carpentry shop and being part of an out same-sex couple), with the knowledge that she had "backup" in case there were any negative repercussions. For Lindsey, the GSA and the relationships she formed in it seem to have made a major contribution to the development of the self-assured voice we hear in her interviews.

While recognizing the tremendous value and potential of GSAs, however, it is also important to note the variations among LGBTQ youth with regard to their experiences in these groups. Ruth, for example, never felt safe voicing the fact that she was lesbian or bisexual in her high school's GSA despite the fact that she was a regular, active member. Travis characterizes his school's GSA, which he says the school administration attempted to keep "on the down low," as being made up of "me and the straight girls," and he contrasts it with a community-based group he also joined while in high school because "it had gay people." Moreover, prior research has suggested that LGBTQ students of color sometimes have difficulty feeling safe participating in their schools' GSAs because of potential racism within a school's LGBTQ community, perceptions that they do not belong, or the fear that they may face rejection by some of their peers of color if they identify too strongly and publicly with the LGBTQ aspects of their identities (McCready 2010).

Jeff Perrotti and Kim Westheimer's groundbreaking 2002 book *When the Drama Club Is Not Enough* was among the first to highlight the benefits of GSAs and other LGBTQ-positive programming in schools. Given the evidence that has accumulated since Perrotti and Westheimer's book was published about the lifesaving value of GSAs, it is unconscionable that most U.S. high schools *still* do not have them, and only a small minority of middle schools do despite evidence that homophobic language and harassment are often worse at this level of schooling than in high school (Kosciw et al. 2010). For schools with GSAs, however, it may be important to consider *when the GSA is not enough*—or, perhaps more accurately, whether it is enough *merely* to have a GSA without examining the relational dynamics taking place within it and ensuring that it is supported by a broader culture of respect and openness throughout the school.

At the surface, the schools that Ruth and Eddie attended were safe and supportive. Both participants reported that anti-LGBTQ language and harassment were minimal, both schools had GSAs, and Eddie's school held annual schoolwide pro-LGBTQ programs. Yet both Ruth and Eddie struggled with the decision to express their voices as out LGBTQ youth at school and questioned whether they would be safe. (Eddie ultimately came out, and Ruth decided not to do so.) While many factors, both developmental and environmental, are obviously involved in a teenager's decision to come out as lesbian, gay, bisexual, transgender, or queer, Ruth's and Eddie's stories suggest the need for schools to conduct a deep assessment how safe they really are for the open expression of LGBTQ identity and where subtle and not-so-subtle messages contribute to a culture of silence. In light of the liberation that coming out ultimately provided for Eddie and for other participants such as Lindsey and Jordan, who thrived at school once they felt freer to express gender and sexuality in their own ways, school staffs should explore this question honestly among themselves: "Would a student *really* feel safe expressing an LGBTQ identity at our school?"

In the cases in which LGBTQ students seem to have enjoyed school and to have felt free to explore and express who they are, traditional taboos and silences with regard to gender and sexuality were broken, often by the youth themselves but at times also by educators. The encouragement Lindsey received when writing a paper for her English class about transgender identity and the informal lessons Jason says his teachers sometimes use to "try to open up [other students'] horizons" about gay people seem to have helped both students feel safer and freer in incorporating a queer voice into their day-to-day work at school. These examples also suggest that their teachers felt safe and comfortable enough to engage in discussion about gender and sexuality with students without fearing that they would lose their jobs.

For David, having a "queer class" in college allowed his voice to resonate with other students concerned about LGBTQ issues and ultimately within a larger conversation. There is no indication that any of the participants had the opportunity to take a similar "queer class" in high school, and while such a notion may seem utopian given the current scrutiny of public education in the United States, the need for educators to provide more than a minimal level of safety for LGBTQ students and truly support their positive development requires rethinking some basic assumptions. As this book went to press, California became the first state in the nation to require the teaching of gay and lesbian history in public schools, an overdue and welcome first step, but only a small minority of students who responded to GLSEN's most recent survey (13 percent) indicated that there was *any* mention of LGBTQ issues in their school curricula.

Moreover, the fact that Lindsey, Travis, Jordan, Eddie, and Jessie (and perhaps others who did not mention it) all turned to openly LGBTQ teachers or school staff when they needed to talk to an adult who, as Travis put it, "knew where I was coming from" suggests that school leaders can support LGBTQ students in an important way by taking active steps to ensure that LGBTQ teachers, counselors, administrators, and staff feel safe coming out at school. (Conversely, David and Ruth expressed a belief that there were closeted LGBTQ teachers at their high schools and that this knowledge contributed to their own sense that it was not safe to come out there.) At the very least, these adults can contribute to the range of "possible selves" (Markus and Nurius 1986) that LGBTQ students might imagine becoming in the future and serve as examples of intelligent LGBTQ adults who lead productive lives; at best, they can serve as mentors and, in appropriate ways, trustworthy confidants to whom students can talk "about anything," and thus provide the foundation and the audience for a young queer voice to grow.

Further, as suggested by the examples Lindsey and Jason shared in which their teachers brought up LGBTQ topics in informal ways and posted "LGB Safe Zone" stickers on their doors, non-LGBTQ teachers can serve as assets by making their support for LGBTQ students known. This, in turn, requires school boards and administrators to establish conditions such that teachers feel safe and supported in being "straight allies" and to provide teachers with educational opportunities that prepare them to discuss LGBTQ issues with students accurately and comfortably. As the various accounts of teacher interactions heard in these interviews make clear, the only alternatives to this kind of public support are hostility and silence.

Clay Tech, where Lindsey, Jordan, and Jason all attended high school, was clearly a learning environment where many supportive elements were in place (although there is no indication that LGBTQ issues were included in curricula, except in informal ways). Yet Jordan's experience there illustrates how transgender issues are a last frontier of sorts even in schools where lesbian and gay issues (and, to a lesser extent, those related to bisexual and queer identities) are addressed. Jordan's experience as transgender, although it was later affected by medical issues, was clearly a central aspect of her self-definition during late adolescence, one through which she was able to find a voice that expressed "the one thing that identifies me the most." As a high school student, however, Jordan was barely familiar (if at all) with the term *transgender*, in part because there was no discussion of transgender issues at otherwise LGBTQ-friendly Clay Tech. As indicated in Chapter 5, transgender students face even greater risk for verbal, physical, and sexual harassment at school than other sexual minority youth (Greytak, Kosciw, and Diaz 2009). It is therefore imperative that in efforts to provide LGBTQ-positive programming in schools and to educate teachers about LGBTQ issues, clear and specific attention is paid to the T within the LGBTQ framework.

The benefits of Clay Tech notwithstanding, it is also important to note that both Jordan and Jason transferred to the school after facing excessive harassment at their comprehensive high school, Smith County Regional, and were thus "tracked" to a vocational/technical school as a result. Although it seems that in all cases in which participants attended Clay Tech it was a highly positive experience for them (and far preferable to Smith County), in general the practice of transferring students from a comprehensive high school to a vocational/technical school for reasons other than academic choice or career preference is highly questionable. While safety was the apparent motivation in both cases of transfer, these students were silenced in the ultimate way—being absent altogether—at the comprehensive high school they had a right to attend, and their college and career trajectories may well have been affected in the process. In cases where an LGBTQ student's voice is being silenced in a homophobic and transphobic school culture, the burden should be on the school to change its culture, not on the student to change schools.

All the recommendations in this section come with one caveat: transforming schools to make them more conducive to the positive development of LGBTQ students' voices is easier said than done. It requires educators, especially those working in more conservative settings, to take some professional risks and to find their own voices as progressive agents of change, voices that are frequently silenced in the current test-driven, risk-averse environment of K–12 schooling. As is the case for LGBTQ youth, the voices of committed educators are found most effectively through relationship, by aligning with colleagues who share their commitment to change and are willing to take the risks associated with making it happen. As I have written elsewhere, support for LGBTQ students is in keeping with the mission statement of virtually any school and aligns with core values such as equal opportunity to learn and a commitment to every student's success. Educators committed to the equal opportunity and success of LGBTQ students can thus advocate for change most successfully by articulating how this work is closely aligned with larger school principles that already exist (Sadowski 2010). As the accounts heard in these case studies illustrate, the only alternative to safe, harassment-free schools in which LGBTQ issues are discussed openly and with respect are those that silence the voices of LGBTQ students at a critical turning point in their lives.

Foundations in the Community: Fostering Communication, Belonging, and Purpose

Numerous participants in this study reported that community-based LGBTQ youth groups served as key sites for relationship building and for their own identity development as LGBTQ youth. On one level, this is not surprising given the fact that participants were recruited for this research at CityYouth, one of the largest LGBTQ youth support groups in the Northeast, and YouthWest, a considerably smaller group based in a largely rural area. Understanding *how* and *why* these community-based groups make a difference in LGBTQ youths' lives, however, is important for designing the kinds of interactions and experiences that can promote queer voice most effectively.

One crucial benefit that both CityYouth and YouthWest provided participants was immersion into an LGBTQ culture that was unavailable to them in their schools and in many cases even their GSAs. Whereas GSAs draw from general school populations and exist within larger school communities, in which considerable anti-LGBTQ attitudes may still exist, most community-based groups are made up primarily of LGBTQ-identifying youth in which acceptance and even celebration of LGBTQ identities are the norm. Ruth speaks for numerous members of CityYouth when she says her membership there led to her becoming "pretty immersed" in queer youth culture (including participation in the city's LGBTQ proms and pride events). Lindsey credits YouthWest with teaching her how to "get really close to people," and she used her involvement there as a springboard toward work as a peer educator. Jordan's close relationship with Jarrett, one of YouthWest's adult advisors who is transgender, presented a unique opportunity for mentorship that Jordan was unable to find at school or at home. Getting involved in either CityYouth or YouthWest was a turning point for these young people; after they discuss their involvement in these groups, many of their voices shift and take on tones of self-acceptance, agency, and pride. David, tortured by persistent antigay harassment in high school, associates his getting involved in CityYouth with his feeling fortunate to be gay:

> I feel, like, really, really good about it [being gay], because—I feel like if I wasn't gay, but I was still different than everyone growing up, I wouldn't have found such a supportive, understanding community to help me deal. But because I was gay, I found this community of loving people who understood what I went through and understood who I was and were there to support me every second. I know I could call anybody at CityYouth if I needed them.

In discussing Eddie's coming-out journey in Chapter 6, I note that "immersion" or "identity pride," whereby a person rejects homophobic and transphobic scripts learned in childhood and for a time commits—almost exclusively, it can seem—to an LGBTQ identity, can be an important stage in development (e.g., Cass 1979; Lipkin 1999). While the young adults profiled in the case studies (Chapters 1 through 6) all live multifaceted adult lives, their experiences as CityYouth and YouthWest members suggest that the immersion experience offered by these LGBTQ-specific groups may have been, at least for some, an important contributor to positive identity development and queer voice. Particularly insofar as the pro-LGBTQ immersion in community-based groups contrasts with the homophobic and transphobic traumas many experienced in earlier adolescence, these groups may serve a uniquely important compensatory function in the development of queer voice, one that complements that of school GSAs and other forms of support in LGBTQ youths' lives.

Like high school GSAs, it is important for the organizers of community-based LGBTQ youth groups to ensure that they are inclusive of all young people under the LGBTQ umbrella. The statewide network under which both CityYouth and YouthWest operate has undertaken outreach efforts in recent years to attract more youth of color, and several groups in the state in which our research was conducted now specifically address the needs of LGBTQ youth of color and of transgender youth, another historically underserved group.

Beyond community-based LGBTQ youth groups, Ruth's story highlights the potential for religious organizations that are LGBTQ-friendly to provide institutional support to young people who may be struggling to find acceptance and voice in other relational contexts. Although Ruth experienced abuse at home and felt unsafe coming out at school, through involvement in her Unitarian Universalist church and its related youth group, Ruth found a community in which she could comfortably come out, an institution whose support for LGBTQ people was unambiguous and well publicized (perhaps unlike that of her high school), and access to a mentor, her church youth group advisor, who continues to provide Ruth advice and support into adulthood. The fact that Ruth has built an academic and professional life around her involvement in the UU church speaks to its strong influence in her development and is reflected in her adult voice as a scholar, educator, and mentor.

For LGBTQ youth, religion can, of course, be a double-edged sword. Clark's experience with an ex-gay "Christian counselor," who told him that homosexuality was a sin and had a conversion agenda, is extremely troubling. Clark seems to have survived this experience with his gay identity, his faith, and his voice all intact, but for young people who lack the assets Clark had (including his membership in CityYouth), such conversion efforts can have a silencing effect on both their religious and their LGBTQ identities (Johnston and Jenkins 2006).

Finally, in discussing the "communities" that support the development of queer voice, the role of the virtual community for the current generation of LGBTQ youth cannot be ignored. Particularly in situations in which youth felt the most isolated—David, living in a rural community where he did not know any other out gay people; Jordan, having little access to other "transgender guys and women"; and Clark, trying to come to terms with being both a gay young man and a person of faith—the Internet provided a virtual lifeline. Most important, in all three of these instances, it served as a springboard to other forms of communication. Given its largely anonymous and relatively faceless nature (although this is changing in the age of Facebook, Skype, and YouTube), the Internet offered these young people a safe place to begin to explore their queer voices and have them "heard" online. With this foundation in place, they were able to speak in more intimate ways with the people and institutions closest to them. Promoting queer voice, then, involves ensuring that LGBTQ youth, particularly those living in the most isolated circumstances, have access to supportive, age-appropriate online resources through which they can connect with their peers and discover how and why their unique voices matter.

Foundations in Families: Learning and Teaching a New Language

For this group of participants, levels of family support with regard to parents' openness about their LGBTQ identities ran a wide spectrum. Kate's parents, for example, reached out to her to talk about LGBTQ topics even when she was uncomfortable doing so, whereas Travis describes his family's approach to discussing his homosexuality as "don't ask, don't tell." As discussed in Chapter 7, none of the youth in this study were forced to leave home or disowned by their families, a risk that far too many LGBTQ youth face after coming out (Lowrey 2010). Moreover, all of the youth profiled here are or were out to their parents as LGBTQ and credit their parents or other immediate family members with providing them at least some level of support. Yet a close examination of these youths' narratives illustrates how wide-ranging family "support" can be.

Both David and Clark, for example, describe their parents as "supportive," yet Clark's parents avoided all discussion of his homosexuality and sent him to a religious counselor, and David's parents failed to address the issue of his sexual orientation when he was experiencing severe antigay harassment at school. As Jordan's story illustrates, and as I discuss at the end of Chapter 5, transgender youth can have an especially difficult time coming out to their parents, since parents may experience the news as the "loss" of a son or daughter (Wren 2002). Thus, the findings herein suggest that (1) when LGBTQ youth report that their parents are supportive, terms such as *support* and *supportive* can have vastly different meanings based on their expectations, and (2) open communication about being lesbian, gay, bisexual, transgender, or queer is frequently absent even from otherwise supportive relationships between LGBTQ youth and their parents.

One disturbing current running across several of the youths' stories about their family relationships is the experience of severe anti-LGBTQ harassment at the hands of siblings and—in a few cases—even parents. David, Lindsey, Matt, Kim, and Phil all report having experienced fairly serious verbal abuse from siblings for reasons associated with their sexual orientation and/or gender identity, and for Phil, these attacks were frequently accompanied by physical assaults. Moreover, Jessie and Lindsey report having been verbally abused by a parent: Jessie says her mother called her a "fucking dyke" when she got a short haircut in eighth grade, and Lindsey says her stepfather verbally abused her to the point where she believes it was a factor in her suicide attempt. Thus, for at least several of these youth, home was not a safe haven from the anti-LGBTQ abuse they experienced at school. Any efforts to address anti-LGBTQ youth harassment must therefore take into account the fact that, at least for some young people, abuse at home can be just as serious a risk as that taking place in school or on the street.

Abusive situations aside, there is much in these narratives to suggest that the parents of the people participating in this study love their children. Jordan, for example, is extremely close to her parents, particularly in adulthood, despite the emotional "war" Jordan experienced while planning to undergo sex reassignment surgery several years earlier. David's mother drives him two hours round-trip to and from school each day so that he can be in a safer environment. After Eddie comes out to his mother, she tells him, "I hope you know that I would always love you no matter what. . . . If you were in the electric chair waiting for the death penalty, I'd be holding your hand, and they'd have to drag me away."

Rather than love, what seems to be lacking in many of these family relationships—among parents, siblings, and even in some cases the LGBTQ youth themselves—is a language for talking about gender and sexuality in ways that are comfortable, open, and respectful. The participants in this research told us again and again how much their families meant to them. Being able to be in true dialogue with the people to whom they feel closest—and having their real voices resonate in these relationships—requires that the traditional silences about sexuality and gender that pervade our society be broken. As Eddie's story illustrates, coming out can be a particularly difficult conversation for LGBTQ youth to begin completely on their own, and many young people will ruminate on the decision—silently and alone—for months or even years. David clearly wanted to talk to his parents about the harassment he was experiencing at school but felt that his parents offered no entrée into the conversation: "What I wish they would've said was, 'What can we do to help you be safe? What have you been going through in high school?'" Also, David's near-miss experience with his father's gun and his disordered eating behaviors, Lindsey's cutting, Jason's overdose, and other risks participants related here point to the need for parents to be attuned to the "language of violence" an LGBTQ child might use when communication by other means seems impossible. Families can turn to a number of organizations and websites for help in beginning supportive conversations about sexuality and gender, including those listed at the end of this book.

Foundations in Society: Clearing the Air

Psychologist Beverly Daniel Tatum, in her widely read book on racial identity development, *"Why Are All the Black Kids Sitting Together in the Cafeteria?" and Other Conversations about Race* (1997), discusses the challenges she has faced persuading college students and participants in her antiracism workshops to acknowledge their own racial prejudices. To explain the unavoidability of prejudice in a society that is deeply racist, Tatum writes:

> Prejudice is one of the inescapable consequences of living in a racist society. Cultural racism—the cultural images and messages that affirm the assumed superiority of Whites and the assumed inferiority of people of color—is like smog in the air. Sometimes it is so thick it is visible, other times it is less apparent, but always, day in and day out, we are breathing it in. None of us would introduce ourselves as "smog-breathers," but if we live in a smoggy place, how can we avoid breathing the air? If we live in an environment in which we are bombarded with stereotypical images in the media, are frequently exposed to the ethnic jokes of friends and family members, and are rarely informed of the accomplishments of oppressed groups, we will develop the negative categorizations of those groups that form the basis of prejudice. (6)

In addition to making a provocative and astute statement about cultural racism and the prejudicial attitudes that inevitably follow from it, Tatum's smog metaphor sheds light on the most difficult challenge we face trying to envision schools, communities, and families that support the development of queer voice and do not silence LGBTQ youth or encourage them to silence themselves. Homophobia and transphobia are not at all the same as racial prejudice—they operate in different ways in our society and have completely different histories and effects—but a useful analogy can be drawn. Just as racism is the "smog" we all breathe living in a deeply racist society that makes attitudes of racial prejudice inevitable, so do the presumed superiority of heterosexuality and of traditional expressions of gender hang in the air and make homophobia and transphobia inevitable. As the participants in this research told us again and again in various ways, this "smog" seeps into the walls of our schools, our homes, and our communities. We all breathe it in, including LGBTQ people ourselves. The creation of a society that is truly supportive of the development of young queer voices, then, requires nothing less than a revision of some of its foundations so that we might finally begin to clear the air.

In each of these chapters, we can hear the effects of government policies that either silenced or supported LGBTQ students. The most notable examples of supportive policies, heard in the background of interview after interview, were those that make gay-straight alliances possible. The state in which most of our participants attended high school has made GSAs a cornerstone of its efforts to combat LGBTQ youth suicide and has provided funding for GSA startups, which has resulted in a proliferation of these groups over a relatively short time frame. State-level policy support and funding for GSAs is extremely rare, yet the current fiscal woes of most public school districts around the country, combined with the strength of anti-LGBTQ political forces in some regions of the country, make it critical that governments step in to provide funding so that GSAs do not (as some might hope) fall to the bottom of schools' priority lists. Similarly, the tremendous promise of community-based LGBTQ youth programs, and the ways they complement rather than replace school GSAs, point to an urgent need to fund these programs at sufficient levels.

Conversely, the persistence of anti-LGBTQ language and harassment in schools suggests that policies need to be in place to ensure that school officials deal with hostile climates effectively or, better still, prevent their silencing effects from ever taking hold. As this book goes to press, only eighteen states have policies specifically protecting lesbian, gay, and bisexual students from school-based discrimination, harassment, and bullying, and only sixteen states protect transgender students (Human Rights Campaign 2011).[3] More state governments, as well as the federal government, need to treat the silencing of LGBTQ students—both through harassment and through their marginalization in school curricula and programs—as a denial of their right to an equal education. As this book goes to press, a federal Student

---

3. States with protections for students based on sexual orientation *and* gender identity are Arkansas, California, Colorado, Connecticut, Illinois, Iowa, Maine, Maryland, Minnesota, New Hampshire, New Jersey, New York, North Carolina, Oregon, Vermont, and Washington, as well as the District of Columbia. Massachusetts and Wisconsin have laws related to sexual orientation only (Human Rights Campaign 2011).

Non-Discrimination Act has been introduced in both houses of Congress, but its status remains pending. Moreover, there is evidence to suggest that the passage of anti-LGBTQ laws (e.g., those banning same-sex marriage) may have serious negative mental health effects on lesbian, gay, and bisexual people (Hatzenbuehler et al. 2010). These laws and the often vitriolic public campaigns and anti-LGBTQ rhetoric associated with them are an undeniable part of the smog that seeps into our schools, communities, and homes on a daily basis and undermine any efforts to create an atmosphere of safety for youth.

For good or ill, the media is another central aspect of the cultural air we breathe—one that influences not only the way we see the world but how we see ourselves. As adolescent psychology pioneer Erik Erikson observed, our identities and self-perceptions are formed within a complex interplay "by which the individual judges himself in the light of what he perceives to be the way in which others judge him" (1968, 22). This self-judgment can be especially acute during adolescence, when self-definition and peer acceptance take on special salience (Erikson 1968; Sadowski 2008a). It does not take a long time while channel-surfing to get one set of messages television producers and advertisers send to adolescents again and again about how to judge themselves and others: heterosexuality is normal, homosexuality and bisexuality are deviant, and expressing gender is primarily about making oneself appealing to the opposite sex.

In music, another cultural medium that adolescents consume freely, messages are mixed. For every Lady Gaga, heroically calling on LGBTQ individuals and others to feel proud that they were "born this way," there is at least one Lil Wayne, peppering song after song with homophobic epithets and expressions of contempt for LGBTQ people. It is obviously beyond the reach of this book to effect changes in the entertainment industry, but those of us who care about LGBTQ youth should be aware of how the media can work to silence their voices in ways even beyond their awareness (which is how the media generally works on all of us) and help youth develop both resistance to false images of sexuality and gender and the wherewithal to create a future consumer culture that rejects them.

Changing the Conversation

The adolescents and young adults I interviewed for this book give me hope that a new kind of cultural discourse about sexuality and gender are possible and, in many respects, has already begun. In David's having the word *sissy* tattooed on his arm in a public gesture of defiance and pride; in Lindsey's desire to become a role model as a lesbian police officer; in Ruth's queering of the field of ethics to incorporate both LGBTQ and black feminist sensibilities; in Travis's rejection of the traditional model of white, upper-middle-class gay life and his focus not on "who you love" but on "how you love"; in Jordan's living gender in her own way; and in Eddie's expansion of his activist passions to challenge inequality across international borders, I hear a new, collective queer voice that makes me optimistic about the future. In much of this chapter, I focus on what "we" (teachers, parents, researchers, youth service providers, and others) need to do to promote the development of queer youth voices, but the voices of agency I hear in all of these cases remind me how much LGBTQ young people are doing for themselves. At some point in every participant's story, they said "no" to a cultural narrative that threatened to silence, oppress, and even annihilate them, and their own voices of resistance have proven to be their greatest assets.

At the same time, just as I wonder in the Introduction how things might have been different had Tyler Clementi's voice been heard before he jumped off the George Washington Bridge, I cannot help wondering what might have happened differently had some of these participants *not* had access to the resources and relationships, imperfect as some may have been, that helped to support their voices' development. What if David's parents had not been able to afford to send him to college early to escape the harassment he experienced in high school? What if Lindsey's high school had not had a GSA? What if Ruth had not found acceptance at church and a mentor who would continue to be a supportive presence in her life through graduate school? What if Travis had not survived his heavy drug use in high school? What if Jordan had not found other people with whom to discuss the complex emotions associated with being transgender? What if Eddie's mother, instead of expressing her unconditional love, had thrown him out of the house when he came out as gay?

As much of the previous research and other writings cited in this book attest, these are more than hypothetical questions. Change the names and some of the details, and those young people are out there. By listening closely now and in the future to LGBTQ individuals who have developed self-affirming queer voices, we all can learn much more than we currently know about how to hear the voices that are still being silenced. We also just might learn a new language for speaking about ourselves and one another based not on who we are told we should be but on who we are.

Afterword

> I finally see how our lives align at the core, if not in
> the sorry details. I still shiver with a kind of astonished
> delight when a gay brother or sister tells of that narrow
> escape from the coffin world of the closet. *Yes yes yes,*
> goes a voice in my head, *it was just like that for me.* When
> we laugh together then and dance in the giddy circle of
> freedom, we are children for real at last, because we have
> finally grown up.
>
> —PAUL MONETTE, *Becoming a Man: Half a Life Story*

More than two decades separate my experiences in adolescence and young adulthood from those of the research participants profiled in this book. It would therefore be easy and convenient for me simply to assume the role of "objective" researcher on the issues affecting LGBTQ youth and view the findings from a purely empirical perspective. I might reasonably justify this stance on the grounds that these young people have grown up in a very different society than the one in which I began my coming-out process at the relatively late age of twenty-one. Certainly, schools, communities, and families are far different now than they were during the 1980s. Temporal differences aside, however, there are ways in which I believe my experiences and those of the research participants "align at the core," if not in the details of time, place, and circumstance, then certainly in their essence.

Most adults who are lesbian, gay, bisexual, transgender, or queer have our own trauma stories to tell about homophobic or transphobic bullying and the silencing and self-doubt that were associated with it when we were growing up. Paul Monette's depiction of a "narrow escape from the coffin world of the closet" rings true as I look back at my own journey of resilience, just as I suspect it might for many LGBTQ adult readers. As I listened to the stories of relentless school-based harassment related by participants such as David, Lindsey, and Jason, I felt fortunate that my own experiences at school were never such that they drew me to a suicidal turning point like those in these young people's accounts. In my case, the harassment generally took the form of one or two assailants at each level of my schooling (the names and faces would change every few years, but they were always boys) who subjected me to daily verbal taunts. These were often spoken in hushed tones, so as not to draw the attention of teachers, as the harassers used epithets such as "faggot," "queer," and "femme" just loudly enough to humiliate me in front of the very peers whose acceptance I sought. This pattern continued even as late as college, when a young man in the dormitory in which I worked as a hall monitor assailed me verbally—again, in pointed but whispered tones to avoid others' attention—whenever he entered the building.

Like Kate, David, Kim, and many of the other participants in this research, I rarely felt safe telling any adults at school what was happening— and I *never* felt safe sharing it with my family. In addition to what Travis aptly terms unwritten "don't ask, don't tell" policies both at home and at school, the shame of being marked as gay (which was certainly not how I wished to be identified at the time) kept me silent. I also believed, as many of the participants here did, that if I told teachers, school administrators, or my family about the harassment I was experiencing, they would take little or no action and would find me at least partly responsible for what was happening.

Hearing Kim's story about the damaging effects of homophobic language used by teachers, which seems to have played a significant role in her decision to drop out of school, brought me back to experiences with adults whose responses to the fact that I was "different" ranged from sincere acceptance to quiet disdain to, in a few instances, open hostility. Kim's account particularly reminded me of an incident during my last year of elementary school involving "Field Day," an Olympics-like event in which all fifth-grade classes competed to determine which would be named best in the school. I'd hoped to use Field Day as an opportunity to be a hero for my class and to show those who had made fun of me for being a "femme" that I could pass the masculinity test. But when Field Day arrived, I wore leather, hard-soled shoes to school, not the sneakers that were required every day for gym class, let alone a special event like Field Day. When Mrs. Welsh, our gym teacher, discovered my error, she made no attempt to hide the contempt she felt for me: "You forgot your sneakers? On *Field Day*? What are you, some kind of a *sissy*? You must be!"

Mrs. Welsh's admonition confirmed the fear I had always harbored but did not dare acknowledge. I was not masculine enough, and it showed. As an early adolescent, this event taught me that I needed to conceal—or, better yet, change—significant aspects of myself if I wanted to be accepted by my peers, my family, and my teachers. Of course, as an adult researcher and educator, I recognize that Mrs. Welsh's behavior exemplifies precisely the kind of silencing and morale-killing words and actions for which teachers should be counseled to leave the profession.

As I listened to Eddie describe his difficulty even uttering the word *gay* before he came out as a teenager, it reminded me of my own silence and shame in the wake of the Field Day debacle and other similar incidents, and David's account of the various strategies he employed to avoid drawing attention to himself ("walk with your head down; walk with your head up") reminded me of my constant efforts to project a heterosexual front in middle and high school. I dated girls a little, tried to become more interested in sports, and adopted for a time a sort of class clown identity, all of which made me at least feel more masculine. Although my performed straightness did help me get through high school and become confident enough to form friendships, some of which continue to this day, I was living what I cite in the Introduction and elsewhere as the *central relational paradox*: I had relationships of a sort, but to maintain them, I projected a false self and kept other central aspects of myself "out of relationship." As Jordan puts it, the need I perceived to be someone I wasn't for the people I loved was "kind of like a war [within] myself."

When college forced the issue of my sexuality—as dating relationships became more intense, more adult, and more sexual—I found it increasingly difficult to feign heterosexuality; however, I was not ready to accept myself as gay. To survive, for a time I simply retreated into myself; I became what Ruth calls a "floater among my peers." I formed few close friendships and for a time literally hid behind darkly tinted glasses, affecting a sort of brooding, distant persona. When I finally did make friends with a group of people made up primarily of women and gay men during my last two years of college, I made sure to distinguish myself as the "straight one" and found other things to do when their evenings out consisted of going to a gay club.

As I look back in light of these interviews and in particular on the important role that gay-straight alliances and community-based LGBTQ youth groups played in so many participants' lives, I realize that this group of friends was in a sense my GSA before such things existed. In the absence of an adult-run, organized group of peers, it was a place for me to begin to learn about and explore LGBTQ culture as well as my own sexual identity (though given the lack of adult supervision, there was a disturbing amount of drinking and partying). It was ultimately to people from this group of friends that I began my coming-out process, a story that mirrors those of many participants herein as one of gradual, though not necessarily linear, self-acceptance through the building of increasingly open relationships in an ever-widening circle.

The process of my coming out to friends, and the ways my family relationships evolved over many years—from denial and rejection to acceptance and open communication—are, again, exceedingly complex and no doubt the subject of another book (perhaps a memoir that I may have the courage to write someday). Suffice it to say for the purposes of this afterword that my own experience bears out what I believe to be the main finding of this study: that supportive, honest, and communicative relationships with the people and institutions central to our lives are the most powerful means by which LGBTQ voices silenced for years, or even decades, can be rediscovered. Most important in this regard is my relationship with my husband of twenty years (legally for seven), Robb, whose unconditional love and constancy has built within me a core of human trust that I'd never believed I could feel. I believe this basic trust of other human beings is one of the things homophobia and restrictive ideas about gender steal from many of us in our youth. In this regard, I am reminded of Lindsey's words with which she contrasts her relationships with others before and after coming out: "I can talk to people now. . . . [Before], I never talked to anybody, and that was hard." Lindsey's story and others in this book, including my own, illustrate that it is only through relationships—deep, honest, and communicative ones—that a silenced voice can begin to feel safe expressing itself.

Of course, old habits of self-doubt and self-silencing die hard. When David, now a successful activist well known in the queer community, told me at the end of his Phase II interview, "How happy I am is different than how happy I am with my life. Happiness is hard," his words struck me in a deeply personal way. I do not think any of us ever completely gets over the residual effects of homophobic taunting and rejection we experience in childhood and adolescence, regardless of the accomplishments we may accrue. Despite a secure faculty position at a nationally known liberal arts college, I am sure I am not alone among middle-aged gay men (or lesbian women, or bisexual or transgender people) in still feeling a bit like the bullied child I once was, the boy who needs to prove himself to the Mrs. Welshes of the world on a virtually daily basis.

The writing of this book is thus a critical turning point in the expression of my own queer voice, and I have deep appreciation for all of my participants not only for making the book possible but for teaching me many valuable lessons along the way. As I complete these final words, I think back on the numerous decisions I have made throughout the process to, like Ruth,

"queer" the conventions of academia, to reject many of the standard practices of scholarly writing and simply focus on the aspects of participants'
stories that I believed needed to be told. With Travis's words echoing in my
ears, "I stopped listening to everyone around me and just listened to myself,"
and I believe the book is the better for it.

As this book goes into production, news of still more LGBTQ youth
suicides are making headlines and reminding me that even if technology and
other aspects of our world have changed since my adolescence, the silencing
continues. Just when I think the wave of such stories surely must be over,
another young person takes her or his own life. Fourteen-year-old Jamey
Rodemeyer, a high school freshman from a suburb of Buffalo, New York,
who had been bullied relentlessly for his sexual orientation both in school
and online for years, committed suicide in September 2011. On the blog
website Tumblr eleven days before his death, Jamey posted, "I always say
how bullied I am, but no one listens. What do I have to do so people will listen?" Jamey had the support of his parents and of many female friends (but
no male friends), as he had expressed in a YouTube video for the "It Gets
Better" campaign four months earlier, but clearly these were not enough to
protect him from the cruelty he endured.

Times have surely changed since I was an adolescent—in some ways for
the better and in some ways not. I never had the opportunity to post a blog
entry or upload a YouTube video to share my voice with a virtual community, so I have no idea if it would have made a difference in how I felt about
myself or when I chose to come out. But I was never cyberbullied either.
Today's young people are clearly still living in what Monette called a "coffin
world" of homophobia and gender straitjacketing, but it is now a virtual one
that follows them into their homes, twenty-four hours a day, seven days a
week. Until we have buried the last of the children who take their own lives
because of what an uncaring school, community, peer group, or society has
done to them, we need to do all we can to hear their living, vibrant voices
and to take action based on what we hear. I thank my participants for add-
ing their voices—voices of wisdom, self-respect, and healing—to this conversation and for the precious opportunity they have given me to hear and
share my own.

Acknowledgments

This book is dedicated to the adolescents and young adults who generously shared their stories with me and with our research team, particularly those who allowed me into their lives a second time many years later. I believe their voices will resonate with many readers who pick up this book—most importantly, lesbian, gay, bisexual, transgender, and queer (LGBTQ) young people who may be struggling to find their own voices in a world of silence. Both to me and to the readers they will inspire, their contributions to this work are immeasurable.

My idea for a voice-centered interview project with LGBTQ youth was born in the early 2000s during my doctoral research at the Harvard Graduate School of Education. I could never have conceived of this book were it not for the work and guidance of two women who led Harvard's Gender Studies program in the department of Human Development and Psychology: Carol Gilligan, whose seminal work provided the foundation for the research and who helped me envision the possibilities for its extension to LGBTQ populations, and Lisa Machoian, who served with me as co–principal investigator on the first phase of the project and who led our team with the utmost thoughtfulness, care, and sensitivity.

I am extremely grateful for the ongoing, enthusiastic support of two particularly important members of our Harvard research team, Stephen Chow and Connie Scanlon, who continued to meet with me years after our official team meetings were completed to review transcripts, discuss interpretations, and help get the work published. Without Connie's and Stephen's insights and constant belief in the importance of hearing the voices of LGBTQ youth, this book would never have come to fruition.

In addition, I acknowledge several current and former Harvard faculty members who played key roles in helping me conceptualize the work in its early stages: Mary Casey, who taught me how to conduct cross-case analysis and cheered me on as a writer; Renée Spencer, who helped guide me toward important foundational literature; and

Jocelyn Chadwick, Michael Nakkula, and Terry Tivnan, a dissertation committee who for years gave generously of their time, advice, knowledge, and expertise.

Although I cannot mention them by name (to protect the anonymity of the research participants), I am immensely grateful to the adult advisors of the two community-based organizations through which I originally met the youth who participated in this project. As the accounts in this book attest, these advisors are heroes for the work they do every day mentoring LGBTQ young people and providing them with a place to be heard.

This work would never have moved from manuscript to book without the enthusiastic support of Mick Gusinde-Duffy at Temple University Press. From my initial contact with Mick, he provided that boost that every writer needs when completing a project—the sense that someone else "gets it" and can envision, as you do, the contribution it can make to the field. I will forever be indebted to Mick for his unwavering belief in this book and his gracious shepherding of it throughout the process. I am also extremely grateful for the meticulous work of project manager Rebecca Logan and for Gary Kramer's enthusiastic and thoughtful marketing of the book, which I know will help it reach its widest possible audience.

I thank the Spencer Foundation and the Harvard Gay and Lesbian Caucus for supporting Phase I of this research; Patrick Neitz of Bits and Bytes Creative Design, who prioritized transcription of the interviews even when he faced countless other deadlines (no doubt from better-paying clients); and Bernie Gardella, who provided excellent advice, as always, for the resource list.

On a more personal note, I thank my family and friends who over the years have helped me find my own voice as both a writer and a person. Thanks to Mom Elsie, to all my brothers and sisters and their families, and to my wonderful friends for their love and support and for always asking, "How's the book going?" That question has cheered me on more than they know. Thanks, too, to the late Jasper, friend and companion for fourteen years, who sat by my side through much of the writing and, more importantly, helped me relive some of my lost boyhood as an adult.

Finally, thanks are not enough for my husband, Robb Fessler, who is, to quote one of my research participants, "the real hero of the story." A dedicated high school/middle school teacher and founding gay-straight alliance advisor, Robb is my daily inspiration for everything we should be doing right by LGBTQ young people. In addition to being my most astute editor, Robb has been the force that has kept me going, both through the writing process and for the last twenty years of my life. He has always—always—believed in me, and if that doesn't help a writer find his voice, I don't know what does.

Note on the
Listening Guide Method

The Listening Guide method (Gilligan et al. 2003) was used for collecting and analyzing all interview data during both phases of this research. Our research team originally chose this method because it is specifically designed to explore such issues as participants' experience of relationships, multiple layers of knowledge or awareness about these relationships, and the "central relational paradox" (Miller and Stiver 1997), as described in the Introduction. With its roots in feminist relational psychology, the Listening Guide is particularly attuned to capturing the experiences of individuals from socially and politically subordinate groups, those whose voices have historically been silenced by and within predominantly white, male, heterosexual societal structures.

The interview protocols consisted of thirty-four questions in Phase I and thirty-five questions in Phase II. In keeping with Listening Guide methodology, however, items in the protocol were used only as a starting point for the actual interviews. The content of the interviews was instead determined largely by "the lead of the person being interviewed and discovering in this way the associative logic of the psyche and the constructions of the mind" (Gilligan et al. 2003, 158). The interviews were recorded and transcribed verbatim, with both utterances and pauses noted.

The interviews were then analyzed in keeping with the Listening Guide's four steps, as outlined briefly here:

1. The first step in the analysis is to determine the "plot" or story of the interview. This step is in many respects like other forms of qualitative analysis, except that a traditional coding system is not used. Instead, using extensive text marking and memo writing, the researcher tracks her or his observation of relevant facts, dominant themes, pauses, omissions, and contradictions, as well as personal reactions to the interview (Gilligan et al. 2003).

2. The second step involves a close, specific examination of the participant's first-person or "I" statements. After highlighting all of the first-person

statements in an interview transcript—the pronoun *I* plus the associated verb and related words—the researcher lines them up like the lines of a poem to note patterns, rhythms, and shifts in voice of which the participant may or may not be aware (Gilligan et al. 2003). For example, a participant's "I" statements might be clear and direct when discussing one relationship or relational context and equivocal or tentative when talking about another.

3. The third "listening" involves an analysis of the "contrapuntal voices" (Brown and Gilligan 1992, 26) that emerge in an interview. The notion that the human voice is made up of multiple voices in counterpoint is based on psychoanalytic theories about the "layered nature of the psyche" (Gilligan et al. 2003, 157). This step consists of listening for, naming, and tracking different "voices"—verbal expressions of particular attitudes, feelings, or aspects of the self—in an iterative way (Gilligan et al. 2003). This step is in a sense a form of coding, with the concept of voice used as a "contextualizing strategy" (Maxwell 1996, 79). Like the "I" statements analysis, however, it is intended to yield subtextual data about the participants' experiences, beyond what they state explicitly.

4. In the fourth step, the researcher examines all three prior "listenings" and interprets them in the context of each other, noting where they both support and contradict one another. Working from the three marked transcripts for each interview as well as numerous memos and summaries written at various points in the analysis, the researcher then writes an overall analysis of each interview participant's narrative, focusing particularly on the ways in which her or his "voices" both emerge and fade as she or he discusses key relationships and experiences.

References

American Psychiatric Association. 1998. *Position Statement: Psychiatric Treatment and Sexual Orientation.* Arlington, VA: APA.

Andersen, A. 1999. "Eating Disorders in Gay Males." *Psychiatric Annals* 29 (4): 206–212.

APA Task Force on Appropriate Therapeutic Responses to Sexual Orientation. 2009. *Report of the Task Force on Appropriate Therapeutic Responses to Sexual Orientation.* Washington, DC: American Psychological Association.

Austin, S., N. J. Ziyadeh, H. L. Corliss, M. Rosario, D. Wypij, J. Haines, and A. E. Field. 2009. "Sexual Orientation Disparities in Purging and Binge Eating from Early to Late Adolescence." *Journal of Adolescent Health* 45 (3): 238–245.

Bilodeau, B. L., and K. A. Renn. 2005. "Analysis of LGBT Identity Development Models and Implications for Practice." *New Directions for Student Services* 111:25–39.

Bochenek, M., and A. W. Brown. 2001. *Hatred in the Hallways: Violence and Discrimination against Lesbian, Gay, Bisexual, and Transgender Students in U.S. Schools.* New York: Human Rights Watch.

Boisvert, J. A., and W. Harrell. 2009. "Homosexuality as a Risk Factor for Eating Disorder Symptomatology in Men." *Journal of Men's Studies* 17 (3): 210–225.

Bornstein, K. 1994. *Gender Outlaw: On Men, Women, and the Rest of Us.* New York: Routledge.

Bronfenbrenner, U. 1979. *The Ecology of Human Development.* Cambridge, MA: Harvard University Press.

Brown, L. M., and C. Gilligan. 1992. *Meeting at the Crossroads: Women's Psychology and Girls' Development.* Cambridge, MA: Harvard University Press.

Butler, J. 1993. "Critically Queer." *GLQ: A Journal of Gay and Lesbian Studies* 1:17–32.

Cass, V. C. 1979. "Homosexual Identity Formation: A Theoretical Model." *Journal of Homosexuality* 4 (3): 219–235.

Coleman, E. 1981. "Developmental Stages of the Coming Out Process." *Journal of Homosexuality* 7 (2/3): 31–43.

Crenshaw, K. 1991. "Mapping the Margins: Intersectionality, Identity Politics, and Violence against Women of Color." *Stanford Law Review* 43 (6): 1241–1299.

de Waal, F. 2009. *The Age of Empathy: Nature's Lessons for a Kinder Society.* New York: Crown.

Duke, T. 2011. "Lesbian, Gay, Bisexual, and Transgender Youth with Disabilities: A Meta-Synthesis." *Journal of LGBT Youth* 8 (1): 1–52.

Elze, D. E. 2003. "Gay, Lesbian, and Bisexual Youths' Perceptions of Their High School Environments and Comfort in School." *Children and Schools* 25 (4): 225–239.

Erikson, E. H. 1968. *Identity: Youth and Crisis.* New York: Norton.

Freud, S. (1925) 1961. "Some Psychical Consequences of the Anatomical Distinction between the Sexes." In *The Standard Edition of the Complete Psychological Works of Sigmund Freud*, vol. 19, translated and edited by James Strachey, 241–260. London: Hogarth Press.

Garmezy, N. 1993. "Children in Poverty: Resilience Despite Risk." *Psychiatry* 56 (1): 127–136.

Gilligan, C. 1982. *In a Different Voice: Psychological Theory and Women's Development.* Cambridge, MA: Harvard University Press.

———. 2002. *The Birth of Pleasure.* New York: Knopf.

———. 2011. *Joining the Resistance.* Cambridge, UK: Polity Press.

Gilligan, C., and L. Machoian. 2002. "Learning to Speak the Language: A Relational Interpretation of an Adolescent Girl's Suicidality." *Studies in Gender and Sexuality* 3 (3): 321–340.

Gilligan, C., R. Spencer, M. K. Weinberg, and T. Bertsch. 2003. "On the Listening Guide: A Voice-Centered Relational Method." In *Qualitative Research in Psychology: Expanding Perspectives in Methodology and Design*, edited by P. M. Camic, J. E. Rhodes, and L. Yardley, 157–172. Washington, DC: American Psychological Association.

Goodenow, C., L. Szalacha, and K. Westheimer. 2006. "School Support Groups, Other School Factors, and the Safety of Sexual Minority Adolescents." *Psychology in the Schools* 43:573–589.

Gray, M. L. 2009. *Out in the Country: Youth, Media, and Queer Visibility in Rural America.* New York: New York University Press.

Greytak, E. A., J. G. Kosciw, and E. M. Diaz. 2009. *Harsh Realities: The Experiences of Transgender Youth in Our Nation's Schools.* New York: Gay, Lesbian and Straight Education Network.

Grossman, A. H., and A. R. D'Augelli. 2006. "Transgender Youth: Invisible and Vulnerable." *Journal of Homosexuality* 51 (1): 111–128.

Grossman, A. H., A. R. D'Augelli, and J. A. Frank. 2011. "Aspects of Psychological Resilience among Transgender Youth." *Journal of LGBT Youth* 8 (2): 103–115.

Grossman, A. H., A. R. D'Augelli, and N. P. Salter. 2006. "Male-to-Female Transgender Youth: Gender Expression Milestones, Gender Atypicality, Victimization, and Parents' Responses." *Journal of GLBT Family Studies* 2 (1): 71–92.

Harper, G. W., D. Bruce, P. Serrano, and O. B. Jamil. 2009. "The Role of the Internet in the Sexual Identity Development of Gay and Bisexual Male Adolescents." In *The*

Story of Sexual Identity: Narrative Perspectives on the Gay and Lesbian Life Course, edited by P. L. Hammack and B. J. Cohler, 297–326. New York: Oxford University Press.

Hatzenbuehler, M. L., K. A. McLaughlin, K. M. Keyes, and D. S. Hasin. 2010. "The Impact of Institutional Discrimination on Psychiatric Disorders in Lesbian, Gay, and Bisexual Populations: A Prospective Study." *American Journal of Public Health* 100 (3): 452–459.

Heck, N. C., A. Flentje, and B. N. Cochran. 2011. "Offsetting Risks: High School Gay-Straight Alliances and Lesbian, Gay, Bisexual, and Transgender (LGBT) Youth." *School Psychology Quarterly* 26 (2): 161–174.

Human Rights Campaign. 2011. *Statewide School Laws and Policies*. Washington, DC: Human Rights Campaign.

Johnston, L. B., and D. Jenkins. 2006. "Lesbians and Gay Men Embrace Their Sexual Orientation after Conversion Therapy and Ex-Gay Ministries: A Qualitative Study." *Social Work in Mental Health* 4 (3): 61.

Kann, L., E. O. Olsen, T. McManus, S. Kinchen, D. Chyen, W. A. Harris, and H. Wechsler. 2011. "Sexual Identity, Sex of Sexual Contacts, and Health-Risk Behaviors among Students in Grades 9–12—Youth Risk Behavior Surveillance, Selected Sites, United States, 2001–2009." *Morbidity and Mortality Weekly Report* 60 (7): 1–133.

Kimmel, M. S. 2008. "'I Am Not Insane; I Am Angry': Adolescent Masculinity, Homophobia, and Violence." In *Adolescents at School: Perspectives on Youth, Identity, and Education*, 2nd ed., edited by M. Sadowski, 99–110. Cambridge, MA: Harvard Education Press.

Kosciw, J. G., E. M. Diaz, E. A. Greytak, and M. J. Bartkiewicz. 2010. *2009 National School Climate Survey: The Experiences of Lesbian, Gay, Bisexual, and Transgender Youth in Our Nation's Schools*. New York: Gay, Lesbian and Straight Education Network.

Kosciw, J. G., E. A. Greytak, and E. M. Diaz. 2009. "Who, What, Where, When, and Why: Demographic and Ecological Factors Contributing to Hostile School Climate for Lesbian, Gay, Bisexual, and Transgender Youth." *Journal of Youth and Adolescence* 38:976–988.

Lee, C. 2002. "The Impact of Belonging to a High School Gay/Straight Alliance." *High School Journal* 85 (3): 13–26.

Lewis, R. J., V. J. Derlega, D. Brown, S. Rose, and J. M. Henson. 2009. "Sexual Minority Stress, Depressive Symptoms, and Sexual Orientation Conflict: Focus on the Experiences of Bisexuals." *Journal of Social and Clinical Psychology* 28 (8): 971–992.

Lipkin, A. 1999. *Understanding Homosexuality, Changing Schools: A Text for Teachers, Counselors, and Administrators*. Boulder, CO: Westview Press.

———. 2008. "What's in a Label? Adolescents and *Queer* Identities." In *Adolescents at School: Perspectives on Youth, Identity, and Education*, 2nd ed., edited by M. Sadowski, 142–146. Cambridge, MA: Harvard Education Press.

Lowrey, S., ed. 2010. *Kicked Out*. Ypsilanti, MI: Homofactus Press.

Macgillivray, I. K. 2008. "My Former Students' Reflections on Having an Openly Gay Teacher in High School." *Journal of LGBT Youth* 5 (4): 72–91.

Machoian, L. 2001. "Cutting Voices: Self-Injury in Three Adolescent Girls." *Journal of Psychosocial Nursing and Mental Health Services* 39 (11): 22–29.

————. 2005. *The Disappearing Girl: Learning the Language of Teenage Depression.* New York: Dutton.

Markus, H., and P. Nurius. 1986. "Possible Selves." *American Psychologist* 41 (9): 954–969.

Massachusetts Department of Elementary and Secondary Education. 2010. *Massachusetts High School Students and Sexual Orientation: Results of the 2009 Youth Risk Behavior Survey.* Malden, MA: Massachusetts Department of Elementary and Secondary Education.

Massachusetts Governor's Commission on Gay and Lesbian Youth. 2004. *Recommendations of the Governor's Commission on Gay and Lesbian Youth Based on Testimony Received at the Commission's Tenth Anniversary Forums.* Boston: Massachusetts Governor's Commission on Gay and Lesbian Youth.

Maxwell, J. A. 1996. *Qualitative Research Design: An Interactive Approach.* Thousand Oaks, CA: Sage.

Mayo, J. B. 2008. "Gay Teachers' Negotiated Interactions with Their Students and (Straight) Colleagues." *High School Journal* 92 (1): 1–10.

McCready, L. T. 2010. *Making Space for Diverse Masculinities: Difference, Intersectionality, and Engagement in an Urban High School.* New York: Peter Lang.

McGuire, J. K., C. R. Anderson, R. B. Toomey, and S. T. Russell. 2010. "School Climate for Transgender Youth: A Mixed Method Investigation of Student Experiences and School Responses." *Journal of Youth and Adolescence* 39 (10): 1175–1188.

Miller, J. B., and I. P. Stiver. 1997. *The Healing Connection: How Women Form Relationships in Therapy and in Life.* Boston: Beacon Press.

Monette, P. 1992. *Becoming a Man: Half a Life Story.* New York: Harcourt.

National Institutes of Health. 1999. *Inclusion of Children as Participants in Research Involving Human Subjects.* Bethesda, MD: NIH Office of Extramural Research.

Pascoe, C. J. 2007. *Dude, You're a Fag: Masculinity and Sexuality in High School.* Berkeley: University of California Press.

Pearson, J., L. Wilkinson, and C. Muller. 2007. "School Climate and the Well Being of Sexual Minority Youth." Paper presented at the annual meeting of the American Sociological Association, August 11, New York.

Perrotti, J., and K. Westheimer. 2002. *When the Drama Club Is Not Enough: Lessons from the Safe Schools Program for Gay and Lesbian Students.* Boston: Beacon Press.

Pollack, W. 1998. *Real Boys: Rescuing Our Sons from the Myths of Boyhood.* New York: Holt.

Pollack, W. S., and T. Shuster. 2000. *Real Boys' Voices.* New York: Penguin Press.

Poteat, V., and D. L. Espelage. 2005. "Exploring the Relation between Bullying and Homophobic Verbal Content: The Homophobic Content Agent Target (HCAT) Scale." *Violence and Victims* 20 (5): 513–528.

Raffo, S., ed. 1997. *Queerly Classed.* Boston: South End Press.

Rauscher, L., and M. McClintock. 1996. "Ableism Curriculum Design." In *Teaching for Diversity and Social Justice*, edited by M. Adams, L. A. Bell, and P. Griffin, 198–231. New York: Routledge.

Resnick, M. D., P. S. Bearman, R. W. Blum, K. E. Bauman, K. M. Harris, J. Jones, J. Tabor, et al. 1997. "Protecting Adolescents from Harm: Findings from the National Longitudinal Study on Adolescent Health." *Journal of the American Medical Association* 278 (10): 823–832.

Rhodes, J. E. 2001. "Youth Mentoring in Perspective." *The Center*, Summer. Republished in *Inf Ed*. Available at http://www.infed.org/learningmentors/youth_mentoring_in_perspective.htm.

———. 2002. *Stand by Me: The Risks and Rewards of Mentoring Today's Youth*. Cambridge, MA: Harvard University Press.

Rhodes, J. E., R. Spencer, T. E. Keller, B. Liang, and G. Noam. 2006. "A Model for the Influence of Mentoring Relationships on Youth Development." *Journal of Community Psychology* 34 (6): 691–707.

Rogers, A. G. 2006. *The Unsayable: The Hidden Language of Trauma*. New York: Random House.

Russell, S. T., A. Muraco, A. Subramaniam, and C. Laub. 2009. "Youth Empowerment and High School Gay-Straight Alliances." *Journal of Youth and Adolescence* 38 (7): 891–903.

Rutter, M. 1987. "Psychosocial Resilience and Protective Mechanisms." *American Journal of Orthopsychiatry* 57 (3): 316–331.

———. 2006. "The Promotion of Resilience in the Face of Adversity." In *Families Count: Effects on Child and Adolescent Development*, edited by A. Clarke-Stewart and J. Dunn, 26–52. New York: Cambridge University Press.

Rutter, M., and H. Giller. 1983. *Juvenile Delinquency: Trends and Perspectives*. New York: Guilford Press.

Ryan, C. 2009. *Helping Families Support Their Lesbian, Gay, Bisexual, and Transgender (LGBT) Children*. Washington, DC: National Center for Cultural Competence, Georgetown University Center for Child and Human Development.

Ryan, C., D. Huebner, R. M. Diaz, and J. Sanchez. 2009. "Family Rejection as a Predictor of Negative Health Outcomes in White and Latino Lesbian, Gay, and Bisexual Young Adults." *Pediatrics* 123 (1): 346–352.

Ryan, C., S. T. Russell, D. Huebner, R. Diaz, and J. Sanchez. 2010. "Family Acceptance in Adolescence and the Health of LGBT Young Adults." *Journal of Child and Adolescent Psychiatric Nursing* 23 (4): 205–213.

Sadowski, M. 2008a. "Introduction: *Real* Adolescents." In *Adolescents at School: Perspectives on Youth, Identity, and Education*, 2nd ed., edited by M. Sadowski, 1–9. Cambridge, MA: Harvard Education Press.

———. 2008b. "Still in the Shadows? Lesbian, Gay, Bisexual, and Transgender Students in U.S. Schools." In *Adolescents at School: Perspectives on Youth, Identity, and Education*, 2nd ed., edited by M. Sadowski, 115–133. Cambridge, MA: Harvard Education Press.

———. 2008c. "The Story of Matt: 'Transgender Superhero.'" In *Adolescents at School: Perspectives on Youth, Identity, and Education*, 2nd ed., edited by M. Sadowski, 136–141. Cambridge, MA: Harvard Education Press.

———. 2010. "Core Values and the Identity-Supportive Classroom: Setting LGBTQ Issues within Wider Frameworks for Preservice Educators." *Issues in Teacher Education* 19 (2): 53–63.

Sadowski, M., S. Chow, and C. P. Scanlon. 2009. "Meeting the Needs of LGBTQ Youth: A 'Relational Assets' Approach." *Journal of LGBT Youth* 6 (1): 174–198.

Saltzburg, S. 2004. "Learning That an Adolescent Child Is Gay or Lesbian: The Parent Experience." *Social Work* 49 (1): 109–118.

Savin-Williams, R. C. 2005. *The New Gay Teenager.* Cambridge, MA: Harvard University Press.

Scales, P. C., and N. Leffert. 2004. *Developmental Assets: A Synthesis of the Scientific Research on Adolescent Development,* 2nd ed. Minneapolis, MN: Search Institute.

Strong, S., D. Williamson, R. Netemeyer, and J. Geer. 2000. "Eating Disorder Symptoms and Concerns about Body Differ as a Function of Gender and Sexual Orientation." *Journal of Social and Clinical Psychology* 19 (2): 240–255.

Szalacha, L. A. 2003. "Safer Sexual Diversity Climates: Lessons Learned from an Evaluation of the Massachusetts Safe Schools Program for Gay and Lesbian Students." *American Journal of Education* 110 (1): 58–88.

Tatum, B. 1997. *"Why Are All the Black Kids Sitting Together in the Cafeteria?" and Other Conversations about Race: A Psychologist Explains the Development of Racial Identity.* New York: Basic Books.

Taylor, J. M., C. Gilligan, and A. M. Sullivan. 1995. *Between Voice and Silence: Women and Girls, Race and Relationship.* Cambridge, MA: Harvard University Press.

Troiden, R. R. 1989. "The Formation of Homosexual Identities." *Journal of Homosexuality* 17 (1/2): 43–73.

U.S. Department of Health and Human Services. 2005. *HIV/AIDS and Transgender Persons.* Washington, DC: HHS Leadership Campaign on AIDS.

Vermont Department of Public Health. 2010. *2009 Vermont Youth Risk Behavior Survey Data.* Burlington, VT: Outright Vermont.

Walls, N. E., S. B. Kane, and H. Wisneski. 2010. "Gay-Straight Alliances and School Experiences of Sexual Minority Youth." *Youth and Society* 41 (3): 307–332.

Warner, M. 1993. "Introduction." In *Fear of a Queer Planet: Queer Politics and Social Theory,* edited by M. Warner, vii–xxxi. Minneapolis: University of Minnesota Press.

Way, N. 2011. *Deep Secrets: Boys' Friendships and the Crisis of Connection.* Cambridge, MA: Harvard University Press.

Werner, E. E., and R. S. Smith. 1982. *Vulnerable but Invincible: A Longitudinal Study of Resilient Children and Youth.* New York: Adams Bannister Cox.

Wren, B. 2002. "'I Can Accept My Child Is Transsexual but If I Ever See Him in a Dress, I'll Hit Him': Dilemmas in Parenting a Transgendered Adolescent." *Clinical Child Psychology and Psychiatry* 7 (3): 377–397.

Yarbrough, D. G. 2003. "Gay Adolescents in Rural Areas: Experiences and Coping Strategies." *Journal of Human Behavior in the Social Environment* 8 (2/3): 129–144.

Yoshino, K. 2006. *Covering: The Hidden Assault on Our Civil Rights.* New York: Random House.

Online Resources for Supporting Queer Youth Voice

In Chapter 8, I outline foundations for the development of queer youth voice in schools, communities, families, and society. Following is a brief list of online resources that I hope will give readers a starting point toward building these foundations and help support their ongoing efforts. While clearly not an exhaustive list of all the local, state, and national organizations doing important work on behalf of LGBTQ youth in the United States, I have chosen these websites specifically as national resources that can help bring queer youth voices out of the silence.

SUPPORTING QUEER VOICE IN SCHOOLS

Gay, Lesbian and Straight Education Network
http://www.glsen.org

The GLSEN website includes resources for combating harassment and creating safer schools, building and maintaining gay-straight alliances, educating teachers and school staff about the needs of LGBTQ youth, and organizing in-school education activities such as the Day of Silence to raise awareness about LGBTQ issues. The site also includes extensive reports on GLSEN's research, which advocates can use to help effect local change.

GSA Network
http://www.gsanetwork.org

The GSA Network provides assistance for starting and maintaining gay-straight alliances and making GSAs sites for youth empowerment, support for antibullying initiatives, and leadership and activist training for youth.

NYQueer's Beyond Tolerance: A Resource Guide for Addressing LGBTQI Issues in Schools
http://www.nycore.org/2010/11/beyond-tolerance-resource-guide

NYQueer, a working group of the New York Collective of Radical Educators, created a free online booklet, *Beyond Tolerance: A Resource Guide for Addressing LGBTQI Issues in Schools*, with links to a range of resources that can be used by both students and educators. Sections of the guide include links to information about LGBTQI-related historical figures and events, literature, commemoration days (such as National Coming Out Day), lesson plans and curricula, and professional reading for teachers.[1]

Safe Schools Coalition
http://www.safeschoolscoalition.org/RG-teachers_highschool.html

A Washington State–based organization that provides support to schools worldwide, the Safe Schools Coalition includes a variety of useful resources on its website, including sample lesson plans and resource lists for incorporating LGBTQ issues into K–12 curricula.

Unheard Voices: Stories of LGBT History
http://www.adl.org/education/curriculum_connections/unheard-voices

A collaboration of the Anti-Defamation League, GLSEN, and StoryCorps, Unheard Voices is an oral history and curriculum project aimed at helping educators incorporate LGBTQ topics into their curricula. The organization's website includes links to audio interviews with background and discussion questions and lesson plans for middle and high school classrooms.

SUPPORTING QUEER VOICE IN COMMUNITIES

BAGLY/GLBT Youth Group Network of Massachusetts
http://www.bagly.org/home/programs/glbt-youth-group-network-of-massachusetts

One of the largest statewide networks of its kind in the country, the GLBT Youth Group Network is also a source of advice and support for individuals anywhere in the country who wish to form effective community-based LGBTQ youth programs.

FIERCE
http://www.fiercenyc.org

FIERCE (Fabulous Independent Educated Radicals for Community Empowerment) is a New York City–based organization dedicated to leadership development, political organizing, and support for artistic and cultural expression among LGBTQ youth of color, both in New York and nationally.

---

1. In the *Beyond Tolerance* guide, LGBTQI stands for lesbian, gay, bisexual, transgender, questioning, and intersex.

No Gay Left Behind
http://www.facebook.com/nogayleftbehind

Given the lack of gay-straight alliances at many schools (and the importance of GSAs for helping LGBTQ youth find their voices), NGLB is a Facebook campaign encouraging alumni of youth in isolated schools to come together and form "virtual GSAs."

SUPPORTING QUEER VOICE AMONG YOUTH AND THEIR FAMILIES

It Gets Better Project
http://www.itgetsbetter.org

As of press time, more than thirty thousand videos have been created for the It Gets Better Project, whereby youth view and share messages of affirmation to counteract the negative effects of bullying and harassment in schools and society.

Parents, Families and Friends of Lesbians and Gays
http://www.pflag.org

PFLAG's "Get Support" section includes resources for families with LGBTQ members, such as a glossary of terms about LGBTQ issues, a "Family Story Center" where visitors can read and submit stories, and information about finding a local chapter.

Point Foundation
http://www.pointfoundation.org

The Point Foundation provides scholarship support specifically to LGBTQ-identifying youth to attend colleges and universities at the undergraduate and graduate levels. It also provides mentorship and training for the next generation of LGBTQ leaders.

TransYouth Family Allies
http://www.imatyfa.org

TYFA forms partnerships with schools, service providers, and others to offer resources and support to transgender youth and their families. Services and resources include educational programs, a discussion group for parents, and advice about advocating for a transgender child's rights at school and in other contexts.

Trevor Project
http://www.trevorproject.org

The Trevor Project is an organization dedicated to the prevention of LGBTQ youth suicide, including an online, confidential Q&A forum; Trevor Chat, a free, secure online messaging service staffed by trained volunteers; and a twenty-four-hour telephone hotline for youth, the Trevor Lifeline (866-488-7386).

SUPPORTING QUEER VOICE IN SOCIETY

American Civil Liberties Union LGBT Youth and Schools Project
http://www.aclu.org/lgbt-rights/lgbt-youth-schools

The ACLU's LGBT Youth and Schools page contains information on how to start a GSA, how to help establish a school antidiscrimination policy, and publications such as "Know Your Rights: A Quick Guide for LGBT High School Students."

Groundspark
http://www.groundspark.com

Groundspark produces films (including the well-known *It's Elementary*) and educational campaigns about the LGBTQ experience, bullying and harassment, and other issues relevant to youth and educators. Through its "Respect for All" project, Groundspark provides media resources, training, and support to educators, youth, and service providers.

Lambda Legal
http://www.lambdalegal.org

Lambda Legal is a nonprofit legal organization dedicated to defending the rights of LGBTQ individuals in a variety of circumstances, including the rights of youth in schools and other settings. Lambda Legal's help desk responds to inquiries by individuals who believe they may have experienced discrimination on the basis of sexual orientation, gender identity and expression, or HIV status.

Index

Michael Sadowski is an Assistant Professor in the Bard College Master of Arts in Teaching Program, based in New York City and Annandale-on-Hudson, New York. He is also the editor of *Adolescents at School: Perspectives on Youth, Identity, and Education*. A former high school teacher, he was an instructor at the Harvard Graduate School of Education, editor of the *Harvard Education Letter*, and vice-chair of the Massachusetts Governor's Commission on Gay and Lesbian Youth.

In a **Queer** Voice

Michael Sadowski

In a **Queer** Voice

Journeys of Resilience from Adolescence to Adulthood

Foreword by Carol Gilligan

Temple University Press
Philadelphia

TEMPLE UNIVERSITY PRESS
Philadelphia, Pennsylvania 19122
www.temple.edu/tempress

Copyright © 2013 by Temple University
All rights reserved
Published 2013

Library of Congress Cataloging-in-Publication Data

Sadowski, Michael.
   In a queer voice : journeys of resilience from adolescence to
adulthood / Michael Sadowski ; foreword by Carol Gilligan.
      p. cm.
   Includes bibliographical references and index.
   ISBN 978-1-4399-0801-3 (cloth : alk. paper) —
ISBN 978-1-4399-0802-0 (pbk. : alk. paper) —
ISBN 978-1-4399-0803-7 (e-book)   1. Gay youth.   2. Gay
teenagers.   3. Gay students.   I. Title.
   HQ76.27.Y68S23 2013
   362.78'66—dc23

                                          2012025885

♾ The paper used in this publication meets the requirements of the
American National Standard for Information Sciences—Permanence
of Paper for Printed Library Materials, ANSI Z39.48-1992

Printed in the United States of America

2 4 6 8 9 7 5 3

Contents

Foreword

Carol Gilligan

> Never again will a single story be told
> as though it's the only one.
>
> —JOHN BERGER

A voice that sounds different may be called just that—a different voice. Or it may be called odd, or deviant, or queer. The implication is that there is a right way to speak and that this different voice is somehow not right. At the time I wrote *In a Different Voice*, women, insofar as they differed from men, were considered to be either less or more than human. Like children, they were seen as not fully developed, or they were regarded as saints. Listening to women at that time, I heard the differences that led Freud to describe women as having "less sense of justice than men" (Freud [1925] 1961, 257–258) and others to question whether women in fact had a sense of self. But I questioned the interpretation. The categories of psychological theory, the conception of self, relationships, and morality, had been framed by listening to men. What could be learned about human experience by listening to women?

My ear had been caught by two things: a silence among men and an absence of resonance when women said what they really felt and thought. "Would you like to know what I think? Or would you like to know what I really think?" a woman asked me one day early on in my research. I had asked her to respond to one of the dilemmas psychologists use to assess moral development. As her question implied, she had learned to think about morality in a way that differed from how she really thought. But as she also revealed, she knew how she really thought as well as how she was supposed to think. This posed a challenge to the methods of psychological research. What are the conditions in which people will say or even know what they really think and feel? What voices are we listening to, and how do we hear them?

The inclusion of women's voices in what had been called the human conversation changed the voice of the conversation by giving voice to aspects of human experience that had been for the most part unspoken or unseen. It shifted the paradigm, changing the categories that shape how we listen and what we see. The voice once heard as deficient and associated with women— a voice that joins reason with emotion and self with relationships—turned out to be a human voice. The splitting of self from relationships and thought from emotion once taken as markers of development turned out to be manifestations of injury or trauma. In his recent book *The Age of Empathy*, the primatologist Frans de Waal calls for "a complete overhaul of assumptions about human nature" (2009, 7). As researchers across the human sciences are discovering, we had been telling false stories about ourselves.

In a Queer Voice joins the series of books that have set out to correct our perception of ourselves by giving voice to those among us who have been driven into silence. I have known Michael Sadowski since he enrolled in my seminar on the Listening Guide method with a particular interest in listening to the voices of gay, lesbian, bisexual, and transgender youth. Within a society infected by homophobia, their voices were heard as queer. Listening to their ways of speaking about themselves and their experiences of being in the world, Sadowski found that their voices queer the categories of sexuality and gender that presume heterosexuality. The analogy to *In a Different Voice* implied by his title captures this shift in interpretation. Like the different voice that joins reason with emotion and self with relationships, the queer voice he asks us to listen to spurs a reconsideration of what it means to be human.

In *Covering: The Hidden Assault on Our Civil Rights*, Kenji Yoshino (2006), writing as a poet and a legal scholar, describes the many ways he felt called on to cover his gay identity and the struggles he faced in seeking authenticity in his personal and professional life. If he could not reveal who he knew himself to be, how could he be loved? And what was the meaning of acceptance? The psychoanalyst D. W. Winnicott and others have written about the costs of assuming a false self. To Yoshino, the demand to cover is the civil rights issue of our time. At a telling moment in his book, he describes the responses he encountered from straight men when he presented his work, their anger at the failure to recognize that they, too, feel pressures to cover who they are. At the root of the problem are the categories of identity often written into the law that force assimilation to a false notion of humanity. Yoshino urges us to challenge these categories rather than sacrifice our desire for authenticity.

The "queer voice" Sadowski describes heeds this challenge. In transforming a corrosive self-silencing into an open protest for equal rights and freedom of expression, it is a voice of resistance. More specifically, it is a voice that resists patriarchal social structures. The gender binary, in which being a man means not being a woman or like a woman, and the gender hierarchy, in which human qualities designated masculine are privileged over those considered feminine, are the DNA of patriarchy—the building blocks of a patriarchal order. In challenging both the binary and the hierarchy, the queer voice articulates an ethic of care and the values of a democratic society: the belief that everyone's voice should be listened to carefully and heard with respect and the recognition that equal voice is a prerequisite for free and open debate. In Sadowski's research, the development of a queer voice is associated with signs of psychological resilience and health.

Like Yoshino, Sadowski reveals the costs of demands to cover—the assault on personal integrity and the sacrifice of authentic relationships. Extending the project of *In a Different Voice*, he brings voices that have historically been silenced into the conversation. As a voice of resistance and resilience, the queer voice is a voice of hope. Listening to the young people in his book, we just might, as Sadowski suggests, "learn a new language for speaking about ourselves and one another based not on who we are told we should be but on who we are."